Norm Violation and Intergroup Relations

Norm Violation and Intergroup Relations

EDITED BY

Richard DeRidder

Department of Psychology
University of Tilburg

and

Rama C. Tripathi

Department of Psychology
University of Allahabad

CLARENDON PRESS · OXFORD

This book has been printed digitally and produced in a standard specification in order to ensure its continuing availability

OXFORD
UNIVERSITY PRESS

Great Clarendon Street, Oxford OX2 6DP

Oxford University Press is a department of the University of Oxford. It furthers the University's objective of excellence in research, scholarship, and education by publishing worldwide in

Oxford New York

Auckland Cape Town Dar es Salaam Hong Kong Karachi Kuala Lumpur Madrid Melbourne Mexico City Nairobi New Delhi Shanghai Taipei Toronto

With offices in

Argentina Austria Brazil Chile Czech Republic France Greece Guatemala Hungary Italy Japan South Korea Poland Portugal Singapore Switzerland Thailand Turkey Ukraine Vietnam

Oxford is a registered trade mark of Oxford University Press in the UK and in certain other countries

Published in the United States by Oxford University Press Inc., New York

Reprinted 2011

ISBN 978-0-19-852249-2

Printed and bound in Great Britain by CPI Antony Rowe, Chippenham and Eastbourne

PREFACE

Several overviews of social-psychological theories and research into intergroup relations have already been published (Austin and Worchel 1979, Turner and Giles 1981, Worchel and Austin 1986, Taylor and Moghaddam 1987, Hogg and Abrams 1988). In our opinion these books deal insufficiently with the historical roots of intergroup relations. Current social-psychological approaches do not take into account the fact that relationships between groups in a society are influenced by norms and other social factors, which foster the maintenance of a certain status quo or peaceful co-existence. It seems as if social psychology has left the study of relations between natural groups to sociologists and cultural anthropologists.

The present book adopts a social-psychological perspective in studying natural groups, focusing on relationships between groups that have been living in the same environment for a long period of time. A theoretical model is proposed concentrating on norm violation as a triggering factor of attributions and reactions between two social groups. In an elaboration of this framework, called norm violation theory, this process is conceptualized as being affected by a number of social-psychological context factors: identification with the own group, intergroup attitudes, perceived differences in power, and feelings of fraternal relative deprivation. Each of these factors can influence the manifestation of negative intergroup behaviour and contribute to a possible escalation of conflict. The theory also proposes that norms of redress, existing between groups embedded within an overall cultural or organizational entity, become operative as soon as an escalating process is set in motion. These norms of redress are assumed to function as a counter-force against tendencies towards escalation.

The theoretical framework advocated supplements existing social-psychological theories. Its scope is demonstrated by cross-cultural empirical research.

The book consists of three parts. In Part I, we review current social-psychological approaches to intergroup relations and present our own theoretical framework. We claim that the relationships specified by the theory will hold across different groups and cultures (Chapter 1). To investigate the plausibility of this claim, we conducted a number of studies with different groups in India and The Netherlands. All studies employed a similar design and similar instruments. Chapter 2 serves as a methodological introduction and overview of the empirical studies.

These studies are reported in Part II. The main body of research assessed the effects of social-psychological context factors on expected intergroup reactions to norm violations. Two types of intergroup relations (ethnic and organizational) were studied in both countries (Chapters 3–6). The main results are summarized and further analysed in Chapter 7. In a second series of studies (two in The Netherlands and one in India, cf. Chapter 8) norms of redress are dealt with. Anthropological evidence and the results of our own studies suggest that norms exist which prescribe how one group should react to another group's norm violation.

In Part III we discuss the strengths and limitations of this research project and formulate our main conclusions. We end with a presentation of the prospects for the understanding and prediction of intergroup relations which the present approach offers (Chapter 9).

This book is the result of an intensive collaboration by members of three institutes: The Centre for the Psychological Study of Social Change and National Development, Allahabad University (Rama C. Tripathi, Emmanuel S. K. Ghosh, Rashmi Kumar), the A. N. Sinha Institute for Social Studies, Patna (Jai B. P. Sinha, Ravi B. P. Singh), and the Department of Psychology, Tilburg University (Richard DeRidder, Xander H. M. Jansen, Ype H. Poortinga, Sandra G. L. Schruijer). It was decided among the editors that Richard DeRidder would take responsibility for the book's final form and content.

Financial support came from various sources. We acknowledge a grant which the Ministry of Education in The Netherlands provided at the very early stages of the project. The University Grants Commission and the A. N. Sinha Institute for Social Studies made the investigations in India financially possible. In The Netherlands part of the funds came from the projects' 'Social Security' and 'Adaptation and Society' at Tilburg University.

Many colleagues and friends supported us over the past six years. We especially appreciate the contributions of Ype Poortinga. He has served not only as one of the founding fathers of the whole research endeavour, but also as an interested and critical referee of many of the chapters in this book. Together with Fergus Healy and Durganand Sinha, Ype was also a valuable facilitator of good cross-cultural communication among the members of the research team. We are indebted to Jan Pijnenburg for the design and production of some excellent figures, and to Rinus Verkooyen who managed to complete the word-processing of the final text under stressful circumstances. Freek de Bruijn and Marion Singendonk spent days on the tedious job of proof reading. We are grateful to them.

During the course of this project we realized that cross-cultural research is not fast, smooth, and easy. We had to deal with differences in orientations and research priorities and with differences in communication styles in the discussion of scientific disagreements. These difficulties come on top of methodological problems inherent in this kind of research. We wholeheartedly agree with the statement that cross-cultural research is 'long, problematic, and difficult' (Roy Malpass, personal communication). However, we would like to add immediately that we found it extremely fruitful both theoretically and empirically. We hope that our book testifies to this.

Tilburg
27 February 1991

R. DE R.
R. C. T.

CONTENTS

PART II EMPIRICAL STUDIES

PART III GENERAL DISCUSSION

CONTRIBUTORS

RICHARD DERIDDER Department of Psychology, Tilburg University, P.O. Box 90153, 5000 LE Tilburg, The Netherlands.

EMMANUEL S. K. GHOSH Department of Psychology, University of Allahabad, Allahabad 211002, India.

XANDER H. M. JANSEN Department of Psychology, Tilburg University, P.O. Box 90153, 5000 LE Tilburg, The Netherlands.

RASHMI KUMAR Department of Psychology, University of Allahabad, Allahabad 211002, India.

YPE H. POORTINGA Department of Psychology, Tilburg University, P.O. Box 90153, 5000 LE Tilburg, The Netherlands.

SANDRA G. L. SCHRUIJER Canterbury Business School, University of Kent, Canterbury CT2 7PD, UK.

RAVI B. P. SINGH A. N. Sinha Institute of Social Studies, Patna 800 001, India.

JAI B. P. SINHA A. N. Sinha Institute of Social Studies, Patna 800 001, India.

RAMA C. TRIPATHI Department of Psychology, University of Allahabad, Allahabad 211002, India.

PART I

Theory, Methodological Concerns, and Instruments

1 Norm violation as a precipitating factor of negative intergroup relations[1]

Richard DeRidder, Sandra G. L. Schruijer, and Rama C. Tripathi

Introduction

The purpose of this chapter is twofold: first, to give a critical overview of current social psychological theories and notions about intergroup relations; second, to present our approach, called norm violation theory, to the study of intergroup relations.

Within psychology several theories have been developed to understand the nature of relationships between groups. The frustration–aggression hypothesis (Dollard *et al.* 1939) suggests that negative intergroup behaviour, e.g. a riot, occurs as a result of explosive tensions built up between groups over years. Adorno *et al.* (1950), with their concept of the authoritarian personality, locate the origin of racial prejudice in the personality structure of individuals. Other theories state that the cause of negative behaviour can be traced back to the groups' desire to achieve a positive group identity (social identity theory; Tajfel and Turner 1979), or to competition over scarce resources between the two groups involved (realistic conflict theory; Sherif 1967). Cognitive approaches, which have recently gained popularity, try to explain intergroup relations in terms of information processing models. (For overviews of existing approaches see Tajfel 1982; Brewer and Kramer 1985; Stephan 1985; Taylor and Moghaddam 1987; Messick and Mackie 1989).

A priori, none of the suggested social-psychological interpretations is necessarily more convincing or more valid than another, nor is there any contradiction among them. This is because each of the proposed theories adopts only a partial view of the complexity of intergroup relations. Moreover, as will become clear in this chapter, some theories address more basic and/or remote social-psychological causes of negative intergroup behaviour, while others focus on more immediate triggering events; some theories employ concepts which pertain to relatively invariant features of intergroup relations, others are more process oriented.

The approach, called norm violation theory, which we advocate and elaborate in this chapter, is integrative since it combines a number of notions and ideas from different social-psychological fields and theories. We employ this integrative framework to understand the relationship between ethnic groups in a society and between groups in organizations which have coexisted over a long period. The approach is based on the observation that over the years each existing group has developed explicit and/or implicit norms that stipulate how its members ought to act and react towards members of the other groups. These norms are known to members of each group. Usually, group members tacitly assume that these norms are respected. Therefore, a norm violation by members of one of the groups is considered to be a potent triggering factor of negative intergroup behaviour.

The main emphasis of the theoretical framework to be presented is norm violation by one party and its immediate cognitive and behavioural consequences for members of the other party. A process of escalation or de-escalation of negative intergroup behaviour is expected to ensue from a norm violation. Its direction (an escalation or de-escalation), intensity, and pervasiveness will depend on processes taking place within the two groups and on a number of relatively invariant group factors, such as the groups' social identity, power, and fraternal relative deprivation. Processes within the two groups involved are thought to be controlled by pre-existing or emerging norms of redress.

In social psychology little attention has been devoted to norms (cf. Pepitone 1976) and even less to norm violation as a potential precipitating factor of negative intergroup behaviour. The present framework attempts to fill this gap. Until now social psychology has been mainly concerned with relatively invariant psychological features of (negative) intergroup relations and with its more basic determinants. An example is the discussion within social psychology of the necessary and sufficient conditions under which intergroup behaviour occurs (e.g. Tajfel 1980), an issue that has attracted a fair amount of attention. As some of these features and determinants are supposed to play a role in our theoretical approach we will review them in the next section.

Before proceeding further, it should be emphasized that our framework is not intended as an alternative to the existing theories about intergroup behaviour in social psychology. It is designed to complement these theories and is proposed as a counter current against the recent individual(istic) cognitive research on intergroup relations.

Definition of concepts

Until now the terms 'intergroup behaviour' and 'intergroup relations' have been employed without further specification or definition. We conceive of 'intergroup relations' as a broader concept than 'intergroup behaviour'. That is, 'intergroup relations' refers to behaviour and to cognitive and affective processes between groups, such as stereotyping, prejudice, ethnocentrism, attributions, and attitudes. Intergroup behaviour refers in our view to instances of concrete and observable verbal and non-verbal actions of individual group members towards members of another group (e.g. discrimination). Sherif distinguished between intergroup relations and intergroup behaviour as follows. 'Intergroup relations refer to relations between two or more groups and their respective members. Whenever individuals belonging to one group interact, collectively or individually, with another group or its members *in terms of their group identification,* we have an instance of intergroup behaviour' (Sherif 1967, p. 12). Tajfel and Turner define intergroup behaviour as 'any behaviour displayed by one or more actors toward one or more others that is based on the actors' identification of themselves and the others as belonging to different social categories' (Tajfel and Turner 1979, p. 40). An important difference between the definitions of intergroup behaviour by Sherif on the one hand and Tajfel and Turner on the other, should be noted here. Sherif uses the concept of *groups* to define intergroup behaviour, whereas Tajfel and Turner use the concept of social *categories.* It would be wrong to equate both these concepts (Rabbie and Horwitz 1988). Sherif defines a group as 'a social unit that consists of a number of individuals (1) who, at a given time, have role and status relationships with one another, stabilized in some degree and (2) who possess a set of values or norms regulating the attitude and behaviour of individual members, at least in the matters of consequence to them. Shared attitudes, shared sentiments, shared aspirations and goals that characterize the closely identified members are related to these properties, especially to the common values or norms of the group' (Sherif 1967, p. 12). Tajfel and Turner, however, conceptualize a group 'as a collection of individuals who perceive themselves to be members of the same social category, share some emotional involvement in this common definition of themselves, and achieve some degree of social consensus about the evaluation of their group and their membership of it' (Tajfel and Turner 1979, p. 40).

For our purposes Sherif's conceptualizations are more adequate than that of Tajfel and Turner. Since we shall be studying natural groups, their members need not only to identify with their social category, they also have to assume that their social category has shared norms and goals. Emphasizing these latter characteristics we shall sometimes refer to the ethnic and organizational groups studied as 'parties'. We employ the concept of intergroup relations to denote cognitive and affective processes within and between groups which elicit and affect intergroup behaviour. The notion also intends to cover our interest in those aspects of the relationship that may trigger, mitigate or facilitate the occurrence of changes in intergroup behaviour. How can one explain, for instance, that after a period of stability some groups suddenly begin to become violent whereas others do not?

Social-psychological theories of intergroup relations

Here we will briefly review the existing social psychological theories and approaches in research. First, we will review the realistic conflict theory, the social identity theory and the theory of relative deprivation. After that, the notions of power, attitudes and attribution—partly taken into account by these theories—will be discussed in more detail along with the most recent advances in research on intergroup relations.

Realistic conflict theory

The work of Sherif on intergroup relations lies at the basis of what is now known as the realistic conflict theory. His extensive research program in real-life settings made Sherif a pioneer in intergroup research.

The main thrust of realistic conflict theory is that intergroup conflict is due to an incompatibility of group goals. Whenever a negative interdependency between groups exists—that is, one group achieves its goals at the expense of the other group's goal attainment—negative intergroup behaviour is likely to emerge.

In a series of experiments, set up as boys' camps, Sherif gathered most of his empirical data (for a description see Sherif 1967). Most of these boys' camps, in which boys aged between 10 and 12 participated unaware of any experimental manipulation, went through three or four phases. In the first phase the boys were allowed to form spontaneous interpersonal relationships. In the second phase the boys were divided in two separate groups. Sherif made sure that boys who became friends in the first phase of the study were placed in different groups. Then, each group engaged in its own activities. During this group formation phase a positive interdependence was created between the boys within each group. Consequently, a leadership and status structure developed, as well as group norms, values, and a group identity. In the third phase, a negative interdependence between the two groups was created, i.e. intergroup competition was introduced. The groups were engaged in games like tug-of-war and baseball, or were otherwise made to compete for scarce resources (e.g. a treasure-hunt). In some of Sherif's studies the intergroup competition phase was followed by a fourth phase. Here, Sherif tried to resolve the intergroup conflict in several ways. One of the most successful to overcome intergroup hostilities proved to be the introduction of superordinate goals. These were goals which could only be achieved by cooperation between the groups (for example fixing the water supply).

Sherif's findings can be summarized as follows. Groups in conflict become more cohesive, task-oriented, and organized. Autocratic leadership emerges and group members are expected to conform and be loyal.

Each group sees the other group as an enemy and negative stereotypes and attitudes develop. Intergroup hostility increases while interaction and communication between the groups decreases. Biases in perception and listening, in favour of the ingroup, occur. The *winning* group finally, becomes even more cohesive, yet loses its task-orientedness and fighting spirit ('fat and happy'). Since their stereotypes of the outgroup are confirmed, no learning takes place, such as reconsidering perceptions and strategies. The *losing* group firstly denies or distorts the reality of having lost. Initially the situation or an outsider is blamed, then scapegoats are sought within the group. Task-orientedness and tension increases ('lean and hungry'), whereas there is low concern for members' needs. Outgroup stereotypes are disconfirmed and hence losers are able to learn about the ingroup and the outgroup and perceive both more realistically. The introduction of superordinate goals led to a decrease in intergroup hostilities, although not immediately.

A number of attempts have been made to replicate Sherif's experimental studies. Sussman and Weil (1960) obtained similar results to Sherif with groups of diabetic children, i.e. a competition over scarce resources led to negative intergroup attitudes and negative intergroup behaviour. Diab's (1970) replication in Lebanon of all four phases of Sherif's study partly failed. The elicitation of negative intergroup behaviour proved to be so successful that it was impossible to reduce the hostilities between the two groups by introducing superordinate goals. The experiment had to be stopped and Diab ended in hospital. In some studies supportive evidence for Sherif's assertions have been found (e.g. Bass and Dunteman 1964). A recent replication of one of Sherif's boys' camp studies, however, did not result in intergroup hostilities nor in increasing ingroup solidarity over time (Tyerman and Spencer 1983). This is probably due to the fact that Tyerman and Spencer used boys who were familiar with one another prior to the experiment and shared an overall identity, namely being a scout.

The experiments of Sherif have been severely criticized on methodological grounds. Rabbie (1982) points out that it is difficult to ascertain whether their results are due to (i) the classification of individuals into distinct groups; (ii) the experience of sharing a common interdependence of fate with other members in the group; (iii) anticipated or actual intergroup interaction; (iv) the (in)compatibility of the group goals, i.e. anticipation of competing or cooperating with one another; (v) the mutually frustrating intergroup interaction during the actual intergroup competition; (vi) the anticipated or actual experience of having won over or lost to the other group; (vii) a combination of these factors. Rabbie and his colleagues (see Rabbie 1982) as well as other social psychologists have pursued the validity of these explanations. Research has mainly focused on two issues.

First, what are the effects of intergroup competition and cooperation on intragroup dynamics? Although the popular view holds that intergroup competition increases intragroup cooperation, it appears that competitive intergroup interaction sometimes increases intragroup cohesiveness, morale, cooperativeness, conformity pressures, status and leadership differentiations, and sometimes it does not (Doise and Lorenzi-Cioldi 1989). Especially important proved to be the (anticipated) outcome of competition. Whether, for instance, an increase in intragroup cohesion takes place seems to depend on whether the group members (anticipate to) achieve the goals they have set for themselves (Rabbie 1982). Intergroup cooperation tends to decrease the social distance between the groups and ingroup–outgroup biases.

A second issue involved the conditions under which the different effects of cooperative and competitive intergroup behaviour occur. According to Turner they 'tend to disappear when social interaction is minimized and the salience of the ingroup–outgroup division maximized; under these conditions all forms of anticipated and actual intergroup behaviour seem sufficient for ingroup–outgroup biases' (Turner 1981, p. 74–5).

In spite of the preceding criticism, Sherif's notion of superordinate goals has been widely applied, for instance, to conflicts between labour and management (Blake and Mouton 1962), to international conflicts (Frank 1967), and to the interaction between children with various ethnic backgrounds in desegregated schools (Aronson 1984). It has been argued, however, that it is very difficult to prevent intergroup conflict, since society (and organizations) is made up of different groups which compete for scarce resources and hence are negatively interdependent. Introducing a superordinate goal might solve a conflict between groups yet at the same time it most likely creates a new intergroup conflict at a higher level.

Another strategy which has been proposed as a means of solving intergroup conflict is locating a common enemy and bringing leaders or subgroups of the competing groups into interaction. Experiential intergroup training has also been used for solving intergroup conflict (Blake and Mouton 1962).

For a proper appreciation of realistic conflict theory, it is necessary to emphasize some of the important features of Sherif's boys' camp studies and of his intergroup theory. In Sherif's view a 'group' is more than a collection of individuals all of whom share a group identification. A group also has an identity, goals, a structure, and a set of norms and values. For this reason Sherif always introduced in his experiments a *group formation* phase, before he introduced intergroup competition. Secondly, it must be noted that no differences in power were taken into account in Sherif's experiments. Last, but not least, the notion of interdependence (positive within groups and negative between groups) forms the crux of his theory. Without such interdependence no groups are formed and no negative intergroup behaviour takes place. In fact, following Sherif's conceptualizations, the introduction of superordinate goals can be considered as a means to dissolve the two competitive groups by imposing a positive interdependence between individuals who previously were members of different groups. When successful, only one group will exist as a consequence of this manipulation.

Social identity theory

While Sherif considered negative interdependence between groups to be the basic cause of negative intergroup behaviour, social identity theory questions its necessity. Tajfel can be considered as the founder of this theory. Using a so-called minimal group paradigm, Tajfel (1970) and Tajfel *et al.* (1971) initiated a series of experiments in order to find out the minimal conditions for the occurrence of discrimination.

Subjects in a minimal group paradigm are arbitrarily divided in two groups and do not engage in face-to-face interaction. They are then asked to divide points between anonymous members of the ingroup and the outgroup. The results show that not only do subjects favour ingroup members in awarding points, yet they tend to maximize the difference between ingroup and outgroup even though this strategy results in a lower absolute ingroup gain possible. Apparently, a mere categorization of individuals into two 'groups' is sufficient to create intergroup discrimination in the allocation of points. Tajfel's experiments on the 'accentuation effect' (Tajfel 1957), as a congnitive explanation of stereotyping, illustrate this point. He showed that, both for physical and for social stimuli, intercategory differences and intracategory similarities are accentuated (e.g. Tajfel and Wilkes 1963; Tajfel 1969). But how does one explain the ethnocentric nature of the discrimination in the minimal group? Similarly, why are outgroup stereotypes generally negative and ingroup stereotypes generally positive? A purely cognitive explanation does not provide the appropriate answers. Concepts like social identity, social comparison, and values have to be introduced to answer this question.

Individuals behave in some situations in terms of their group membership because the group to which they belong can be important to them. Dividing people in groups (*social categorization*) not only orders the social environment; it also defines a person's position in society. Tajfel and Turner assume that individuals strive for a positive self-image. Such a positive self-image can be obtained via the group to which one belongs. Individuals define and evaluate themselves, to a smaller or larger extent, in terms of the group(s) to which they belong; groups which can be positively or negatively valued. Tajfel and Turner use within this context the concept of *social identity*, i.e. 'that part of an individual's self-concept which derives from his knowledge of his membership of a social group (or groups) together with the value and emotional significance attached to that membership' (Tajfel 1981*a*, p. 255). Individuals strive for a positive social identity and they try to attain this by comparing their own group with a relevant other group on a dimension which is important for the group making the comparisons (*social comparison*). If the outcome of this comparison is favourable, that is, one's group distinguishes itself positively from the other group on that important dimension, a positive social identity is experienced.

For social identity theory it is essential that an individual's social identity should be salient. Individuals will only engage in an intergroup comparison on a specific dimension in situations where they consider their group membership as an important part of their self-image. Moreover, the other group should be perceived as a relevant comparison group (often determined by salience, proximity, and similarity of that group (Austin 1977)). Under these conditions, individuals will try to achieve positive group distinctiveness on the comparison dimension adopted. Applied to the minimal group paradigm this reasoning implies that individuals, categorized in two groups by the experimenter, engage in the only available dimension of comparison which is the distribution of points. The maximization of differentiation favouring the ingroup produces positive distinctiveness.

Group members will experience a negative social identity if an intergroup comparison results in negative distinctiveness of one's own group as compared with the other group on an important dimension. To effect a change in negative social identity, group members could do the following according to Tajfel and Turner (1979, pp. 43–4).

1. Group members might try to leave or dissociate from the group they belong to. This is a purely individual action and Tajfel and Turner therefore label it *individual mobility*. Whether an individual engages in this strategy or not is related to his/her perception of his/her possibilities to change his/her group membership for another which would provide the individual with a positive social identity. This perception is related to the individual's belief system concerning the ease with which this can be achieved. This belief system can range from social mobility to social change. A social mobility belief system refers to an individual's belief in the permeability of group boundaries. In contrast, when an individual perceives group boundaries as fixed and impermeable, he/she is characterized by a belief system of social change. A social mobility belief system will lead a group member to adopt a strategy of individual mobility (be it at an actual or psychological level). Another possibility is for the individual to engage in intragroup comparisons. Neither way results in the position of the ingroup *vis-à-vis* the comparison group being fundamentally changed.

Apart from this individual strategy, the following group strategies exist in which those group members who are characterized by a belief system of social change could engage.

2. Group members might choose another comparison dimension; they could change their evaluation of the ascertained negative distinctive-

ness, and they could change their comparison group. These three behavioural options are called *social creativity* by Tajfel and Turner and will be chosen by those individuals who cannot conceive of alternatives to the present state of affairs. Whether one is able to think of alternatives to the present status quo or not, is determined by the perceived (il)legitimacy and (in)stability of the status quo. When no cognitive alternatives are conceived of, that is, the system is perceived as stable and/or legitimate, even positive attitudes towards the superior group can exist.

3. A third behavioural option is *social competition*. Here, group members may directly confront the comparison group on that dimension which initially resulted in a negative distinctiveness. This strategy, opted for by those group members who *do* perceive alternatives to the status quo, will most likely lead to intergroup conflict.

The perception of (il)legitimacy and (in)stability is subject to change: inferior groups which tolerated a negative social identity for a long period of time can sometimes quite suddenly strive for a positive social identity by way of direct confrontation with the superior group. An often mentioned illustration of this 'becoming conscious' is the women's liberation movement.

Initially, many studies were undertaken using the minimal group paradigm. The predictions deriving from social identity theory have been applied in field settings, using other methodologies and studying other than minimal groups. We mention the study of racial prejudice among blacks and whites, intergroup bargaining between management and labour, the role of language in ethnic group relations. Also, issues like status differences, relationships of power and subordination, and of stability and change in intergroup relationships have been studied. The macrosocial context in which groups relate is considered to be very important when explaining and predicting intergroup behaviour. It is beyond our scope to review these or other studies which have been conducted from a social identity theory perspective. We therefore refer the interested reader to other relevant work (Tajfel 1978*a*, 1981*a*, 1982; Turner and Giles 1981; Turner *et al*. 1987; Hogg and Abrams 1988).

The social identity theory is not without criticisms. The minimal group paradigm has been criticized, not only for methodological reasons (Aschenbrenner and Schaefer 1980), but also because of the fact that categories are studied within this paradigm and not *groups* (in Sherif's terms) (Rabbie and Horwitz 1988). Some authors note that the empirical evidence for the core ideas of Social Identity Theory is weak (Schiffman and Wicklund 1988; Messick and Mackie 1989). Schiffman and Wicklund (1988) also raise conceptual problems in the theory. One of the problems they raise is the preoccupation of social identity theory with conflict between groups. As such, it can be characterized as belonging to a conflict-structuralistic approach. Considered in this perspective, the theory is unclear on how conflicts between groups can be solved or prevented. Perhaps social creativity could be conceived of as the mechanism that is responsible for peaceful co-existence of groups. Crossed category memberships (Deschamps and Doise 1978), has also been proposed as a means of solving conflict (Brewer and Kramer 1985). One can also be doubtful whether a firm link between society and the individual is indeed established as the social identity theory appears to claim. Furthermore, it is unclear how the 'objective' world is translated into perceptions of this world and consequent (inter)group behaviour (Schruijer 1990*b*). According to the theory, salience of social identity is situationally dependent, but the theory does not make sufficiently explicit which situational factors foster salience (DeRidder 1988). It also does not specify the conditions under which individuals or groups will adopt (what) different strategies to bring about social change (Taylor and Moghaddam 1987). Finally, as Brown (1986) points out, in none of the minimal group experiments has a group been found actually *expressing dislike or hostility* towards the outgroup.

Relative deprivation theory

The theory of relative deprivation shares with social identity theory a focus on social comparison processes, yet takes as its starting point feelings of resentment, unhappiness, anger or moral outrage. These feelings are thought to arise from unfavourable outcomes relative to those of other people or group(s); and these outcomes are perceived as *unjust or illegitimate*. People experiencing relative deprivation may perceive themselves as victims of distributive and/or procedural injustice.

The term 'relative deprivation' was first used in a sociological study by Stouffer and his colleagues (Stouffer *et al.* 1949) in the American army. The authors attempted to explain the unexpected finding that Air Force personnel were more dissatisfied than the Ground Force personnel, although they had better opportunities for promotion. It was suggested that the Air Force personnel felt deprived, because they felt they were less well off relative to the people with whom they compared themselves (the other men in their own ranks).

Following Stouffer *et al.* a number of authors have developed theories of relative deprivation. Crosby (1982) presents an account of the theories proposed by Davis (1959), Runciman (1966), Gurr (1970), Williams (1975) and compares them with the theory which she herself proposed. Feelings of relative deprivation, she suggests, surface in the form of resentment, discontent, dissatisfaction or anger. There is the overall cognition that one is poorly off in comparison with others or that one's own group is poorly off in comparison with another. All relative deprivation theorists agree that for it to be present an individual must want or desire a certain object or a certain state. Except for Gurr (1970) all theorists specify that the individual should compare his/her own fate or state with that of others. Similarly, with the exception of Williams (1975), relative deprivation theories postulate that the individual should also feel she/he deserves or is entitled to obtain the desired object or state. Theorists disagree about the effects of expectations on feelings of relative deprivation. Some (Runciman 1966; Crosby 1976) propose that relative deprivation will follow when an individual's expectations of obtaining the desired outcome are high, others (Gurr 1970) feel that it will result when they are low.

Based on the nature of the comparisons made, Runciman (1966) made a distinction between egoistical and fraternal relative deprivation. Egoistical relative deprivation is said to exist when the comparisons one makes with own group members are found unfavourable (i.e. my gains are less than those of my fellow group members). Fraternal relative deprivation is said to be the result of comparisons of ingroup with outgroup, where the gains of ingroup members are found to be less (favourable) than those of outgroup members. Theoretically, fraternal relative deprivation presupposes a certain degree of identification with the group to which individuals belong.

Irrespective of the type of relative deprivation, it can be argued following Cook *et al.* (1977) that it has two components, one cognitive and the other affective. These two components may be differentially related to behaviour. Guimond and Dubé-Simard (1983), for instance, found that only the affective component of fraternal relative deprivation correlated with an overall index of nationalism in Francophone Québécois. The notion of fraternal relative deprivation appears particularly relevant for intergroup relations. Unfortunately, as Walker and Pettigrew (1984) pointed out, research in this area has mainly focussed on egoistical relative deprivation. Since this type of relative deprivation involves only intraindividual and interindividual comparisons it cannot, according to these authors, explain social phenomena occurring between members of different groups.

Theoretically, fraternal relative deprivation is proposed to lead to constructive individual and collective behaviour, as well as to destructive or negative forms of it (cf. Crosby 1976). The empirical evidence for the relation between fraternal relative deprivation and negative intergroup behaviour is mixed, however. In some studies feelings of fraternal relative deprivation have been found to be predictive for collective negative intergroup behaviour. Caplan, for instance, found that individuals scoring high on fraternal relative deprivation were more likely to participate in riots (Caplan and Paige 1968; Caplan 1970). Abeles (1976) reports a positive correlation between fraternal relative deprivation and militancy and Dubé and Guimond (1986) found that group discontent rather than personal prospects related to student participation in protest behaviour on the campus. Other studies (e.g. McPhail 1980; Tripathi and Ansari 1980; DeCarufel 1981; Martin *et al.* 1984) did not find the expected relation between fraternal relative deprivation and intergroup behaviour. In the Tripathi and Ansari study on modes of conflict resolution for communal riots; Muslims showed a preference for compromise, followed by withdrawal and forcing as strategies, irrespective of the feelings of fraternal relative deprivation measured.

A sense of injustice about the actual state of affairs of one's group in comparison with that of another group appears to be crucial for fraternal relative deprivation. This sense of injustice is accompanied by negative feelings, like anger and resentment. In this respect fraternal relative deprivation theory adds an important element to social identity theory, in which the cognitive consequences of (il)legitimacy are emphasized (see Tajfel 1981*a*, pp. 266–7). It attempts to provide some essential elements for an understanding of collective negative action.

The evidence thus far collected within fraternal relative deprivation theory suffers from one major deficiency. None of the studies known to us are really *predictive* of negative intergroup behaviour. All of them either employed measures of collective action which are supposedly related to intergroup behaviour, but which may be more properly called attitudes (e.g. the tendency to vote for a black mayor and nationalism in the Vanneman and Pettigrew (1972) study), or these studies have employed the theory to explain *post hoc* collective actions like participation in riots.

Power, attitudes, attribution

We have encountered the notions of power and attitudes in the theories of intergroup relations reviewed above. Differences in power delimit the range of phenomena which the social identity theory and fraternal relative deprivation attempt to explain. Both theories focus on individuals who are members of the disadvantaged group. Negative attitudes towards the other group has been a main dependent variable in the studies inspired by the realistic conflict theory (Sherif 1967). It has also been taken as a dependent variable in studies on fraternal relative deprivation (e.g. Tripathi and Srivastava 1981) and in a number of experiments based on social identity theory (e.g. Turner 1978). The importance of causal attributions for intergroup relations was clearly recognized by Tajfel (1969, see Tajfel 1981*a*, pp. 138–9), Apfelbaum and Herzlich (1970–71), and Deschamps (1973), but it was much later that more extensive accounts of the role of attribution processes in intergroup relations were proposed (Pettigrew 1979; Hewstone and Jaspars 1982). We will discuss attribution processes, attitudes and power in more detail here because of their importance for intergroup behaviour.

Power Power is a widely used concept in the social and political sciences (see Ng 1980 for a review). It is embraced as useful for understanding social conflict and stratification by sociologists (e.g. Weber 1947).

In social psychology, power has been considered essential by many theorists for understanding the social influence between individuals within groups (e.g. Asch 1952; Sherif 1962; Deutsch 1973; Ng 1980).

Some authors, however, have strongly objected to the use of a power concept. They propose that it should be excluded from the domain of study of minority influence (e.g. Moscovici 1976).

In the area of intergroup relations few researchers have been interested in the effects of power inequality. The contrast beteen the sociologists' conviction of the importance of power and the social psychologists' neglect of it appears so evident that it led Apfelbaum (1979, p. 118) to exclaim 'where has all the power gone?'. She strongly argues that social psychologists should devote their attention to processes of domination and subordination between groups and no longer leave these essential (inter)group phenomena outside their theories and research. A similar viewpont is taken by Ng, who criticises the research paradigm employed in experiments inspired by social identity theory, stating that 'out-group discrimination is not a necessary outcome of social categorization, but is contingent upon a permissive intergroup power relation' (Ng 1982, p. 204). In other words, there may be a number of causes of discrimination or negative intergroup behaviour, such as competition over scarce resources or social categorization, but these factors are insufficient for the *manifestation* of such behaviour. What is needed additionally is a power relation between groups which makes such discrimination possible. Ng (1982) was able to show experimentally that a stable majority treated their own group more favourably than two groups with equal power or one in which individuals were members of a minority. He concludes that 'there can be no minimal and sufficient cause [of discrimination] apart from one which is embedded in, and mediated by, the social arrangement of power' (Ng 1982, p. 202; see also Sachdev and Bourhis 1985, 1987).

The main difference between the arguments of Ng (1982) and those put forward by Apfelbaum (1979) appears to be one of focus. Ng's main focus appears to be the introduction of the power variable into research inspired by the social identity theory and to suggest the importance of power for the study of minority influence (Ng 1980, pp. 169–72). In contrast, Apfelbaum, considers the power of the dominant group(s) in society to be the force *par excellence* by which a dominant group is able to shape and/or dismantle the identity and thereby threaten the very existence of subordinate groups in that society. Both authors agree, however, that power inequality is an important factor in intergroup relations.

Intergroup power is a relative concept. In a situation where two groups are involved it can be defined as the capacity each group or party has to exert influence over the other or to control the other party's outcomes (cf. Cartwright 1959; Thibaut and Kelley 1959). Essential in this definition are the elements 'capacity to influence' and 'control over the other party' and 'each'. The capacity to influence refers to the different bases on which influence can be based (see French and Raven 1959, for discussion of the social-psychological bases) or to the different resources a group has access to (cf. Tedeschi *et al.* 1973). The notion of control refers to the existing behavioural dependence of each group on the other and 'each' emphasizes that this behavioural dependence is mutual (see Ng 1980, pp. 119–85 for an extensive review of the different conceptualizations of power in social psychology).

Power inequality of two groups is a matter of scope and quantity. It may be that one group has more intergroup power compared with the other because it has access to a greater number of different resources, or that it has access to the same resources as the other group but to a greater extent. In co-existing groups in a society or organization, the scope of power of the dominant or superior group is not limited to social resources, such as reward or referent power. It is also extended to other domains, such as economics and politics.

Social-psychological research on power has almost exclusively focused on interpersonal influence in dyads where a direct exchange relationship exists (see for instance Deutsch 1973, on interpersonal conflicts; Thibaut and Kelley 1959, on interpersonal exchange). In this kind of research the consequences of one person's use of power are short term and immediately visible for the two persons involved. In co-existing groups in an organization or a given society, however, power may be exerted in a variety of indirect and disguised manners (cf. Blau 1964; Apfelbaum 1979). An objective assessment of intergroup power is therefore in our view problematic. For this reason, and also because of our conviction that people respond to their subjective representation of reality, the focus of our study will be *perceived* power.

Intergroup attitudes Based on one of the most popular conceptions of the term, we conceive intergroup attitudes as predispositions of members of each group to respond with certain classes of responses to members of the other group (cf. Rosenberg *et al.* 1960). The classes of responses refer to the different components of this so-called three-component definition of attitude: a cognitive one (beliefs, opinions about the other group), an evaluative one (feelings of liking and disliking) and an action tendency component (tendency for certain behaviours towards members of the other group). In research and later theoretical work on attitudes, the first two components of attitude, opinions/beliefs and evaluation/affect are emphasized (cf. Petty and Cacioppo 1981). Following Fishbein and Ajzen (1975) intergroup attitudes can be defined as the sum of the beliefs members of each group hold about the other group multiplied by the evaluation of each belief (Fishbein and Ajzen 1975).

Although a number of exceptions is reported in the literature (e.g. Milner 1975; Jaspars and Warnaen 1982), it is generally postulated and found that members of a certain group have a more positive attitude towards their own group than towards the outgroup (Sherif 1967; Tajfel and Turner 1979). The attitude towards the outgroup is one of the main dependent variables in the theories of realistic conflict and social identity, and the theory of fraternal relative deprivation. As an independent variable, however, it is conspicuously absent in studies originating from these theories. It seems likely that a group having a negative attitude towards a particular outgroup will be more prone to manifest negative behaviour towards this outgroup.

There appear to be two main reasons why treating attitude as an independent variable has received little attention. Since LaPiere's (1934) classic study on the relationship between attitude and behaviour, the research has been plagued by inconsistent findings. It is only sometimes that people were found to behave in accordance with the attitude they had expressed (see Fishbein and Ajzen 1975; McGuire 1985, for reviews). These inconsistent findings led to a disinterest among researchers to study attitudes as an independent variable in intergroup relations. A second reason appears to be that intergroup researchers tend to focus on stereotypes rather than on attitudes (see Taylor and Moghaddam 1987). In this kind of study the main question concerns the idea or implicit personality theory which members of a certain group entertain about members of another group (e.g. which idea do males share about females?). The past research on stereotypes used to be rather descriptive. More recently, however, researchers have tried to extend this line of research by attempting to predict how stereotypes are formed and maintained from a general cognitive perspective (Messick and Mackie 1989).

The present state of affairs is to be regretted, as Deutsch's general statement about interpersonal conflict is equally valid for intergroup relations. Deutsch argues that 'characteristic processes and effects elicited by a given type of social relationship . . . tend also to elicit that type of social relationship' (Deutsch 1973, p. 365). If, for instance, competition over scarce resources between two groups elicits negative intergroup attitudes, then it is also likely that negative attitudes may in turn elicit such a competition.

Intergroup attribution Although attribution theory is a well established area of theorizing and research within social psychology, social and sociological aspects of attribution have been neglected (Pettigrew 1979; Deschamps 1982; Jaspars *et al.* 1983; Crittenden 1983; Hewstone 1989). The main focus has been on causal explanations of individual behaviour, outside of its social context. Recent studies, however, have demonstrated the importance of societal variables for understanding attributional behaviour. The influence of variables like race, sex, social class, and age on the outcome of causal attribution processes has now been well documented (e.g. Deaux and Emswiller 1974; Mann and Taylor 1974; Taylor and Jaggi 1974; Duncan 1976; Stephan 1977; Branco and Williamson 1982). In many of these studies group members opt for explanations which put their own group in a favourable light. These results are in line with the predictions made by the realistic conflict and social identity theories and have been referred to as a group-serving bias (Taylor and Doria 1981). However, it was found that only majority groups engaged in this group-serving bias. Minorities in some studies did not look favourably on their own group, yet they gave explanations favouring the majority! Sagar and Schofield (1980) showed that explanations given by both black and white subjects might be taken as evidence of an anti-black bias. Similarly, Deaux and Emswiller (1974) found that male task success is attributed to skill by both males and females, whereas both sexes attribute female success on the same tasks to luck.

It has been argued that the sociostructural position of a group in society *vis-à-vis* other groups plays an important role in intergroup attribution (Deschamps 1982; Hewstone 1989, pp. 187–9). A minority group which is exposed to a continuous devaluation and discrimination by the dominant majority, might internalize these negative evaluations. Consequently, such a group may not engage in an ingroup bias but may even favour the outgroup (Apfelbaum 1979; Deschamps 1982). Field studies on language and intergroup behaviour (Giles and Powesland 1975) and on racial identification of black children (Milner 1975), as well as laboratory studies on outcome distribution using a minimal group paradigm (Paicheler and Darmon 1978), supported the view of Deschamps and Apfelbaum. Sometimes, however, minorities do favour their ingroup (Bornewasser 1985; Hewstone and Ward 1985) and majorities are not always more positive about their ingroup than about a minority outgroup; they sometimes favour the subordinate outgroup (Bornewasser 1985; Howard and Pike 1986).

Social attribution theory (Hewstone and Jaspars 1984) attempts to synthesize these apparently conflicting results by stating that social attributions 'will tend to serve functions for the perceiver's social group'. Positive behaviour by ingroup and negative behaviour by outgroup members will be internally attributed; negative behaviour of ingroup and positive behaviour of outgroup members will be externally attributed (cf. Pettigrew 1979). However, 'under certain conditions social attributions will not function to provide a positive ingroup identity, e.g. certain minority–majority group relations (where members of the minority group perceive no alternatives to the existing system)'. In this case, members of the 'objectively inferior group will make attributions which tend to devalue the ingroup and favour the outgroup' (Hewstone and Jaspars 1984, p. 398).

The preceding reasoning implies that in order to explain and predict intergroup attributions, the specific social context of a particular intergroup relationship should be taken into account: persons belonging to different societal groups will, under certain conditions, make different attributions about similar behaviour.

It can be concluded that group membership and the position of groups *vis-à-vis* one another (e.g. majority–minority status) are important factors influencing attribution processes. However, the existing literature makes it very difficult to predict the extent and direction in which these factors affect attributions.[2] Unfortunately, no research on the relationship between social attributions and subsequent intergroup behaviour has been carried out, although there is evidence in other areas, e.g. health, that attributions do affect behaviour (e.g. Bulman and Wortman 1977; Dalal and Pande 1988).

Recent developments

Reviews of recent developments in the area of intergroup relations demonstrate the impact of a general cognitive information-processing model on research (see Stephan 1985; Messick and Mackie 1989). The cognitive information-processing approach of intergroup relations, deals with 'intergroup cognitions' (Stephan 1985) and is interested in information processing origins of e.g. perceptual ingroup and outgroup biases, of stereotypes, etc. Its interest lies in the formation and content of cognitive representations of social categories and its relationship to the attention, encoding, and retrieval of information. Topics which at present are being studied within this approach are e.g. the role that categorization processes play in the formation of stereotypes; the influence of stereotypes, schemata, scripts and expectancies on information processing; the phenomenon of 'illusory correlation' showing that uncommon groups are rather quickly coupled to uncommon behaviours. A proper understanding of the cognitive underpinnings of intergroup behaviour is important, although there is much more to it than just individual information processing (see e.g. Tajfel 1981*b*). A review of the cognitive literature falls beyond the scope of this chapter, since we shall be dealing with natural groups and are hence primarily interested in the *social* processes involved, and the influence of the larger macrosocial context in intergroup relations. We refer the interested reader to Hamilton (1981) and Stephan (1985) for reviews of the cognitive approach.

The interest in predictions derived from the social identity theory is continuing (see Oakes and Turner 1980; and Van Knippenberg and Ellemers 1990), although methodological and theoretical criticisms have been raised (Aschenbrenner and Schaefer 1980; Schiffmann and Wicklund 1988).

Both the cognitive approach as well as the social identity theory generally neglect the dynamic features of intergroup behaviour. Moreover, the link between cognitions and *behaviour*, although assumed, is hardly studied. Furthermore, no attention is paid to the importance of critical incidents which may trigger negative intergroup behaviour. This criticism may be raised not only against the recent developments discussed above, but equally against the realistic conflict and social identity theories and fraternal relative deprivation. More generally, whereas the realistic conflict theory to some extent displays an interest in the processes occurring within groups, such as a changing group structure after losing or winning, none of the predominant theories pays explicit attention to the process or dynamics between and within groups as a result of a particular intergroup relationship.

Norm violation theory, which will be presented in the next section, is cognitive in its orientation yet attempts to overcome some of these deficiencies.

Norm violation theory: towards a model of intergroup dynamics[3]

'Groups in transaction with one another over a period of time rarely remain neutral toward one another. Between them and their individual members, there develop reciprocal states of friendship or hatred, trust or mistrust, aggressive intent or willingness to give a helping hand. This is an undeniable fact of social life', wrote Sherif (1967, p. 61). Any social scientist attempting to study relationships between co-existing groups, or 'groups in transaction' as Sherif called them, has to take into account the past history of such groups. While Sherif tried to 'trace the course of these intergroup states from their inception' (1967, p. 61), Norm Violation theory has a more modest objective and limited focus. It takes norm violation as the triggering factor of changes from one state to another. More particularly, it focuses on the conditions under which—in two co-existing groups—a norm violation by members of one of them leads to negative attributions, negative intergroup behaviour and eventually mutual distrust. It takes norms, which have developed over a period of time within and between the two groups, as its starting point. Consider the following real-life example.

A pig in the Eidgah Moradabad is a middle-sized town in the state of Uttar Pradesh. Compared with other towns in Uttar Pradesh, the Muslim population here is considerable. Muslims in the town are engaged in a variety of trades, but a large number of them are artisans and work in the famous brassware industry for Hindu traders. In the late sixties and early seventies quite a few of the Muslims found employment in the Gulf countries. Consequently, their economic conditions changed and they were able to start their own businesses. Their relationship with other Muslims outside the country also helped them to develop a 'pan-Islamic' identity. One of the Islamic countries gave a large grant to start a World Islamic University near Moradabad. Against this background, the following events took place.

It is the day of Eid, August 1980. This day marks the end of the holy month of Ramadan for the Muslims. This morning a large number of Muslims congregates in the Eidgah (an open ground reserved for the saying of the Eid prayers). They are all dressed in impeccable white dresses. It is only when the prayers have just begun that a pig, an animal intensely disliked by the Muslims, is sighted inside the Eidgah.

The Muslims complete their prayers, but they are outraged that such a holy occasion is defiled. They attribute the incident to Hindus living near the Eidgah. 'These Hindus', they say 'have driven the pig into the Eidgah to disturb our prayers.' They also blame the police for their connivance with the Hindus.

Soon a large group of Muslims starts marching towards the police station. They attack it with stones. Some policemen are injured. There is a rumour that someone has been stabbed. Then arson begins. Shops are looted. The police resorts to shooting. The fleeing crowd sets shops and houses on fire.

A communal riot has broken out. Hindus stab Muslims and Muslims stab Hindus. Groups of Hindu and Muslim youngsters roam around their neighbourhoods. They seek out members of the rival group, enter houses and attack the inmates. Armed police are brought in to control the riots. They raid the houses of the rioters in search of arms and bombs. A large number of arrests is made.

It took almost a month for the town to return to normalcy.

The main message that the preceding example is intended to convey is that any concrete incident which involves a perceived norm violation may lead to a chain of cognitions and behaviours between and within the two groups. The course which events will take largely depends on historically grown features of each group and of the groups' relationship.

Norms and intergroup relations

The study of the impact of norms on (inter)group behaviour in social psychology was popular in the fifties and sixties. Examples of social psychologists studying norms at the time are Lewin (1948), Homans (1950), Newcomb (1950), and Sherif and Sherif (1953). After this period, along with a focus on individual cognition, researchers lost 'the group' as an object of study (see Steiner 1974) and thereby lost sight of (group) norms. The current interest in norms was revitalized by the writings of Gergen (1982) on 'social constructivism' and Moscovici (1981) on 'social representations'.

Norms can be studied from different perspectives, at different levels of aggregation, and in past treatments the very notion of norm itself has been given different meanings. Thibaut and Kelley (1959, p. 126) distinguish several perspectives from which norms can be studied: *how* do norms develop, *which* norms apply in a certain situation, what are the short-term *consequences* of norms, and what long-term *function* do they serve? Although no study can treat norms from any of these perspectives in complete isolation from the others, a failure to state explicitly the major focus of a given approach creates confusion. Furthermore, norms can be and have been studied at the level of cultures (e.g. Gergen *et al.*

1980), groups (e.g. Sherif *et al.* 1961), dyads (e.g. Thibaut and Kelley 1959), and individuals (e.g. Schwartz 1977; Harvey and Enzle 1981). Moreover, the concept of norms has been defined in different ways (cf. Rommetveit 1955). Some authors (e.g. Sherif and Sherif 1969) refer to a norm as a shared perceptual or cognitive framework, a 'frame of reference', while others (e.g. Zajonc 1966) employ the concept of norms to designate a certain 'uniformity of behaviour in groups'. Most often, however, norms are used to construe a collective obligation or some kind of an 'ought' quality (Heider 1958; Thibaut and Kelley 1959; Homans 1961). The obligatory character of norms was also identified by Lautmann (1971) as one of the most distinctive features of the concept of norms. Lautmann, who made an extensive analysis of over 100 definitions of norms and values in the social sciences, adds as a second characteristic that norms pertain to behaviour. These two aspects distinguish norms from values. Values, according to Lautmann's analysis, refer not only to behavour, but also to a range of other objects (such as opinions and goals) and values do not indicate what is obligatory, but rather what is desirable. Moreover, norms imply sanctions.

In the present discussion, only a general treatment will be given to problems such as which characteristic features can be attached to norms and to the development of norms. The main emphasis will be on short-term consequences of norm violation. Norms and norm violations are studied at the level of individual group members. Therefore, we define norms as opinions or beliefs of individual members of a group about how they *should or ought to behave* in a specific situation. These norms must be clearly distinguished from expectations. While quite often norms imply expectations about the frequency of occurrence of a certain behaviour, the reverse is not true. It may well be the case, for instance, that many employees in a company steal small materials for private use and that the statistical expectation of stealing is therefore high. The preceding does not imply that employees ought to steal. Or, to give another example, one might expect that the chances of a certain group starting a riot are considerable; nevertheless, it would be considered a norm violation if it were to do so.

Attributes of norms

A number of classifications of norms have been proposed (e.g. Morris 1956; Gibbs 1965). Gibbs's typology follows the elements distinguished in his generic definition of a norm. A norm 'involves: (1) a collective evaluation of behaviour in terms of what it *ought* to be; (2) a collective expectation as to what behaviour *will be*; and/or (3) particular *reactions* to behaviour, including attempts to apply sanctions or otherwise induce a particular kind of conduct' (Gibbs 1965, p. 589). All norms which fulfill the first and third criteria Gibbs mentions, fit the definition of norm employed by us. Collective conventions, collective moral norms, customs, rules and laws can be used to describe what certain group members ought to do in a certain situation.

Morris's (1956) typology is only relevant here insofar as his criteria specify some of the features in which norms may vary. He classifies norms with respect to the degree to which they (i) are known; (ii) are accepted; and (iii) are applicable to specific groups or situations. In a two party intergroup situation the norms which are primarily relevant are those which group members apply to members of the other group (*outgroup norms,* pertaining to behaviour of the outgroup towards the ingroup) and those which group members apply to themselves (*ingroup norms,* pertaining to ingroup behaviour towards the outgroup). The ingroup and outgroup norms may be identical or different. The norms may range from very general, e.g. 'We should not destroy the other group's properties and they should not destroy ours', to very specific, e.g. 'We, Hindus, should not offer tea to a Muslim in the daytime during the Ramadan period'. Whether norms are known and/or accepted in reality is a matter for empirical study. Often, for instance, the existence of a norm that group members hold only becomes evident from their reactions to norm violations (cf. Collett 1977). Therefore, we propose that, for outgroup norms, members of a group need only to assume that members of the other group know and accept the norms they apply to them. A similar statement can be made for ingroup norms.

In summary, group norms can be described in terms of 'if . . ., then . . .' statements: *if* a certain situation is present for a member of the ingroup or outgroup, *then* this group member is obliged (should, ought) to perform a certain behaviour or abstain from a certain behaviour. If a group member is not behaving in accordance with a norm, that norm is being violated. With reference to the attributes of norms described by Shaffer (1983), our conception of group norms can be summarized as follows.

1. Group norms do not describe behaviour of group members, they prescribe or proscribe it.
2. Norms are opinions or beliefs of individual group members which they assume are shared (i.e. known and accepted) by members of their own group (ingroup norms), members of the outgroup (outgroup norms) or by both.
3. Norms vary in importance and generality; they can range from very important to insignificant and from fairly general to very specific.
4. Norms are conceived to set latitudes of acceptable or objectionable behaviour; the more important the norms, the smaller these latitudes.
5. Members of a group must either be able to articulate which norms exist or be aware when a norm violation occurs.
6. Sanctions to norm violations range from unspecified (non)verbal signs revealing disappointment or uneasiness to precise rewards and punishments.

Norm development

Among anthropologists and researchers of groups there is general agreement that norms exist or emerge within and between groups (e.g. Sherif 1967, p. 154; Turner and Killian 1972). In psychological terms the existence of group norms can be explained as a consequence of socialization practices, in which modelling and reinforcement play a central role. When dealing with existing groups one also has to take into account that these groups themselves are embedded within an overall societal and/or organizational structure. Often it is this 'superordinate' body which sets at least part of the norms that group members hold. Here it suffices to note that many of the norms group members hold are rather invariant, they survive generations. Some norms, however, may develop through communication between group members and are limited to a certain situation, e.g. a demonstration, and have a short time span.

Once norms exist within and between groups they will govern the behaviour of group members. In our view, the assumed existence of such norms provides the basis for coordination and communication within and between groups. Violations of norms therefore have a number of immediate consequences.

Norm violation and intergroup behaviour: a theoretical framework

The origin of norm violation theory is a model for aggressive behaviour between two individuals or parties proposed by DeRidder (1980, 1983). Our presentation will strictly follow that of Schruijer *et al.* (1986), which implies that a strong emphasis will be placed on attribution processes. In Schruijer *et al.* (1986) a framework is developed for behaviour between two co-existing groups. This framework consists of a central chain or sequence which operates within a set of contextual factors. We will discuss the central chain first (see Fig. 1.1, p. 26).

An elementary sequence The starting point is a norm violation by members of one of the two groups, called group A. Norm violation by members of group A triggers an attribution process in which members of group B try to find sufficient reasons to explain the norm-infringing behaviour. Behaviour which is in accordance with the norms does not start the attribution process because it is already explained or understood by the groups' a priori considerations.

The preceding statement is summarized in the following hypothesis.

Hypothesis 1. When members of a group perceive behaviour manifested by members of the other group as a norm violation, this appraisal will lead to an attribution process in which these members will try to find a sufficient reason to explain this behaviour.

The attribution process itself is conceived of as a hypothesis-testing activity (DaGloria 1975; DaGloria and DeRidder 1977; Snyder and Swann

1978). Members of group B compare the event actually occurring in a situation (the norma violation) with alternative representations in which members of group A would have respected the norm, and test hypotheses which might sufficiently explain this discrepancy. The hypotheses members of group B take into consideration are drawn from their past experience with group A or similar groups in similar previous situations.

The subjective validity of the hypothesis that group A's behaviour is inspired by malevolent intent or is due to negative traits of group A depends on the *a priori probabilities* members of group B attribute to that hypothesis and on the *amount of evidence* favouring it compared with the a priori probabilities and evidence of alternative hypotheses taken into account by them (e.g. the behaviour is due to environmental constraints acting on group A). These a priori probabilities are dependent on group B's earlier experience with members of group A and similar other groups in similar situations and on group B's stereotypes and prejudices.

Whenever a norm violation occurs between existing groups it is supposed that the kind of explanation at which group members arrive is mainly determined by their prior ideas (stereotypes) about the other group. When intragroup communication is possible, members of group B will attempt to gain support for their explanation, arrive at a consensual attribution and devise a 'proper' reaction. When intragroup communication does not take place, members of group B will assume that their attributions of group A's norm violation are shared by their other group members.

In general, group B's attribution process will be negatively biased, i.e. the chances that norm violations committed by the outgroup are attributed to negative intentions or attributes of the other group are high. This statement is in line with the suggestion made by Pettigrew (1979) who argued that negative outgroup behaviour is more likely to be attributed to negative characteristics or dispositions than the same behaviour manifested by ingroup members. It is also consistent with the findings of Taylor and Jaggi (1974) and those of Duncan (1976). Therefore the following hypothesis was formulated.

Hypothesis 2. When members of a group perceive behaviour manifested by members of the other group as a norm violation, the attribution for this behaviour at which they will arrive is likely to be negative, i.e. they are more likely to attribute it to negative characteristics or bad motives of the outgroup than to transient states or environmental factors.

The explanation at which members of group B arrive determines their reaction towards group A members. When attributions are negative, i.e. malevolent intentions or negative characteristics of group A, negative reactions are likely to take place. When these reactions of group B members, in turn, constitute a norm violation in the view of group A members, they will try to explain it; and thus the sequence continues.

The relationship between attributions and reactions is specified in the following hypothesis.

Hypothesis 3. When members of a group attribute a norm violation by members of the other group to negative characteristics or bad motives of the other group, they are likely to react with negative behaviour towards (members of) the other group.

In summary, as depicted in Fig. 1.1, norm violation by group A is likely to lead to negative attributions by group B which, in turn, leads to negative behaviour of group B towards group A. When the latter constitutes a norm violation in the view of group A members, the sequence continues.

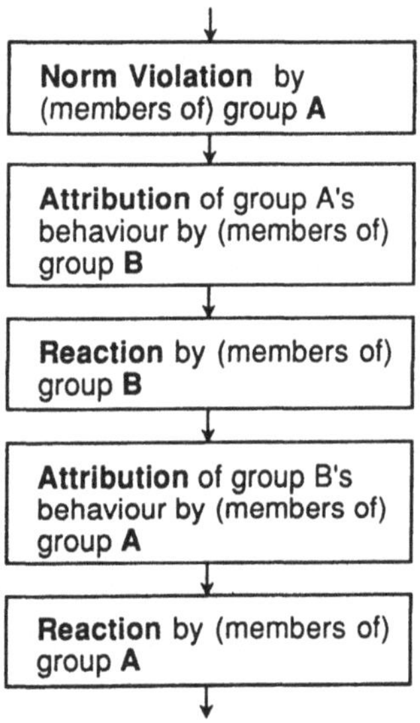

Figure 1.1 An elementary sequence

In terms of the Hindu–Muslim example (pp. 20–1), our analysis will start with the 'victim' group's perception of the norm-violating incident 'How serious an infraction will Muslims consider the pig inside their place of worship?' Next 'Who is to blame for it?' Once the Muslims consider the Hindus as being the causal agent with negative intentions ('They want to defile our holy place of prayers'), an escalating process of intergroup behaviour may be set in motion. Whether it escalates or not will depend on factors related to the Muslim community (such as the Muslims' identification with their own community and their feelings of relative deprivation), and on the Muslims' ideas about the proper ways of retaliation against the supposed agents of the incident, the Hindus.

Within the sequence of 'norm violation–attribution–reaction' depicted in Fig. 1.1, there are a number of ways in which an escalation or de-escalation of negative intergroup behaviour can be understood. The following conditions may lead to de-escalation.

1. Although group A violates the norm group B applies to them, it is not perceived as such by members of group B. In this case the cycle of attribution, reaction, etc. is not started.[4]
2. Group A's norm-violating action is not attributed to the bad character or negative motives of its members but to transient and/or environmental factors. In this case it is not likely that group B will give a negative (norm-violating) reaction.
3. Group B's reaction is not perceived as a norm violation by members of group A.

It can be argued that if neither of these conditions holds, an escalation of negative intergroup behaviour is likely to occur. For co-existing groups such an argument loses some of its validity. Such groups are embedded within an overall organization or society which is likely to set limits to a possible escalation of negative intergroup behaviour (Pospísil 1971; Deutsch 1973). Moreover, the groups involved will have learned from their past history that such an escalation is costly to both of them. Therefore, one can assume that co-existing groups would have developed norms, rules, and procedures to prevent such an escalation of negative intergroup behaviour. We will call them '*norms of redress*' because, in our view, the function of these norms is to maintain, restore or redress the intergroup relationship, to the way it existed *before* the norm violation occurred.

In situations where no norms of redress exist, or where these norms stipulate revenge or a 'tit for tat' reaction (e.g. Kuschel 1987), intergroup behaviour will escalate when none of the three conditions mentioned above are met.

Assumptions of the elementary framework The chain of events described is assumed to be applicable to intergroup behaviour only under certain conditions. First, the groups A and B mentioned can be considered as two separate parties. By this we mean that each of the groups has its own norms and goals. These goals may be circumscribed formally and/or may be highly specific (such as is often the case in formal organizations), or informal and vague (such as those of an ethnic group in a given society). What is minimally required is that members of each group desire to maintain a separate social entity. It is of course possible that members of one or both groups involved differ in the degree to which their own and/or the other group are recognized as separate parties. On the basis of earlier research it can be said that such a recognition depends on (i) the clarity or ease with which people can be defined as being a member of either the ingroup or outgroup (linguistic differentiators and labels play an important role in this respect); (ii) the permeability of the groups' boundaries; (iii) the degree of identification of individuals with their own group; (iv) the degree to which one of the two groups is threatened in their existence; (v) the extent of intergroup contact; etc. Second, it is assumed that members of each group come into contact (either directly or indirectly) with one another. By direct contact we mean that members of the ingroup and outgroup actually meet face to face. Indirect contact can take several forms, i.e. the means of contact may be more indirect (only non-verbal or in writing) or only the consequences of the other group's behaviour are felt. Third, it is also assumed that for the group which experiences norm violation by members of the other group, the other group is an important comparison group.

The first and the third of the preceding three statements, suggest that the application of norm violation theory intergroup behaviour postulates that for members of the two groups concerned the conditions relevant for social identity theory are fulfilled. Additionally, the assumption related to the contact between the two parties is a necessary condition for the study of relations between co-existing groups.

An elaborated framework It would be naïve to apply the elementary process described above to behaviour between members of existing groups without further specification. It would suggest, for instance, that once members of one of the groups start with a norm violation and no norms of redress exist, negative intergroup behaviour is likely to occur and thereafter will never stop. In reality, a number of factors—group identification, existing attitudes, perceived differences in power, and fraternal relative deprivation—is supposed to affect this sequence.

As the importance of these factors for intergroup relations has been treated in the previous section of this chapter, we shall here address only the effects of each of them on the elements of the elementary sequence.

Own group identification refers to the degree to which individuals identify themselves with the group to which they belong. Own group identification is expected to affect the likelihood that behaviour of group A members is (i) perceived as norm infringing; (ii) attributed to dispositions of group A; and (iii) retaliated.

Individuals with a strong group identification are likely to perceive many of the other group's behaviours which imply negative consequences for their own group as norm violations. This assertion echoes the accusation of 'discrimination', which minority members frequently make when they feel badly treated by members of the majority. It is further proposed that the stronger their identification will be, the more likely it is that such group members will commit what Pettigrew (1979) called the 'ultimate attribution error'. In other words, group members with a strong own group identification will attribute the other group's norm violation to negative dispositions of this group. Independent of the preceding, individuals with a strong identification with their own group are thought to react negatively to the outgroup because they will perceive the other group's norm violation as a possible threat to their own group's integrity.

The preceding statements are formulated in the following hypotheses.

Hypothesis 4. The more strongly individuals identify with their group, the more likely it is that they will perceive a behaviour of members of the outgroup, which has negative consequences for ingroup members, as norm infringing.

Hypothesis 5. The more strongly individuals identify with their group, the more likely it is that they will attribute a norm violation by members of the outgroup to negative characteristics and bad motives of the outgroup.

Hypothesis 6. The more strongly individuals identify with their group, the more likely it is that they will react negatively to a norm violation by members of the outgroup.

Intergroup attitudes refer to the total of positive and negative opinions members of each of the two groups hold about members of the outgroup. Such attitudes are supposed to influence the kind of attributions made about the outgroup's norm violation and reactions to this violation.

When negative attitudes towards the outgroup exist, the *a priori* probability of the group member's hypothesis that bad motives or negative characteristics of the other group inspired the occurrence of norm violation will be greater (cf. Greenberg and Rosenfield 1979). When positive attitudes exist, an attribution of outgroup norm violation to relatively transient states of the outgroup members or to environmental factors, is more likely. Therefore the following hypothesis is formulated.

Hypothesis 7. When members of a group hold negative attitudes towards the other group, they are more likely to ascribe a norm violation by members of that outgroup to negative characteristics and bad motives of the outgroup than when they hold positive outgroup attitudes.

A combination of this hypothesis and hypothesis 3 implies that attitudes will have an indirect influence on reactions to norm violation. A direct effect of attitudes on reactions is also expected.

Hypothesis 8. When members of a group hold negative attitudes towards the other group, they are more likely to react with negative behaviour towards (members of) the other group than when they hold positive outgroup attitudes.

Perceived power refers to the capacity groups have to exert influence or to control the other group's outcomes, in the view of the members of the groups involved. In the case of co-existing groups two general classes of power are distinguished. A first class, called *resource power*, refers to the social, economic and political means or resources each of the groups is perceived to possess by which they are able to exert influence. A second class is labelled *retaliation power*. This denotes all the means attributed to groups which enable them to become militant, organize themselves in violent or non-violent ways to resist the other group's influence attempts. For these two classes of power the following hypothesis is formulated.

Hypothesis 9. The greater is group B's perceived power advantage over another group A, the more negatively will group B members react to a norm violation by members of group A.

Fraternal relative deprivation refers to a sense of injustice and its accompanying feelings of dissatisfaction of resentment which members of a group have about the actual state of affairs of their group in comparison with that of the other group. This sense of injustice was shown to be related to negative attributions (Naqvi and Tripathi 1980) and is theoretically expected to lead to negative intergroup behaviour. This is formulated in the following two hypotheses.

Hypothesis 10. The more members of a group experience feelings of fraternal relative deprivation, the more they will attribute a norm violation by members of the other group to its negative characteristics and/or bad motives.

Hypothesis 11. The more members of a group experience feelings of fraternal relative deprivation, the more negatively will they react to a norm violation by members of the other group.

The effects of own group identification, intergroup attitudes, perceived power and fraternal relative deprivation spelled out in hypotheses 4–11 are summarized in Fig. 1.2.

In our Hindu–Muslim example, an escalating sequence is likely because Muslims in this particular town can be considered as having a strong and positive feeling about their own group and because they feel that such a serious norm violation should be properly revenged. It might also be the case that, knowing the Hindu–Muslim relationship in India (see Chapter 4), feelings of relative deprivation, power differences and intergroup attitudes influence the Muslim attributions and reactions.

Summarizing the effects of the factors mentioned on the elements of the elementary sequence, the following can be stated. Once one group starts with a norm violation, an escalation of negative intergroup behaviour is likely, when

(1) members of both groups strongly identify with their own group;
(2) negative intergroup attitudes exist;
(3) the perceived differences in power between the groups are small;
(4) members of the victim group feel their group suffers seriously from fraternal relative deprivation.

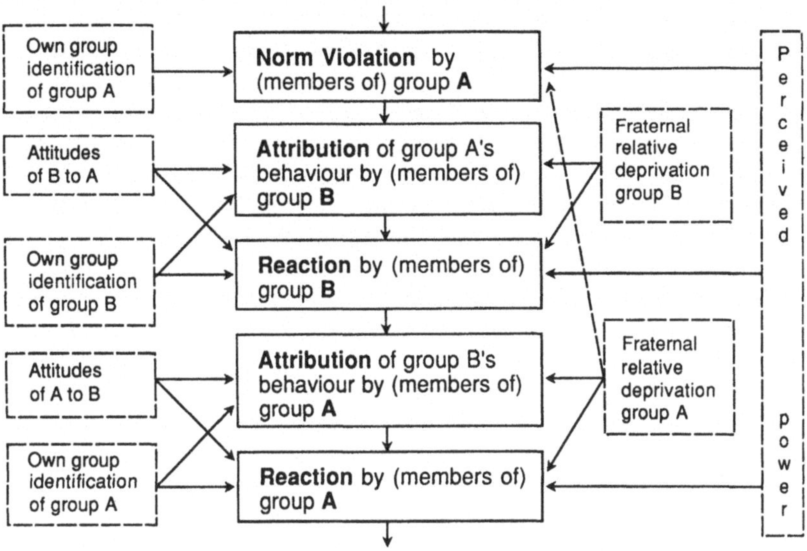

Figure 1.2 Norm violation theory: an elaborated framework

Such an escalation can be prevented, attenuated or turned into de-escalation of negative intergroup behaviour more easily, when

(1) the identification of members of the two groups with their own group is weak;

(2) positive intergroup attitudes exist;

(3) the perceived differences in power between the groups are large;

(4) members of the victim group do not suffer from fraternal relative deprivation.

As an additional factor the existence of norms of redress may again be mentioned. When such norms stipulate the use of constructive means to solve conflicts, an escalation of negative intergroup behaviour is less likely.

Apart from the direct effects of the four factors mentioned on the elementary sequence of norm violation, attribution, reaction, etc., many indirect and/or long-term effects of these factors can be imagined. Some of these will be mentioned briefly when we discuss the limitations of the present framework. Let us first turn to the empirical evidence collected thus far.

Empirical evidence

Some empirical evidence related to the preceding hypotheses can be mentioned. With respect to hypothesis 1, it was found that subjects, when asked, do make attributions about norm-violating behaviour by outgroup members (Taylor and Jaggi 1974; Duncan 1976; Sagar and Schofield 1980). The important question, however, is whether they would have done so when *not* being asked to explain the stimulus behaviour. People are likely to engage in attributional activity when a person exhibits unexpected behaviour, negative behaviour, or when an event takes place which is stressful, unknown, or important (Wong and Weiner 1981). We expect norm-violating behaviour to be negative and unexpected, although it might be the case that negative behaviour is more expected by an outgroup member than by an ingroup member, implying that more attributional behaviour is stimulated in the latter case.

Hypothesis 2 is supported by, for example, the results of Taylor and Jaggi (1974) and Duncan (1976). In The Netherlands a study has been conducted which measured explanations of norm-violating ingroup and outgroup behaviour with Dutch and Turkish high school students as subjects (Schruijer 1990*a*). The results indicated that both the Turkish and the Dutch subjects engaged in group-serving biases, though the former did so to a much larger extent. On some variables the Dutch even engaged in biases favouring the outgroup. It also appeared to be a phenomenon which is dependent on the importance of the norm and/or seriousness of the violation: when an unimportant norm was violated less ingroup and more outgroup biases were found in the Dutch subjects' responses as compared with their evaluations and explanations of a more serious norm violation.

Partial evidence for hypothesis 3 is found in a study we did in The Netherlands in which Dutch subjects were presented with a norm violation engaged in by an ingroup or an outgroup (Turkish) member (Schruijer 1989). The kind of attribution given by the victim was manipulated by presenting the explanation in the vignette. Results show that the kind of attribution presented was important in determining the subsequent reaction of the victim, as anticipated by the subjects.

Kerssemakers and DeRidder (1989) conducted a vignette study with Hindu and Muslim students. In this study the seriousness of norm violation and the mutual attitudes were manipulated. In support of hypothesis 7 it was found that more blame was attributed to the norm-violating group when negative attitudes existed than when positive attitudes prevailed. That study also provided some support for hypothesis 3 as significant correlations between attributed blame and negative intergroup behaviour were obtained. In the Schruijer study (1990*a*), it was found that those Dutch subjects who held a negative attitude towards the integration of Turks in Dutch society, engage in an ingroup bias in their attributions, whereas those with a positive attitude do not differentiate in their explanations between norm-violating behaviour by a Turkish or Dutch actor. Those with a positive attitude towards Turkish integration show an outgroup bias where subjects with a negative attitude do not differentiate between ingroup and outgroup. These results are supportive of hypothesis 7.

There is too little research available to draw firm conclusions about the relation between fraternal relative deprivation and negative intergroup behaviour (see the section on relative deprivation). The absence of the predicted effect of fraternal relative deprivation in the work of Tripathi and Ansari (1980) may be partly due to the stability of the existing power relations between the groups studied. It might be suggested that stable power relations decrease the chances of any future change and that therefore Muslims might well desire a change, and feel entitled to an improvement of their relative state, but have little hope that a change may come in the near future. As another reason it can be suggested that the effect of fraternal relative deprivation on negative intergroup behaviour is not direct. It is mediated by intergroup attitudes and attributions (hypothesis 10). Suggestions for such an indirect relation between fraternal relative deprivation and intergroup behaviour can be found in studies by Tripathi and Srivastava (1981) and Naqvi and Tripathi (1980). Tripathi and Srivastava found that Muslims with high fraternal relative deprivation entertained a more negative attitude towards Hindus than Muslims with low fraternal relative deprivation. Naqvi and Tripathi showed that Muslims with higher fraternal relative deprivation attributed greater blame to Hindus for communal riots. Also, Pettigrew's studies (Pettigrew 1964, 1967; Vanneman and Pettigrew 1972) provide evidence for a positive relation between fraternal and relative deprivation and negative intergroup attitudes. These studies on fraternal relative deprivation suggest a direct effect of feelings of fraternal relative deprivation on intergroup attitudes and attributions. To the extent that people have the idea that current power differences are changeable, that they feel angry and resentful against the powerful group, and that they blame this group for their own deprived state, fraternal relative deprivation will increase negative intergroup behaviour.

Norm violation theory in perspective: limitations and related approaches

Norm violation theory as presented in this chapter has some limitations and is related to some of the existing approaches to intergroup relations and aggression.

Limitations

The limitations of norm violation theory for intergroup behaviour pertain to (i) the kind of groups to which it applies, (ii) the kind of norm violations taken into account, (iii) the focus of the theory on negative intergroup behaviour, (iv) the factors included in the framework which are thought to affect the escalation and/or de-escalation of negative intergroup behaviour, and (v) the relative emphasis placed on processes between members belonging to two different groups. Each of these limitations deserves some explanation.

Norm violation theory is designed for a situation where members of two different groups come into contact with one another. Each of these groups is postulated to have goals and a set of norms which regulate intergroup behaviour. Situations involving more than two groups and those groups which do not have goals or norms are excluded. That is, many of the 'groups' studied from a social identity theory framework in a so-called minimal group paradigm fall outside the domain of the theory.

Norm violations can be of different kinds. Group members can deviate from a norm in a positive and in a negative direction. An example may help to clarify this. Suppose that a subordinate has promised to do something for his supervisor, then the subordinate may not do what he promised or do more than he promised. Both instances can be considered as norm violations, the first as a negative norm violation the second as a positive one. Only norm violations in the negative direction are considered in the discussion of the theoretical framework we presented, although in principle it seems possible to apply the framework to 'positive' norm violations as well.

The focus on negative intergroup behaviour constitutes a third limitation of the framework presented. Therefore, the theory does not qualify as a general theory of intergroup behaviour. This focus is based on the findings that norm violations appear to be important precipitating factors of negative intergroup behaviour, such as riots (Lieberson and Silverman 1965). It is our aim to present a social-psychological framework to understand under what conditions such norm violations lead or do not lead to negative intergroup behaviour.

The preceding focus implies that only those factors are included in our theoretical framework which, on the basis of previous theories and research, are likely to facilitate and/or mitigate the emergence of negative intergroup behaviour, namely own group identification, intergroup attitudes, feelings of fraternal relative deprivation and perceived power. Although these factors can be distinguished at a theoretical level they are probably related. For instance, the similarity between perceived power and fraternal relative deprivation is that both concepts start from a consideration of the position of one's own group in the domains of politics, economics and social matters. The difference between them is that for feelings of fraternal relative deprivation to occur, a sense of injustice or illegitimacy about the relative position of one's group compared with the other group is essential; for perceived power it is not. It seems implausible, however, that members who perceive their own group to have more power than the other group will feel fraternally deprived. Thus, both perceived power and fraternal relative deprivation are probably highly correlated in empirical research. Moreover, research, for example by Vanneman and Pettigrew (1972), suggests that feelings of fraternal relative deprivation lead to negative attitudes towards the relatively gratified group. A direct link between own group identification and attitudes towards the outgroup is suggested by research stemming from social identity theory. An extensive discussion of such relations is beyond the scope of the present chapter.

Although it cannot be considered as a limitation inherent to norm violation theory, we devoted only little attention to processes which take place within each of the groups concerned. We emphasized that existing groups hold norms which stipulate how members of the other group ought to behave towards them and about their behaviour towards members of the other group. What occurs within each group was only briefly mentioned. On the one hand it can be said that members of a group will try to validate the attributions they make about the outgroup's norm violation by communication with those of their own group. As it appears plausible that such validation efforts will only take place when people doubt why the norm violation occurred, and that in most instances group members' attributions about such violations are most frequently based on their a priori ideas of the outgroup, no need was felt to treat intragroup processes in the present chapter. On the other hand, we assumed that group members develop, on the basis of a history of past conflicts, norms of redress. Such norms can also emerge in experimentally created groups as Lodewijkx (1989) recently reported. He was able to show that the amount of retaliatory aggression depended on the dominant orientation towards the other group which emerged in the experimental groups he created. Lodewijkx based his research on the 'emergent norm approach' proposed by Turner and Killian (1972). They postulated that in groups—which may range from experimentally created groups to collective crowds—a norm emerges which encourages 'behavior consistent with the norm, inhibits behavior contrary to it, and justifies restraining action against individuals to dissent' (Turner and Killian 1972, p. 22). An integration of processes of communication and/or norm development occurring within groups appears possible. This leads us to the more general point of the relationship of norm violation theory and the existing approaches of intergroup behaviour.

Related approaches to intergroup behaviour

The proposed theoretical framework contains some of the elements of previous theories on intergroup relations and on aggressive behaviour.

It shares with Sherif's realistic conflict theory a focus on individuals who belong to groups that have goals and norms. However, norm violation theory does not focus on incompatibility of goal achievement as a causal factor for negative intergroup behaviour. Such incompatibility is from our perspective not viewed as a necessary condition for negative intergroup behaviour. In contrast to Sherif and social identity theory, norm violation theory focuses on the conditions which precipitate such negative intergroup behaviour between co-existing groups. Membership of such groups is clearly recognized by individuals belonging to the ingroup and outgroup and, therefore, factors and processes indicated by social identity theory, such as the choice of comparison group, the salience of intergroup differences, and the boundaries between the two groups, form the boundary conditions of the framework presented. For this reason, the individuals' identification with their own group was incorporated in the framework as an important factor. While both the realistic conflict and social identity theories consider attitudes, they figure in these theories only as dependent variables. In consonance with general social psychological theories, attitudes occupy a more predominant place in the proposed framework as independent variables.

In addition to the elements norm violation theory shares with realistic conflict and social identity theories, it considers power and fraternal relative deprivation as important for intergroup relations. Inequality of power between groups forms an essential reality for co-existing groups (Apfelbaum 1979; Ng 1980). Fraternal relative deprivation suggests that a sense of injustice adds to this power inequality, feelings of resentment and anger.

Anger has been a central concept in aggression theories (cf. Zillmann 1979). In fact, as mentioned earlier, the framework proposed originates from a recent tradition in aggression research. While the central sequence of the elementary model (Fig. 1.1) is taken from DeRidder (1980, 1983), similar approaches have been suggested (e.g. Pepitone 1981; Mummendey *et al.* 1984*b*). The main difference between the approaches studying the relationship between norm violations and aggression, and our framework, is that studies based on aggression focus on two individuals only. The only exceptions are studies by Rabbie and his colleagues on norm violation and intergroup aggression (e.g. Rabbie and Lodwijkx 1986; Lodewijkx 1989). As we have argued earlier, the central idea of this approach, 'emergent intragroup norms', can be easily integrated into our framework.

It may be noted that parts of norm violation theory bear resemblance to treatments of conflicts in primitive societies which cultural anthropologists have described (e.g. Evans-Pritchard 1940; Gluckman 1963). Our point of departure, norm violation as a triggering factor, and our assumption of the existence of certain 'norms of redress', indeed, are ideas which can be found in the anthropological literature. Beals *et al.* (1977), for instance, acknowledge that among many peoples 'repeated violations of behavioral standards are considered symptomatic of deadly and malevolent intent' (p. 446). These authors also expect that for violations of important consequence to the entire group 'various appropriate actions that will be taken when they are violated [will be enunciated]' (Beals *et al.* 1977, p. 459). This point will be elaborated further in Chapter 8.

Concluding comments

The approach advocated in this chapter is thought to be more adequate than the previous social psychological theories of intergroup behaviour because it takes into account the historical and dynamic nature of intergroup relations. It is also applicable to different intergroup contrasts (ethnic groups, organizational groups, etc.) in a range of different situations.

It is, moreover, expected that the dynamics as represented in the model and the effect of the group contrast factors on reactions to norm violations by (members of) another group and norms of redress are similar across different cultures.

The main purpose of the studies in this book is to check the plausibility of some of the preceding assertions. A fair amount of empirical evidence already exists for the hypotheses predicting relationships between norm violation, attitudes and relative deprivation on the one hand and attributions on the other (see Schruijer 1990*a*). Also, we have obtained some support for the relationship between attributions and reactions. Therefore, we decided to devote most of our research to studying reactions to norm violations by the own group and by the other group, as well as to the influence of fraternal relative deprivation, power, own group identification, and intergroup attitudes on these reactions. It appeared especially relevant to us to study the relative impact of the four factors on reactions to norm violations in different groups and cultures. Moreover, we wanted to find out whether general norms of redress exist among co-existing groups. The studies reported here will indicate the plausibility of our theoretical framework.

Notes

[1] Thanks are due to Sik Hung Ng and Ad Van Knippenberg for helpful comments on a previous draft of this chapter.

[2] For an extensive review of the social attribution literature the reader is referred to Schruijer (1990*a*).

[3] Parts of this section are taken from DeRidder (1983).

[4] This point can be further elaborated in two directions. First, the possibility exists that from the viewpoint of group A or a third party, group A's behaviour constitutes a violation of a norm they think that group B attributes to them, but this attributed norm is not shared by members of group B. Therefore, from group B's perspective, group A's behaviour is not a norm infraction. Second, it may be either that group A's behaviour does constitute a violation of a norm group B applies to group A but the violation is not noticed by members of group B, or group A's behaviour is noticed but members of group B disagree among one another whether it must be evaluated as a norm violation or not.

2 Methodological concerns, choice of groups and instruments

Ype H. Poortinga, and Jai B. P. Sinha

To investigate the framework described in Chapter 1 four major studies were carried out, two in India and two in The Netherlands, as well as three smaller scale projects on norms of retaliation (Chapter 8). In this chapter the research methods are described, as far as they were common to the four main studies (Chapters 3–6). First we pay attention to methodological concerns. Then we discuss the selection of the pairs of groups from which subjects were recruited. In the last section we present the various instruments that were used.

Methodological concerns

In a cross-cultural study the ideal is to use instruments that give strictly comparable or equivalent results. This implies that scores of an equal value obtained in culturally different groups have the same meaning in terms of the psychological characteristics inferred from the scores. There is substantial evidence, particularly from the domain of cognitive tests, that for groups culturally as far apart as the Indians and the Dutch, this ideal of comparable scores is unrealistic (e.g. Poortinga and Malpass 1986). This means that a direct comparison between the scores of subjects in India and The Netherlands had to be avoided.

Such a direct comparison is not necessary to meet the objectives formulated in Chapter 1. There are two main questions:

(1) whether the framework has explanatory value for group contrasts in different societies;

(2) whether there are differences across groups and societies in the relationships between the various components in the framework.

An affirmative answer to the first question requires a valid measurement of each of the components in the framework. A minimal requirement is that the observed direction of the postulated relationships (positive or negative) is in accordance with the predicted direction.

An answer to the second question implies that differences in relationships between corresponding variables can be meaningfully interpreted. This means that we can explain why a correlation has a higher (or lower) value in India than in The Netherlands. In this case one still does not need a direct comparison across studies of scores on separate variables.

However, requirements for psychometric equivalence are more stringent than for the first question, because we have to assume that the different values of correlations are not due to some bias in the procedures and instruments. (For a review of scale properties of variables needed for various forms of comparison, see for example Van de Vijver and Poortinga 1982; Poortinga 1989.)

Strictly speaking, an answer to the two questions does not require identity in the form and item content of instruments across studies. One can meaningfully predict equal correlations between variables in the framework even when different instruments are used cross-culturally. Therefore, the first requirement was that the items and the task format had to be suitable for each subject group, both according to the opinion of the (local) researchers, and in terms of the results of preliminary investigations. This led to various deviations from the common format. In Chapters 3–6 which deal with the four main studies of the project the reasons for these deviations will be given.

However, when an unpredicted difference in correlations is observed there are in principle two interpretations, namely that this difference is reflecting a valid difference in the pattern of relationships between variables, or that it reflects a difference between measurement procedures. In other words, there is uncertainty whether (unpredicted) cross-cultural differences in relationships between variables are valid or due to instrument and procedure artefacts. Therefore, we considered it important that measurement procedures across group contrasts and cultures were as closely matched as possible in terms of administration procedures, item format and item content. For this reason the construction of instruments was discussed extensively in joint meetings between Indian and Dutch project participants.

Group contrasts

Because groups within a society can be differentiated in terms of a large number of criteria, the choice of groups was a difficult issue. Most interesting seemed the distinctions between groups which permeate into all aspects of social behaviour. However, the interpretation of results is more difficult as a larger number of plausible reasons which can account for observed differences is available.

In order to make the analysis of intergroup relations in India and The Netherlands more meaningful, we decided to study two pairs of groups. We tried to find pairs for which the determinants of their interrelations were quite different. We also tried to identify group contrasts that are found in The Netherlands as well as in India. It turned out that the matching of pairs in the two countries on the basis of similar threats to positive interrelationships was only partly possible. Numerous other arguments were considered in the choice of a specific pair of contrasting groups, but societal relevance was the most important criterion in the end. The main issues and the groups for which we chose were the following:

1. *Differences in hierarchy*. Both in India and The Netherlands this issue is relevant for the relations between labour and management in industry, although it was exected that in India the polarization between the two groups might be stronger (Hofstede 1980). It can be argued that the relationships in the industrial organization as a behaviour setting are more similar cross-culturally than for any other major group contrast (Child, 1981).

2. *Different ethnic groups in a society*. In The Netherlands this issue is represented by the relationship between immigrants from the Mediterranean countries and the Dutch autochthonous population. Among the various migrant groups, subjects of Turkish origin were chosen. In India the Muslim–Hindu contrast is the most obvious choice. In both cases the two groups in the pair differ in religion, and in economic and political representation. There are few confusions about identity and the boundaries betwen groups are fairly impermeable. Moreover, each of the two contrasts is among the strongest in its national society.

Subjects within groups

As indicated, the criteria for group membership in the case of Hindus and Muslims as well as in the case of migrants from Turkey and autochthonous Dutch were not a major point of concern. Self-identification, that is the recognition of subjects that they belong to a particular group, was almost the sole criterion.

The distinction between workers and managers turned out to be more diffuse, particularly in The Netherlands. The two studies on this contrast differed, in the sense that in India subjects were recruited from one organization (a mining company). The participants were identified primarily by qualifications in their work environment (i.e. someone works in a supervisory capacity if the name of his function so indicates). In the Dutch study employees from different companies and organizations participated. By means of a set of scales, completed by the subject, the status of supervisor or subordinate was assessed.

Instruments

The framework developed in Chapter 1 required measurements of the following variables: reactions to norm violations, own group identification, intergroup attitudes, differences in perceived power, and fraternal relative deprivation.

Some [X] youth throw stones at the cultural and religious centres of the [Y]. How will the [Y] react?

1 Complain to the parents of the [X] youth (R−)
2 Pay no attention to it (R0)
3 Riot against the [X] (R≡)
4 Forgive the [X] youngsters and tell them to show more respect for the religion of others (R+)
5 Throw stones at the religious and cultural centres of the [X] (R=)

Figure 2.1 An example of an item in the Norm Violation Inventory. The same item but with [X] and [Y] reversed was also presented to all subjects in a group contrast. The 5 levels of retaliation are indicated in brackets.

Norm violation inventory

For the assessment of reactions to norm violations a questionnaire was used. Each item in this questionnaire contained a brief description of a norm violation. An example of an item is given in Fig. 2.1. Each item was presented to a subject in two versions, one version with members of group A (own group) as actors and members of group B (a specified other group) as victims, and the other version with group membership of actors and victims reversed.

The formulation of each item had the following format: 'members (a member) of group A engage in a certain behaviour (or omit to carry out a behaviour) towards members of group B'. From the context it was obvious that the actor was aware, or at least should have been aware, of the norm-violating character of the action (or omission). It was also implied that A's action had negative consequences for members of group B, although this was not always stated explicitly. The items merely described a behaviour, reference was made neither to possible causes of the action (circumstances, intentions, motives), nor to previous events. An item stem such as 'members of A shouted at a member of B, *because* they had been offended *previously*' would have been unacceptable for both reasons.

The situation descriptions in the items were phrased (with a few exceptions) in a single sentence. They were of an intermediate level of generalty, referring to concrete events in real life (cf. Cantor 1981; Van Heck 1989). The items did not refer to abstract principles and concepts. Such items tend to solicit reactions how one ought to behave on the basis of normative principles and values. The items also did not refer to a single historical occasion. The latter restriction implies that situations have been avoided that were likely to be associated by the subjects with a specific event that happened in the past.

With each item the subject was given five response alternatives from which the reaction had to be chosen which the respondent considered the most likely reaction by the victims.[1] Since each item was presented in two versions the subjects gave the expected reaction of their own group as well as the reaction they anticipated on the part of the other group. Many of the responses were specific to the kind of situation on which the item stem was based. All response alternatives matched the seriousness of the offence in the item stem. This means that in principle the same behaviour could have a weak negative meaning in one item but a strong negative meaning in the case of another item. For example, scolding someone for not greeting you is rather strong compared with scolding someone for endangering your life. Nevertheless, a common scale for all items was constructed. The alternatives were chosen for each item to form a five-point response scale with the following steps:

(1) a (mildly) positive reaction, reconciliatory, covering up, etc.;
(2) no reaction, shrug one's shoulders, etc.;
(3) a mildly negative retaliation;
(4) retribution as strong as the preceding norm violation, 'tit for tat' retaliation, an eye for an eye;
(5) strongly negative retaliation.

In comparison with the previous norm violation the last three response alternatives were respectively less, equally, and more serious or negative. In later chapters we shall refer to the five scale points as R+, R0; R−, R=, and R≡ respectively.

The alternatives for the two versions of an item usually differed only in the group identity of actors and victims (i.e. the names of the groups A and B were reversed). Changes in the stem or response alternatives were made when a mere reversal of actor and victim led to an unrealistic item. For example, in the relationship between labour and management there are actions that someone in the position of a subordinate cannot or is unlikely to engage in, but that are not unusual for someone in a position of leadership and control (cf. Chapter 5).

Ample consideration was given to the selection of items. It was impossible to construct an instrument that represented all facets of real life. A general taxonomy of socially relevant situations was not available. It was decided to select three domains and to vary the seriousness of norm violations over items within each domain.[2] The three domains each covered an important aspect of direct and indirect contact between people belonging to different groups in a society. They have been labelled, social contacts, institutional contacts, and social responsibility.

The term *social contacts* refers to interactions between members of different groups in which the actors engage in a private capacity. Positive contacts in this sphere require at least a certain degree of respect for and acceptance of the partners in the interaction. An overt sign of disrespect (which implies an infringement of the social status of the others), constitutes a norm violation. Disrespect can be shown to members of another group as persons (e.g. verbal abuse), but also to their property or to institutions and symbols they value.

With the term *institutional contacts* we refer to interactions that take place between members of different groups in organizational settings. The clearest example of such a setting is the work place. Other settings include societal institutions, such as meetings of community councils, sports matches, and the public transport system where passengers belonging to different social groups are bound to be present. Norm violations amount to infringements on rights and privileges which persons in a certain capacity are entitled to. These rights can be the result of formal agreements, but more often they are based on historically grown modes of interaction.

The third domain, *social responsibility*, is based on a notion of concern for all members of a society; it refers to interests not only superordinate to the individual, but also to the own group. A norm violation occurs when some person or group unduly profits from common resources and facilities. The infringements in this area can range from (alleged) minor forms of misuse of resources to downright criminal acts.[3]

It was stipulated that the design of the norm violation inventory for assessing expected reactions to norm violations should meet the following demands. The scale was to consist of a minimum of 18 items, six for each of the domains of social contacts, institutional contacts, and social responsibility. Each item was to be presented in two versions, with the own group and other group as victim. Thus, the number of reactions per subject was $18 \times 2 = 36$. It may be noted that more extensive instruments, up to 36 items, were used in some studies (see Chapter 3).

Scale scores were obtained by the addition of item scores. Strictly speaking, this requires that in each item response scale (i) the order of the alternatives and (ii) the distance between pairs of successive alternatives, are the same for all subjects for whom the scores are compared. The seriousness of the norm violations described differed considerably over items and for this reason the wording of the various reaction alternatives had to be matched to the item stem. However, this did not prevent us from specifying for each item a response scale that had conceptually the same five points on a dimension from positive to strongly negative reactions. Through a pilot study we investigated the requirement that the relative seriousness of the five alternatives in each item response scale was similar in the case of samples with different cultural backgrounds (i.e. the samples of Turkish migrants and Dutch subjects reported in Chapter 3, Schruijer and DeRidder 1988).

Finally, it should be noted that the present operationalization implies a modification of the framework in Chapter 1, where reactions of victims are emphasized. With the present procedure we asked for *expected* reactions by the victim group. Also the cyclic character of the framework, indicating a continuing action and reaction sequence, is not studied in

Responses by group X	Responses by group Y	
own group	own group	X (own) versus Y (own)
other group	other group	X (other) versus Y (other)
X (own versus other)	Y (own versus other)	X (own) versus Y (other) and other diagonal comparison

Figure 2.2 Comparisons (underlined) that can be made on the basis of the scores of variables in the Norm Violation Inventory.

this way. However, subjects from both groups were asked for expected reactions for both own group and other group. The primary purpose of the project, namely to study relations between groups, appeared to be well served by this design which allows comparisons between own group and anticipated other group reactions as illustrated in Fig. 2.2

Scale for own group identification

Own group identification was conceptualized as the degree to which individuals identify themselves with the group to which they belong. There are few existing measures for this concept. Earlier work by Tripathi and Srivastava (1981) formed the basis for the procedure used in the present project. Subjects were required to give ratings for adjectives (a number of approximately 30 was specified in the design). Part of the items were selected along the dimensions mentioned by Wish *et al.* (1976). In the various studies other items were added that appeared important for the intergroup context concerned on the basis of earlier research or pilot studies.

This checklist was administered four times. During the first administration the subject was asked to indicate for each item to what extent it was applicable to himself, the second time the applicability of the item to the own group was rated, the third time the applicability of the item to the other group, and the last time the subject indicated to what extent he saw it as desirable or undesirable to be described in terms of each of the adjectives. In all four administrations the response scale for each item had five points (not at all, a little, quite a bit, much, very much). This was not the case in the study on the labour–management contrast in India, where a dichotomous item response scale was used (cf. Chapter 5). The item scale points were given values from 1 to 5. Items with a desirability rating of less than 2.5 were reversed.

Own group identification was operationalized as the difference between the applicability ratings of an item for oneself and for one's own group. The score of a subject was the average of the absolute differences calculated over the adjectives in the scale.

Scale for attitudes towards the other group and own group

Following Fishbein and Ajzen (1975), other group attitude was defined as the beliefs members of each group hold about some other group, taking into account the positive or negative evaluation of each belief. An index for attitude towards the other group in a pair was also derived from the ratings on the adjectives, after reversal of the items with low desirability ratings. This attitude score was based on the ratings for the other group. The scale score for each subject was the average of all item scores (or part of the items in the case of scores for subscales).

Parallel to other group attitude, own group attitude can be defined as the beliefs members of a group hold about their own group. The ratings on the applicability of each item to the own group were seen as a measurement of this attitude. The scores are computed in the same way as for other group attitude.

Scale for perceived power

In Chapter 1 it was argued that power is a relative concept. Each of two groups to some extent can exert influence on the other and control the other party's outcomes. A distinction was made between resource power and retaliatory power. Power differences as they are perceived by social groups are seen as an important determinant of the readiness to engage in (re)actions that may lead to (further) retaliations by another group. In the items of this scale subjects were asked to indicate to what extent the own group had the power to influence the interests of the other group, and vice versa.

The items referred to three types of resources: political, economic, and social power. The meaning of these terms was described to the subject prior to the completion of the items concerned. Political power was described as the 'power to impose and implement rules and decisions', economic power as the 'power to decide on the distribution of money and jobs', and social power as 'possession of social status, authority, and influential relations'. Power to retaliate was assessed by questions concerning the scope for members of one group to make life miserable for the other group, and the preparedness to bring sacrifices for the ideals of one's own group, if these were threatened by the other group. An example of an item, including the kind of response scale that was used is given in Fig. 2.3. The scale consisted of pairs of items, one asking for relative power of group A over group B and the other asking for the power of group B over group A.

Internal consistency analyses were performed for the resource and retaliatory power scales in the main studies (Chapters 3–6). In Chapter 7 an overall power score for each individual subject was calculated by averaging item scores, after the deletion of items which were found to be unreliable.

Political power

(power to impose and implement rules and decisions)

To what extent does [X] have political power that can be used to affect the interests of [Y]?

very little	little	somewhat	much	very much
____	____	____	____	____

Figure 2.3 Example of an item for Perceived Power.

Scale for fraternal relative deprivation

The scale was based on the conceptualization of fraternal relative deprivation by Runciman (1966). A distinction was made between the economic, political, and social domains.

In the format of the items and the response scale we followed Tripathi and his associates (Naqvi and Tripathi 1980; Tripathi and Ansari 1980; Tripathi and Srivastava 1981). Items were constructed in which the relative position of the own group and the other group were compared. An example of an item is given in Fig. 2.4. The example shows that the perceived position of the own group (X) had to be compared with that of the contrast group (Y). The subject marked his response for each item on a five-point scale in the form of a ladder that was the same for all items. There were three composite questions referring to the economic, political, and social spheres. In each question there were at least two items, respectively asking for the present position and for the satisfaction of the subject with this position. In some studies (Chapters 3 and 4) subjects also rated their expected future position. Each item asked for an

At what level are Turkish migrants in The Netherlands located as far as their economic position is concerned?

Compared to the Dutch, the Turks are placed:

much higher

somewhat higher

at the same level

somewhat lower

much lower

Figure 2.4 Example of an item in a Fraternal Relative Deprivation scale.

absolute judgement on a five-point scale (from very low to very high), also presented in the form of a ladder.

For the scoring, scale points were given values from 1 (much higher) to 5 (much lower) with 3 indicating equality. Scale scores were computed in the same way as for the perceived power scales.

To conclude this chapter we would like to emphasize that the four main studies, two conducted in India and two in The Netherlands, had a common design. Conceptually the same variables were measured; there were only minor differences in the measurement procedures.

Notes

[1] In some studies not only the most likely, but also the least likely expected reaction had to be selected. These results are not described in this monograph.
[2] As a criterion for evaluating which norms are important we used a classification put forward by Mischel (1973) as a first approximation. He made a distinction between *powerful* situation, which will evoke similar reactions among all the individuals within a group, and *weak* situations which lead to divergent reactions. The powerful situations can be seen as situations in which norms clearly prescribe and/or proscribe behaviour. Weak situations are those in which individuals apparently can choose their own course of action without social sanctions. We elaborated somewhat on this scheme and used it in the selection of items. Because of overlap with the dimension of seriousness of norm violations the scheme was abandoned early in the analysis and will not be reported further.
[3] In this monograph we shall not concern ourselves with differences in results between domains. In a separate paper this is done for the contrast between Turkish migrants and Dutch subjects (Poortinga *et al.* 1990). The description of the domains has been included to make clear how the concept of norm violations was operationalized.

PART II

Empirical studies

3 On what happens when Dutchmen and Turks violate each other's norms: a perfect match of mutual expectations?

Sandra G. L. Schruijer

Introduction

The Netherlands is inhabited by many ethnic minorities (Schumacher 1987). The biggest group of non-Dutch allochthones is the Turks: their number is about 160 000 (CBS 1986), which is slightly more than 1 per cent of the Dutch population. The present chapter reports a study investigating the relationship between these Turks and autochthonous Dutch. Before reporting the actual study, which is conducted within the framework presented in Chapter 1, the historical and sociological context of the relationship between Turks and Dutch in The Netherlands is presented.

Turkish immigration: a historical overview

The Turks, like many others from the Mediterranean countries, came to The Netherlands in the sixties mostly for economic reasons. The Dutch economy needed unskilled labourers, whereas unemployment existed in the Mediterranean countries. Moreover, the education level of the Dutch had risen making them unwilling to do unskilled, unpleasant work. In 1964 a contract was signed by Turkey and The Netherlands, which resulted in the recruitment of Turkish men between the age of 25 and 30, mainly coming from rural areas (66 per cent compared with 33 per cent from urbanized areas, according to Wentholt (1982)). The intention of the Turkish men was to work for a few years, earn money, and subsequently return to their families in Turkey. It became clear, however, that the presence of the migrants was permanent. They had no money to return and settle in their country. This was due to large-scale unemployment and less than expected savings, caused by the economic recession. Recruitment of the Turks stopped in 1975. The population of migrants, however, still grew, because of family reunion in The Netherlands and also because of a relatively high birth rate. The growth in population has now more or less stabilized.

Thirty-four per cent of the Turks live in the four biggest cities of The Netherlands (Amsterdam, Rotterdam, Utrecht and The Hague), as compared with only 14 per cent of the Dutch (CBS 1986). Their living conditions are poor (Van Praag 1981). They inhabit the old neighbourhoods near the centre, where housing is bad and relatively cramped. Several families generally live together. This situation is mainly due to their low income, as well as to their motive to save as much money as possible for their families back home.

Education, (un)employment, and family life of Turkish immigrants

The level of education of the Turkish immigrants is low: 63 per cent have obtained a maximum of 5 years of formal education (Wentholt 1982) and only 75 per cent received primary school education (Woonsituatie 1982). This low level of education decreases their chances on the labour market. Moreover, language is a big problem. Their mastery of Dutch is generally poor. Several factors are responsible for this state of affairs: (i) the low level of education, (ii) illiteracy, (iii) their jobs, which require little communication, (iv) social isolation, (v) lack of motivation, and (vi) difficulty of the Dutch language. The second-generation Turks have a much better mastery of the Dutch language. The employment situation of the Turks is related to their level of education. The unemployment among Turks is high: approximately 40 per cent of the Turkish working population is unemployed (Ministerie van Binnenlandse Zaken 1987), compared with 14 per cent of the autochthonous Dutch working population. Turkish entrepreneurship is emerging (butchers, teahouses and coffeehouses, small companies), although it is still not very flourishing (Schumacher 1987). Eighty-five per cent of the employed Turks do unskilled or semi-skilled work (Penninx 1988) in industry. Their formal position is lower in comparison with autochthones, mainly owing to the level of education, age and years of service (Brassé, *et al.* 1986). These authors report problems in the interaction between allochthones and autochthones at the work place. The Turks are strongly under-represented in governmental jobs. If they are to be found, they belong to the lower levels of organizations (Penninx 1988). Apart from the problems mentioned above, the Turks experience family problems as a result of the different norms and values of Dutch society. Turkish women who keep on living according to Turkish cultural norms find themselves in a very isolated position. However, if they take over a Western attitude they come into conflict with their husbands. The second-generation Turks are also in a problematic situation (Eppink 1981). While at school and with friends they are expected to and reinforced to behave in a Dutch way; at home they are raised according to Turkish norms and traditions.

Turks and Dutch: discrimination and integration

In the sixties the Turks were generally welcomed by the Dutch. They were needed by the Dutch economy to do work which the Dutch did not want to do themselves. More than the minimally required interaction between the Turks and the Dutch hardly ever existed. The Turks remained socially isolated from the Dutch. Furthermore, the number of Turks was then relatively small. The recession caused a larger interdependence between the groups, albeit a negative one. Competition was perceived to exist on the labour and housing markets and within education. The initially tolerant and disinterested attitude of the Dutch changed into a rejecting and negative one. Several sources report that discrimination against Turks and other ethnic minorities increased (Bovenkerk 1978; Dubbelman 1984; Walraff 1985; Schumacher 1987; Gruisen *et al.* 1987). Although Lucassen and Penninx (1985) assert that, apart from some incidents, the discrimination is hardly expressed by verbal or physical aggression, newspapers as well as other sources regularly report occurrences of verbal and physical violence. The political climate for foreigners seems to be deteriorating, as indicated by the recent popularity of extreme right-wing political parties.

Because of the many problems mentioned above, it appears that integration will not be achieved soon. Economic development plays a critical role in whether and how soon integration is realized. As yet, the labour market perspectives are grim, and the educational level of the Turks is low. Moreover, many still express the wish to remigrate although a very low percentage of Turks actually does so (Penninx 1985). Until 1979 no explicit policy had been formulated concerning the Mediterranean immigrants because it was assumed that their stay was temporary and therefore only limited facilities for receiving and supporting them were needed. Since 1979 more fundamental attention has been devoted to problems related to immigration, reflected in explicit governmental policy with respect to immigration (for a discussion see Penninx 1983, 1985; Entzinger 1984).

Predictions

In line with the overall predictions of norm violation theory, we expect that Turks will generally react negatively to Dutch norm-violating behaviour. These reactions will be more negative, the more power they feel they have over the Dutch; the more negative their attitude towards the Dutch, the stronger their identification with their own group and the more they feel relatively deprived. The overview of the Turkish–Dutch relationship given above shows that Turks will most probably experience a lack of power and will feel relatively deprived. From several sources one can infer that their identity, at least for some subgroups, is quite strong (e.g. Vermeulen 1985), strengthened by a gain in political influence (which is still very small indeed and only at a municipal level) and by increasing organization of the Turks (e.g. Topragin and Van Baardewijk 1987). Very little is known concerning the Turkish attitude towards the Dutch. So, two factors clearly contribute to a prediction of negative reactions (relative deprivation, own group identification), yet one factor would predict an inhibition of norm-violating reactions (lack of power). Since we have little information concerning the relative importance of the four factors, we cannot give precise hypotheses on this issue.

The Dutch will in general engage in negative reactions towards Turkish norm-violating behaviour. And, as our model predicts, they will do so more strongly, the more power they perceive they have over the Turks, the less they experience feelings of relative deprivation, the more negative the other group attitude, and the stronger their own group identification. We expect the Dutch to feel powerful over the Turks and to have a negative attitude towards them. On the other hand, the Dutch will feel non-deprived or relatively gratified. It is to be explored how strongly the Dutch identify with their own group. It is therefore not possible to predict accurately how negative the reactions of the Dutch will be to Turkish norm-violating behaviour.

Method

Instruments

Norm violation inventory The norm violation inventory consisted of 36 descriptions of hypothetical situations (see Appendix 3.1). These situations were selected from an initial pool of 69 situations. The selection was based on the judgments of 14 Turkish informants (persons who, because of their profession, status, knowledge, activities or otherwise, have insight into the culture of their own group) and 29 Dutch informants who evaluated the situations, in which an other group actor violated a norm towards an own group victim, on a number of characteristics. They judged which percentage of their group would consider the behaviour depicted as norm infringing; to what extent the actor would be considered as being aware of the fact that he had violated a norm; whether the actor's behaviour would be interpreted as having been caused internally or externally. Moreover, the informants indicated how they thought members of their own group would react. Each situation was evaluated by at least three Turkish informants and three Dutch informants. The following situations were excluded from the final questionnaire: situations which were considered as implausible or unrealistic by the Turkish and/or Dutch respondents; situations in which the actor's norm-violating behaviour was attributed to external factors by both the Turkish and Dutch respondents: situations which were not considered to be norm violating. The 36 remaining situations were equally sampled from the three domains involving social contacts, institutional contacts and social responsibility (see Chapter 2). Each situation of the norm violation inventory was presented in two versions: in one version an other group actor violates a norm towards an own group victim; in the other version an own group actor violates the same norm, to the same extent and in identical circumstances, towards an other group victim. For each situation five response alternatives were provided, describing possible actions of a member of the victim group. These five response alternatives formed the following scale:

(1) positive action, R+ (e.g. conciliatory actions, talk it out, negotiating in order to improve the situation);

(2) no action, R0 (e.g. ignoring the situation, leaving the field);

(3) retribution of a lesser intensity than the original norm violation;

(4) retribution at the same level, R= (an eye for an eye);

(5) retribution at a higher intensity, R≡.

A second pilot-study showed that these five response alternatives could be treated as forming a five-point scale ranging from very appropriate (R+) to very inappropriate (R≡) (see Schruijer and DeRidder 1988, and Chapter 8).

The same response alternatives were used in both versions; only the group membership of actor and victim was changed. The following is an example.

A Dutch shopkeeper refuses to sell to Turkish clients. How does a Turk react?

a. Invite the Dutch shopkeeper to a Turkish cultural event in order to get better acquainted.
b. Go shopping elsewhere.
c. Stand in front of the shop with a banner stating that this shop discriminates.
d. Smash the windows of the shop.
e. Organize a boycott of the shop so that sales are nil.

A Turkish shopkeeper refuses to sell to Dutch clients. How does a Dutchman react?

a. Invite the Turkish shopkeeper to a Dutch cultural event in order to get better acquainted.
b. Go shopping elsewhere.
c. Stand in front of the shop with a banner stating that this shop discriminates.
d. Smash the windows of the shop.
e. Organize a boycott of the shop so that sales are nil.

Both versions appeared on the same page of the norm violation inventory. Which version had to be responded to first was determined by chance. Also, the order of reaction alternatives to be presented was randomly determined. The same order was used for both versions. Eight different versions of the norm violation inventory were created, each containing the 36 situations in a different, randomly determined order. All situations were formulated such that *one* group member violated a norm towards *one* other group victim (in some of the social responsibility situations, society at large was the victim).

These 36 situations were the input for computing an overall own group reaction and an overall anticipated other group reaction. The α coefficient for own group reaction of the Turks was 0.70 (n = 97), and of the Dutch 0.83 (n = 118). The α coefficients for anticipated other group reaction were 0.77 for the Turks (n = 96) and 0.84 for the Dutch (n = 113). For the Turks the α values are acceptable and they can be considered good in case of the Dutch.

Own group identification A list consisting of 25 adjectives was administered to each subject three times. During the first administration the subject indicated for each adjective the extent to which it was applicable to himself; the second time the applicability of each adjective to members of the other group was rated. During the third administration, the subject indicated the applicability of each adjective to members of the own group. Five response alternatives were provided: not at all applicable, somewhat, quite a bit, much, very much.

Of the 25 adjectives presented, 15 were considered to cover the most important dimensions of relations between people (Wish *et al.* 1976). These were: impulsive, helpful, aggressive, tolerant, intelligent, egotistic, friendly, lazy, authoritarian, arrogant, honest, polite, quarrelsome, corrupt, narrow-minded. Ten other items were added being specific to the Dutch, the Turks, and/or their relationship. These 10 specific items were provided by a pilot study in which Turks (interviewed by a Turkish interviewer) and Dutch (interviewed by a Dutch interviewer) were asked how they would describe their own group, in what way their own group was similar to the relevant other group, and in what way the own group differed from the other group. The 10 adjectives mentioned most frequently, were selected. They were: conservative, proud, prejudiced, grateful, profiting, sociable, uncivilized, religious, dirty, reliable.

An own group identification score was calculated by adding per individual the absolute difference between self and own group ratings over the 25 adjectives and subsequently dividing this sum by 25. The value of α belonging to 25 difference scores was 0.79 for the Turks and 0.80 for the Dutch.

Intergroup attitudes To assess intergroup attitudes, the adjective checklist was administered a fourth time. The subject was asked to indicate the desirability of each adjective. A score for other group attitude per individual was computed by multiplying the applicability of each adjective with its corresponding desirability, summing the results of these 25 multiplications and finally dividing it by 25. Before multiplying, each desirability rating was subtracted with three, so that the resulting scores could vary between −10 (a very negative other group attitude) and +10 (a very positive other group attitude). A similar procedure was followed to assess the own group attitude. The latter measure was computed mainly as a standard of comparison with other group attitude. The corresponding values of α were 0.71 for the own group attitude towards the Turks (n = 122), 0.69 for the other group attitude towards the Turks (n = 112), 0.72 for the own group attitude towards the Dutch (n = 120) and 0.66 for the other group attitude towards the Dutch (n = 114). These α values are all at an acceptable level.

Perceived power Subjects were asked to indicate how much power the Turks had over the Dutch and vice versa. Two domains of power were chosen: (i) resource power, consisting of economic power, political power and social power; (ii) retaliatory power, consisting of the power to act and to retaliate. Economic power was described as the power to decide on the distribution of money and jobs. The item formulated was: 'To what extent do the Turks in The Netherlands have economic power which enables them to harm the interests of the Dutch' (and a complementary item which assesses the perceived power of the Dutch over the Turks). Political power was described as making and implementing rules and decisions. The items were formulated analogous to the items concerning economic power. Social power was described as the possession of social status, authority and influential relationships. Retaliatory power was operationalized by the items: 'To what extent are the Turks in The Netherlands able – if they want to – to embitter the life of the Dutch' (and vice versa); 'To what extent would the Turks in The Netherlands be prepared to make sacrifices for their ideals if these were threatened by the Dutch' (and vice versa). The response alternatives for all items were: very little, little, quite somewhat, much, very much.

We computed a composite score for resource power (sum of economic, social, and political scores divided by three), for the own group and other group separately, since Cronbach's α values were sufficiently high. Their values were: 0.76 and 0.81 for resource power of the own group and the resource power of other group respectively, as judged by the Turks (n = 148 in both cases), and 0.80 and 0.68 for the resource power of own group and resource power of other group as judged by the Dutch (n = 147 in both cases). The two variables measuring retaliatory power did not correlate. Therefore these scores were not combined.

Fraternal relative deprivation Feelings of fraternal relative deprivation were assessed from a social, an economic and a political point of view. For each domain subjects had to indicate twice the level at which the own group was located in comparison with the other group, first concerning the present and next with respect to the future. They also indicated the extent to which they were satisfied with progress made thus far. The scale of response alternatives consisted of a scale ranging from 'much higher' to 'much lower' for the first two questions, and from 'very high' to 'very low' for the last question.

For each individual we calculated an average fraternal relative deprivation score with respect to the present for the three domains. The same procedure was followed with respect to future deprivations, and with respect to satisfaction with progress made thus far. The values of α for present, future, and satisfaction were for the Turks (n = 148) respectively 0.68, 0.70, and 0.78, and for the Dutch (n = 142) 0.42, 0.59, and 0.54. The α values of the Turkish measures attained an acceptable level, yet those for the Dutch did not (see results section).

Other dependent variables At the end of the questionnaire subjects were presented with questions concerning their age, marital status, (dependable) children, place of birth, town of residence, education, profession, religion, frequency of contact with the other group, kind of contact with the other group (and for the Turks, the number of years they had been living in The Netherlands).

Sample

One hundred and forty-nine male Turks and 147 male Dutch completed the questionnaire. Both the Turkish and the Dutch subjects were living either in Tilburg and surroundings (48 Turks and 47 Dutch), in Utrecht and surroundings (51 Turks and 50 Dutch), or in Leiden and surroundings (50 Turks and 50 Dutch). All the Turkish subjects were born in Turkey.

The questionnaire was first administered to the Turks. Dutch subjects were then matched to them, with respect to age, level of education, profession, and employment status. Table 3.1 presents the distribution of the Turkish and Dutch subjects on these criteria.

Table 3.1 Characteristics of the Turkish and Dutch sample

	Turks (n = 149)	Dutch (n = 147)
Mean age	30.3 years	32.3 years
Socio-economic status		
unemployed	45.6%	44.9%
employed	50.3%	52.4%
student	4.1%	2.7%
Mean duration of stay in The Netherlands	10.5 years	
Completed education		
no education	7.3%	2.7%
secondary school	34.9%	22.4%
high school	46.3%	63.3%
higher education	8.1%	6.8%
Type of work		
unskilled	15.4%	12.2%
semi-skilled	22.8%	31.3%
skilled	7.4%	6.8%

Since the questionnaire was phrased in Dutch, only Turkish subjects who had mastered the Dutch language participated. The data for the Turkish subjects were collected by Turkish research assistants who were fluent in both languages. In the case of language difficulties, these bilingual assistants were available for explanation and clarification. Dutch research assistants collected the questionnaires for the Dutch subjects. It took subjects 2–4 hours to complete the questionnaire. Subjects were given a small gift for their participation.

Results

First we present the results of the norm violation inventory, and subsequently the results of own group identification, intergroup attitudes, perceived power differences and feelings of fraternal relative deprivation. Finally the relationships between each of the four group factors on the one hand and reactions to norm violations on the other will be presented.

Reactions to norm violation

We eliminated 32 Turks and 15 Dutch from the analyses as they gave on more than eight consequent situations the same prediction for the most likely reaction of the own group, as well as for the other group member. We considered this may have been due to fatigue or boredom and decided that such data had to be discarded. Answers given before the occurrence of the eight identical responses for own and anticipated other group reaction were, however, included in the analyses.

Before presenting the results of the aggregated reactions of the own and the other group (see method), we will briefly consider the results for each situation separately, as well as comment on the percentages with which R+, R0, R−, R=, and R≡ were chosen. Table 3.2 provides the mean own group and other group reactions by the Turks and the Dutch separately for each situation individually.

As can be seen, the Dutch were almost always expected to react more negatively than the Turks, by both the Turkish and the Dutch respondents. In only two situations was the Turkish own group reaction significantly more negative than the Dutch own group reaction, namely in case of the girl telling her parents that she is marrying a man from the other group, and in case of a political leader asserting that intergroup marriages should be discouraged. Also interesting is that in all situations except three, the Turks anticipated the other group reaction to be more negative than their own group reaction. In the three exceptions (obtruding on a married woman, pestering a girl, and a girl of age who tells her parents that she is going to marry a man belonging to the other group), the Turkish own group reaction was *more* negative than their anticipated

Table 3.2 Reactions to 36 norm violations: mean for Turks and Dutch (situations are represented by a key word, see Appendix 3.1 for full details)

Situation	Turkish observer: Own group victim	Turkish observer: Other group victim	Dutch observer: Own group victim	Dutch observer: Other group victim
religion	2.00^{a}	2.64^{bc}	2.70^{c}	2.34^{b}
obtruding	2.96^{b}	2.55^{a}	3.34^{c}	3.42^{c}
pestering	2.48^{b}	2.15^{a}	3.04^{c}	3.37^{c}
present	2.45^{a}	2.76^{b}	3.12^{c}	2.59^{1b}
accident	2.15^{a}	2.50^{b}	2.80^{c}	2.66^{bc}
marriage	3.61^{b}	2.60^{a}	2.77^{a}	3.41^{b}
dish	1.49^{a}	1.83^{b}	1.53^{a}	1.37^{a}
parking	1.99^{a}	2.68^{c}	3.24^{d}	2.38^{b}
music	1.97^{a}	2.31^{b}	2.57^{b}	1.99^{a}
greeting	2.39^{a}	2.89^{b}	3.55^{c}	2.83^{b}
seat	1.88^{a}	1.99^{ab}	1.83^{a}	2.13^{b}
handshake	2.21^{a}	2.31^{a}	3.17^{c}	2.75^{b}
personnel manager	1.89^{a}	2.78^{b}	2.89^{b}	2.01^{a}
football player	2.89^{a}	3.12^{ab}	3.59^{c}	3.31^{b}
market trader	2.67^{a}	2.77^{a}	3.14^{b}	3.23^{b}
shopkeeper	2.33^{a}	2.63^{b}	2.65^{b}	2.36^{a}
bus driver	1.79^{a}	2.38^{b}	2.82^{c}	2.23^{b}
teacher	1.87^{a}	2.33^{b}	2.58^{b}	2.39^{b}
physician	3.34^{a}	4.21^{b}	4.06^{b}	3.30^{a}
factory	2.25^{a}	3.00^{b}	3.43^{c}	2.43^{a}
police-officer	3.22^{a}	3.55^{b}	3.52^{b}	3.26^{a}
shop attendants	2.76^{a}	3.52^{b}	3.75^{b}	2.98^{a}
employee	2.54^{a}	3.03^{b}	3.10^{b}	2.47^{a}
butcher	2.09^{ab}	2.50^{c}	2.33^{bc}	1.93^{a}
heroin	2.42^{a}	2.98^{b}	3.39^{c}	2.51^{a}
smoking	1.86^{a}	2.15^{b}	2.27^{b}	2.10^{ab}
moonlighting	2.26^{a}	3.13^{b}	3.00^{b}	2.23^{a}
queue	3.06^{b}	3.29^{c}	3.41^{c}	2.79^{a}
ticket	2.10^{a}	2.75^{c}	2.32^{b}	2.19^{ab}
stealing	1.92^{a}	2.39^{b}	2.55^{b}	2.37^{b}
holiday	2.14^{a}	3.04^{b}	3.17^{b}	2.18^{a}
coming late	2.01^{a}	2.64^{b}	2.64^{b}	2.20^{a}
handicapped	1.52^{a}	1.88^{b}	2.33^{c}	1.79^{ab}
heart attack	2.40^{a}	2.66^{b}	2.69^{b}	2.55^{ab}
political leader	2.74^{bc}	2.92^{c}	2.38^{a}	2.61^{ab}
insurance company	2.28^{a}	2.95^{b}	2.86^{b}	2.10^{a}

Scale employed for both own group and other group reaction: 1 positive, 2 no reaction, 3 mildly negative, 4 moderately negative, 5 strongly negative. Row values which do not have a superscript in common differ significantly (t-test, $p < 0.05$).

other group reaction. In two situations the Dutch anticipated the other group reaction to be more negative than the own group reaction, namely in the case of the girl telling her parents to marry a man from the other group and where a regular seat was taken by an other group member.

Figure 3.1 presents the mean percentages (computed over 36 situations) for each of the five reactions for own group reaction and anticipated other group reaction by Turks and Dutch.

From Figure 3.1 it can be seen that a high similarity existed between Dutch anticipated other group reaction and the Turkish own group reaction on the one hand, and the Turkish anticipated other group reaction and the Dutch own group reaction on the other. Both groups apparently had a fair idea of what they could expect from one another and these ideas coincide. Inspection of this figure also shows that, in general, the Dutch were expected to react mildly negatively to a norm violation and that the Turks were expected to do nothing or to react positively.

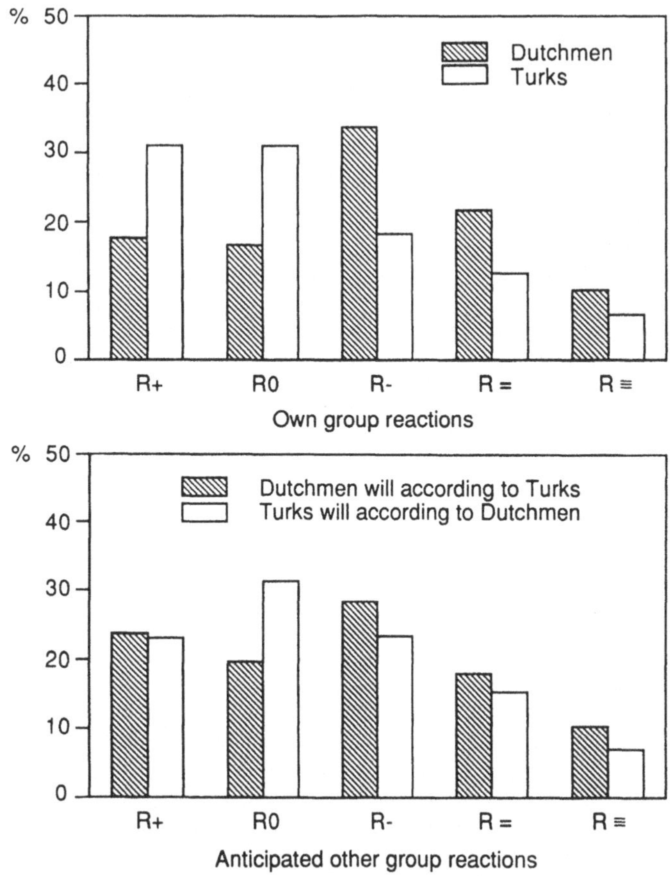

Figure 3.1 Reactions to norm violation by Dutchmen and Turkish immigrants

Table 3.3 Own group and anticipated other group reactions: means for Turks and Dutch combined over 36 situations

Reaction	Turks	Dutch	*t*
Own group	2.32	2.89	−10.54***
mean	0.33	0.40	
SD	97	118	
n			
Other group	2.75	2.51	4.44***
mean	0.38	0.41	
SD	96	113	
t			
t	−9.34***	8.23***	

Scale employed: 1 positive, 2 no reaction, 3 mildly negative, 4 moderately negative, 5 strongly negative.
*** $p < 0.001$.

Next we computed the mean own group and anticipated other group reaction, over 36 norm-violating situations, for the Turks and the Dutch separately (Table 3.3).

Analysis of variance (ANOVA) using a between-subjects factor (Turkish/Dutch group membership) and a within-subjects factor (own group/other group), revealed a significant interaction effect for the mean reaction over 36 situations ($F_{1,197} = 149.05$, $p < 0.001$), as well as a significant main effect for group membership ($F_{1,197} = 17.14$, $p < 0.001$). On the whole the Turks predicted more positive reactions irrespective of the group membership of the victim. The Turkish own group reaction was less negative than their anticipated other group reaction. The Dutch appeared to agree with these Turkish expectations: their own group reaction was more negative than their anticipated Turkish reaction. However, intergroup perceptions did not fully coincide. The Dutch anticipation of the Turkish reaction was more negative than the Turkish own group reaction ($t_{208} = 3.36$, $p < 0.01$). On the other hand, the Turks anticipated the other group reaction to be less negative than the Dutch anticipated their own group reaction to be ($t_{212} = 2.50$, $p < 0.05$).

Context factors

Own group identification The mean own group identification for the Turkish subjects was 0.82 (SD = 0.35) and for the Dutch subjects 1.06 (SD = 0.36). This difference was statistically significant ($t_{286} = -5.77$, $p < 0.001$). The Turks identified more strongly with their own group than the Dutch did with their own group.

Intergroup attitudes In Table 3.4 the results for the own and other group attitudes of the Turks and the Dutch are presented.

Table 3.4 Own group and other group attitudes: means and standard deviations for Turks and Dutch

Attitude	Turks	Dutch	*t*
Own group			
mean	0.33	−0.48	6.62***
SD	1.00	0.89	
n	122	120	
Other group			
mean	−0.04	−0.35	2.57*
SD	0.93	0.88	
n	112	114	
t	4.24***	−1.33	

The attitude score can vary between −10 (very negative) and +10 (very positive).
* $p < 0.05$, *** $p < 0.001$.

ANOVA revealed a main effect for group membership ($F_{1,206} = 25.96$, $p < 0.001$), and a main effect for own group/other group ($F_{1,206} = 4.25$, $p < 0.05$) which, however, was due to a highly significant interaction effect ($F_{1,206} = 14.72$, $p < 0.001$). The Dutch attitude scores were significantly more negative than the Turkish scores. The Dutch did not appear to distinguish between the own group and the other group in this respect. The Turks thought much more positively of their own group than the Dutch did of their own group. The Turks had a neutral attitude towards the Dutch and a positive own group attitude. Finally, the Turks had a less negative view of the Dutch than the Dutch had of the Turks. Note that the Dutch had a more negative attitude towards the Turks than the Turks had towards themselves ($t_{234} = 5.51$, $p < 0.01$). The Turks, however, had a less negative view of the Dutch than the Dutch had of themselves ($t_{230} = 3.67$, $p < 0.01$).

Perceived power The means of the composite resource power variable and the two retaliatory variables are presented in Table 3.5.

For each of the power aspects we performed ANOVA using group membership as the between-subjects factor and the own group/other group distinction as the within-subjects factor. A significant interaction effect was obtained for resource power ($F_{1,293} = 412.72$, $p < 0.001$), and for power to harass ($F_{1,291} = 252.10$, $p < 0.001$), but not for 'willingness to make sacrifices'. For the last two variables we did, however, find a main effect for groups ($F_{1,291} = 9.45$, $p < 0.05$ and $F_{1,291} = 12.03$, $p < 0.001$ respectively), as well as a small effect for the own group/other group distinction ($F_{1,291} = 4.33$, $p < 0.05$ and $F_{1,291} = 6.50$, $p < 0.05$). These effects, however, have to be attributed to the highly significant interaction effect.

The perceptions of the Turks and the Dutch concerning their resource

Table 3.5 Resource and retaliatory power: means and standard deviations for Turks and Dutch

Power		Turks	Dutch	t
Resource power				
own group	mean	1.82	3.42	−16.68***
	SD	0.73	0.90	
	n	148	147	
other group	mean	3.39	1.78	16.21***
	SD	1.02	0.65	
	n	148	147	
Retaliatory power ('harass')				
own group	mean	2.01	3.70	−13.71***
	SD	1.08	1.05	
	n	144	146	
other group	mean	3.63	2.46	8.80***
	SD	1.19	1.00	
	n	144	146	
Retaliatory power ('sacrifices')				
own group	mean	2.60	2.97	−2.67**
	SD	1.16	1.27	
	n	148	146	
other group	mean	2.85	3.16	−2.52*
	SD	1.03	1.10	
	n	147	146	

Scales employed (for both resource and retaliatory power): 1 very little, 2 little, 3 quite somewhat, 4 much, 5 very much.
* $p<0.05$, ** $p<0.01$, *** $p<0.001$.

power over each other, and the extent to which they can harass each other, were generally in agreement. The Dutch were judged as having more resource power than the Turks and were perceived as being able to harass the Turks more than vice versa.

Fraternal relative deprivation The means of the measures of fraternal relative deprivation are presented in Table 3.6.

ANOVA using group membership as a between-subjects factor, and type of fraternal relative deprivation (present future) as a within-subjects factor, resulted in a main effect for group membership ($F_{1,288} = 1195.83$, $p < 0.001$), a main effect for type of fraternal relative deprivation ($F_{1,288} = 34.85$, $p < 0.001$), and an interaction ($F_{1,288} = 117.72$, $p < 0.001$). The Turks felt more deprived than the Dutch did. This was so for the present and for what they expected of the future. Their satisfaction with progression was less than the satisfaction of the Dutch. The Turks expected a considerable improvement in their conditions in the future in comparison with the present (2.32 versus 1.75, $t_{147} = -10.85$, $p < 0.001$);

Table 3.6 Fraternal relative deprivation (FRD): means and standard deviations for Turks and Dutch

	Turks	Dutch	t
FRD-present			
mean	1.75	4.42	−38.32***
SD	0.64	0.55	
FRD-future			
mean	2.32	4.25	−24.43***
SD	0.72	0.63	
FRD-satisfaction			
mean	2.43	3.09	−8.08***
SD	0.82	0.57	

Scales employed for FRD-present and FRD-future: 1 much lower, 2 somewhat lower, 3 equal, 4 somewhat higher, 5 much higher. Scales employed for FRD satisfaction: 1 very low, 2 rather low, 3 moderate, 4 rather high, 5 very high.
*** $p < 0.001$.

the Dutch, however, expected a deterioration (4.25 versus 4.42, $t_{141} = 3.94$, $p < 0.001$).

In the method section it was noted that the α coefficients for the combined scores for the Dutch were rather low (0.42, 0.54 and 0.59). We therefore also computed the differences between the Turks and the Dutch in feelings of fraternal relative deprivation for each variable separately. For all variables, the Turks felt significantly more deprived than the Dutch ($p < 0.001$). Furthermore, the Turks expected a significant improvement in the future for each domain ($p < 0.001$), whereas the Dutch expected a deterioration in the economic ($p < 0.001$) and political domains ($p < 0.001$), yet no change in the social domain.

Relationship between reactions to norm violation and context factors

For the Turks and Dutch separately we performed step-wise multiple regression analyses with the own group reaction and anticipated other group reaction as dependent variables. The following variables were used as predictors: own group identification, other group attitude, present feelings of fraternal relative deprivation, own group's resource power, other group's resource power, own and other group's willingness to make sacrifices, own and other group's capacity to harass.

The only significant predictor of own group reaction by the Turkish subjects was the own group's resource power over the Dutch ($\beta = 0.37$, $t = 3.31$, $p < 0.01$), $R^2 = 0.14$). The Dutch subjects' anticipation of the other group reaction was predicted by the Turkish resource power as well ($\beta = 0.42$, $t = 4.25$, $p < 0.001$), $R^2 = 0.18$). In other words, in the opinion of both the Turkish and the Dutch subjects, the greater the resource power of the Turks, the stronger the Turkish reaction to norm-violating behaviour. The other group attitude of the Dutch contributed negatively to their own group reaction ($\beta = -0.26$, $t = -2.39$, $p < 0.05$, $R^2 = 0.07$). The more negative their attitude towards the Turks, the more negatively they expected a Dutch victim to react towards the Turkish actor.

Discussion

The results can be summarized as follows. Both the Turkish and the Dutch subjects expected the Turks to react less negatively to norm-violating behaviour than the Dutch. Turks mostly were anticipated, by both themselves and the Dutch, to do nothing. The Dutch were expected, again by both groups, to react with a minor norm violation. The Turkish subjects identified more strongly with their own group than the Dutch. Attitudes of the Dutch were equally negative towards the own group and the other group. The Turks thought of themselves in much more positive terms than the Dutch did, although their view of the Dutch was less negative than the view the Dutch had of themselves. The Dutch subjects' attitude towards the Turks was more negative than the Turkish subjects' own group attitude. Both the Turks and the Dutch agreed that the Dutch have more resource power over the Turks than vice versa, and can harass the Turks more than the Turks can harass the Dutch. Finally, the Turks felt more deprived in comparison with the Dutch; now and, as they expect, in the future. It was found that the Turkish reaction to norm violations could be predicted by their resource power, i.e. both Turks and Dutch anticipated a Turk to react more negatively, the more resource power the Turks were perceived to have. The own group reactions of the Dutch were predicted by other group attitude. It must be noted, however, that the explained variances were quite small.

The extent to which intergroup perceptions with respect to predicted reactions and intergroup resource power coincided is striking. It seems that views held of the other group were validated by the views of the other group and that a perfect match of intergroup perceptions was established. However, differences were found. The Dutch subjects anticipated Turkish victims to react *more* negatively than the Turkish subjects predicted own group victims to react. Yet, the Turks expected Dutch victims to react *less* negatively compared with the Dutch prediction of own group reactions. So, the Dutch had a more negative view of the Turks than the Turks had of themselves. The Turks had a less negative view of the Dutch than the Dutch had of themselves. Similarly, although the Dutch had an equally negative attitude towards the own and the other group, their attitude was considerably more negative towards the Turks than the Turkish attitude was towards their own group. Yet, the Turkish attitude towards the Dutch was much less negative than the Dutch own group attitude. (One should keep in mind here that the Dutch tended to have a negative attitude irrespectively of group membership). The point is that intergroup perceptions were not as symmetric as one might conclude at first glance. On the surface the Dutch were very lenient towards the Turks in predicting relatively positive reactions and by not differentiating between them and themselves with respect to attitudes. Yet they were more negative towards the Turks in their evaluations and predictions compared with how the Turks thought of themselves. The Turks, by being more positive towards the Dutch, compared with the Dutch own group evaluations, perhaps identified (at least to some extent) with the powerful Dutch, which in Tajfel and Turner's (1979) terms might hinder a strategy of social competition becoming truly effective.

It appeared that the four group factors differentially predicted reactions to norm violations for the Turks and the Dutch. The single predictor for Turkish reactions to norm violations was their resource power. Furthermore, a positive correlation (see Appendix 3.2) between two relative deprivation indicators, namely present feelings and satisfaction with progress made, and own group reaction existed for the Turks (although this relationship did not emerge from the regression analyses). The stronger these feelings of relative deprivation, the more negative the own group reaction to norm violations. In contrast, only the other group attitude was found to be predictive of the Dutch own group reaction to norm violations. Perhaps power differences and relative deprivation are only related to reactions when one *lacks* power or when one indeed *does* feel deprived, in other words in the case of a minority group. The fact that the Dutch are more powerful is much less salient to the powerful Dutch themselves. For the Dutch the differences in power and feelings of relative deprivation might be so large that the Turks cannot be treated as a relevant comparison group. This can be illustrated by pointing to the lower correlation coefficient for the Dutch compared with the Turks between present and future feelings of relative deprivation on the one hand and satisfaction on the other (the correlations of the anticipated future deprivation and satisfaction of the Dutch were even lower). Also, no relationship for the Dutch was obtained between the relative power measures and satisfaction. Their satisfaction was apparently less related to their future comparative feelings of deprivation and not at all to their relative power.

The Dutch own group reaction seemed to be determined by the respondents' other group attitude. The more negative the Dutch attitude towards the Turks, the more negative the Dutch own group reaction to a Turkish norm violation! The underlying dynamic of this phenomenon is not quite clear. Do Dutch subjects generalize their own other group attitude to other Dutchmen (the victims in the norm violation inventory)? Or, have people (unconsciously) predicted how a Dutch victim *should* react? New studies are needed to address this issue.

In this study we have been concerned with differences between Turks and Dutch in their evaluations and expectations of own and other group members' behaviour. It can be argued that this emphasis on differences is not fully justified by the pattern of data obtained. As can be seen in Appendix 3.2, high correlations exist between own group and anticipated other group reactions (the more negative the anticipated other group reaction, the more negative the own group reaction, and vice versa), and between the other group and own group attitude (the more positive one's attitude towards the own group, the more positive it is towards the other group, and vice versa), both for the Turks and for the Dutch. Of course this does not exclude the possibility that there are differences in own group and other group ratings, yet it does show that these ratings are positively interdependent.

Before ending we want to point out some weak aspects of the present study. First, the reaction alternatives embody different dimensions. Not only the degree of positive/negative reaction is reflected in the scale, but also the degree of assertiveness, verbal or non-verbal reactions, the extent to which third parties are involved, etc. Second, although the results of the second pilot-study (see Chapter 8) revealed that the rank ordering of the reaction alternatives of the 36 norm-violating situations was overall according to our view, for many individual situations we found a different rank ordering of the five reaction alternatives from that we had predicted and, moreover, the judgments of the Turks and the Dutch did not coincide for a number of situations. Finally, the degree of fluency in the Dutch language constituted a difference between the Turkish and Dutch subjects. By selecting only those Turks who had a good mastery of Dutch we tried to reduce this problem; it, however, meant that our Turkish sample was not representative of the total population of Turkish allochthones in The Netherlands. This should be kept in mind when considering the results obtained.

Nevertheless, we feel it is worth drawing attention to several interesting speculations. We have seen that the Turks are less likely to react to norm violations than the Dutch. Avoidance behaviour in an intergroup relationship might imply that conflicts are not likely to escalate. The only situations in which the Turks will react with a norm violation is when a Turkish girl is pestered or a Turkish woman is obtruded upon by a Dutch man. This is also likely to happen when a Turkish girl is willing to marry a Dutch man, although in this particular example the girl herself will be the target of reaction. Thus, in these three situations an escalation of intergroup conflict is possible. However, in the great majority of cases nothing is likely to happen which would disrupt the intergroup relationship.

In Western society people are not expected to avoid or ignore conflict, or to react positively to it. Instead, we are taught to turn the other cheek when we are being hit or to retaliate (see Chapter 8, however). Also, the concept of assertiveness might be quite typical for the West. In other words, the Turkish victims' absence of reactions to norm violations would be considered 'abnormal' by Westerners. Apart from being abnormal, such behaviour is not very beneficial to the Turks themselves. It seems as if they passively undergo the other group's violations, yet by doing so the status quo is very unlikely to be altered. The present study suggests that only when the Turks gain resource power will they stand up for themselves.[1]

In the case of social responsibility situations the Turks are also not inclined to react. Whereas passive behaviour in social contact and institutional contact situations has predominantly negative consequences for the victim, and will therefore be tolerated by the Dutch, society at large suffers when norm violations enacted within the domain of social responsibility are not corrected. Hence, inertia in these types of situations is undoubtedly considered to be inappropriate in our society. It might, however, well be the case that the Turks are quite willing to react to these norm violations, but feel that they lack the power to do so adequately.

Notes

[1] It should be said here that these thoughts are highly tentative. It might well be that the Turks likewise would not react to norm violations, if they were committed by a Turk. Unfortunately, we have not measured reactions to norm violations by a member of the own group.

4 The communal cauldron: relations between Hindus and Muslims in India and their reactions to norm violations

Emmanuel S. K. Ghosh, Rashmi Kumar, and Rama C. Tripathi

Introduction

The Hindu–Muslim equation has puzzled social scientists in modern India considerably. India is committed to 'unity among diversity' as an ideal of a secular, democratic republic. However, in practice the linguistic, regional, ethnic, and religious diversities have tended to pose numerous problems for its integrated national growth and development. Of these many diversities, the relations between Hindus and Muslims have been markedly salient. Though the Hindu–Muslim contact dates back to more than a thousand years, it has been marked with growing violence between the two ethnic communities in recent years. Firstly, a study of demographic data underlines the problem. Muslims in India constitute the largest single minority of about 11–12 per cent of the total population, which is approximately one hundred million people. This is practically equal to the total Muslim population of West Asia and is more than the Muslim population of Pakistan. After Indonesia and Bangladesh, India has the largest concentration of Muslims. There are few nations with such a large minority in relation to its total population. Nearly 50 per cent of this Muslim population of India live in Uttar Pradesh, Bihar and West Bengal. Uttar Pradesh alone accounts for about a quarter of the Muslim population of the country. The urban Muslim population is 16.28 per cent against 9.82 per cent in rural areas. The confrontations between Hindus and Muslims have been largely in urban areas where relatively large numbers of Muslims concentrate (D'Souza 1983). It has also been suggested that urban areas with a Muslim minority population ranging between 20 and 40 per cent of the total population are more disturbance prone (Engineer 1984; Saxena 1984; Krishna 1985).

Secondly, historical data on the Muslims in the subcontinent show that their presence can be traced to migration, conquest or conversion. Their influx into India was sporadic and intermittent. Initially, Arab immigrants came to the coastal areas and Arab conquerors settled down in Sindh. Later, the period between the thirteenth and eighteenth centuries was characterized by invasions of Turks, Afghans and Mughals. Thus, Islam came to India at different times and was brought by diverse races and cultures and added to the plurality of the environment of the subcontinent. The Muslim community, while viewed generally as one group, is composed of various subgroups which are distinct from each other. The criteria of theology, rites, regional cultures and history, linguistic and ethnic variations account for variable patterns of relations.

Thirdly, in the political context, despite regional linguistic, ethnic, economic and other differences, it is relevant to consider Muslims as one community. In the last hundred years or so, the communal Muslim identity has been considerably reinforced.[1] The British historians laid the foundation for a communal interpretation of Indian history and this provided historical justification for the two-nation theory (Thaper 1981). The partition of the country along religious lines was marked by riots and bloodshed between the Hindus and Muslims. Frequent communal riots have further reinforced this identity. Recently, Hindu communalism has been on the rise. A number of new Hindu political organizations, such as Vishwa Hindu Parishad and Shiva Sena, have emerged and become politically powerful. The nature and origins of communal violence have marked differences before and after partition (Engineer 1981). The cause of communal conflict before partition was a struggle for a greater share of political power and control of economic resources. This cause ceased to exist after partition. But with the Jabalpur riots in 1961, a new phase of communal violence was witnessed in post-partition India. A variety of local factors now play a major role in pushing conflict to violence. Targets of communal riots seem to be specific properties and places marked out beforehand and riots appear preplanned and goal oriented. Pointing to local economic inequalities and rivalry, Rustomji observed 'a riot does not occur in a sleepy little village of Uttar Pradesh where all suffer equally, nor in a tribal village of Madhya Pradesh where all live safely in their poverty. It occurs in Moradabad where the metal workers have built up a good industry; it occurs in Aligarh where the lock makers have made good; it occurs in Bhiwandi where power-loom rivalries are poisonous; it occurs in Hatia and Ahmedabad and Hyderabad and Jamshedpur where there are jobs to get, contracts to secure, houses and shops to capture; it occurs in Agra at Ferozabad and in all other towns where economic rivalries are serious and have to be covered with the cloak of communalism' (Rustomji 1980, cited by A. K. Singh 1988, p. 175).

The figures for communal violence showed a sudden rise in 1964–70; a downward trend from 1972–76 and thereafter it has again been increasing. The annual all India figures of communal riots involving Hindus and Muslims from 1978 to 1982 were 230, 304, 427, 319 and 474 (A. K. Singh 1985). Krishna (1985) has given a detailed analysis of communal violence involving Hindus and Muslims. During 1961–80, 10 437 incidents of communal violence killing 655 Hindus and 3163 Muslims and injuring 10 808 Hindus and 10 821 Muslims were reported. A higher incidence of communal violence was reported in the urban (5372) than in the rural (2592) areas. The incidents of communal violence in larger cities were higher than in the smaller cities.

Thus, the Hindu–Muslim relations are clearly characterized by violence. While it is true that in many areas of the country they co-exist in a peaceful manner, by and large the Muslims tend to maintain an exclusiveness from the majority community of Hindus and attempt to preserve their past traditions and religion. The change in status for the Muslims from an earlier position of political and social dominance for about four hundred years to their present position of economic and social disadvantage in post-partition independent India has resulted in their sense of alienation from the majority community.

In recent years, a large number of historical and sociological analyses of the Hindu–Muslim relations have been made (e.g. D'Souza 1983). A. K. Singh (1988) has reviewed a large number of social-psychological studies done in India on intergroup relations and social tensions. The review showed that, on the whole, Hindus as well as Muslims viewed their own groups more positively but held a somewhat negative view of each other's group. Muslims also tend to feel greater fraternal relative deprivation than Hindus (Naqvi 1980; Tripathi and Ansari 1980; Tripathi and Srivastava 1981).

The setting of the present study

The present study focuses on Hindu–Muslim relations in samples drawn from a medium-sized North Indian city of Uttar Pradesh with a history of communal clashes and riots, though not too frequently. The city has a 20–30 per cent population of Muslims who are in business, professions, and industries. Many of them work as skilled or semi-skilled workers or as craftsmen. Politically, because of its sizeable numbers and 'block' voting potential, the Muslim community is very much wooed by vote seekers and political strategists. On the whole, a policy of appeasement and due respect is generally followed by governmental machinery in day to day administration of the Muslim communities' interests. Socially, however, the relationship between Hindus and Muslims is marked by exclusiveness, and intergroup contact is found only in the institutional or professional context of business, trade, and occupation. Separate distinctive festivals, religious rituals, clothing, and dress mark the two ethnic groups as somewhat distinctive in the life of the city.

Hypotheses

In view of the foregoing description of Hindu–Muslim relations the following hypotheses are offered for Hindus' and Muslims' reactions to norm violations.

Hypothesis 1. Both Hindus and Muslims will have negative reactions to norm violations by members of the other group.

Given that relations between Hindus and Muslims have been characterized by mutual violence, there is reason to believe that both groups are likely to make negative attributions about the other party's norm violation which will lead to negative reactions (see Hypotheses 2 and 3, Chapter 1).

Hypothesis 2. The anticipated other group's reaction will be more negative than that of the own group.

As a general other group bias of Hindus and Muslims appears to have been building up over the past years we expect that both groups anticipate more negative reactions from the other group than from their own group. This will be especially true for Hindus as they believe that Muslims are by religion and education 'violent' and 'fighters'.

Hypothesis 3. The degree and strength of reactions to norm violation will be a function of other group attitudes, own group identification, perceived power, and fraternal relative deprivation.

It was predicted that the larger the perceived differences in power, the more likely it is that the high power group will react more negatively to the low power group's norm violations, and further, that the low power group will abstain from negative anticipated reactions to norm violations by the other group. Similarly, the higher the felt fraternal relative deprivation, the more likely it is that negative own group and anticipated other group reactions would be given. Greater own group identification and negative other group attitude were expected to be associated with stronger negative anticipated other group reactions (see Chapter 1).

Method

The development of the norm violation inventory

The basic instrument used for the present study comprised a questionnaire containing 21 situations. Two pilot studies were conducted for the development of the questionnaire.

The first pilot study was conducted to find out the possible range of reactions of Hindu and Muslim respondents. Seventy norm-violating situations were presented and free responses were obtained as reactions to such situations. For instance, a situation 'Hindu boy teases Muslim girl' was presented to Muslim respondents and their free responses as reactions were obtained. By reversing the contrast groups in the situation, Muslims' anticipated responses for the other group were similarly collected. These situations represented norm violations of varying degrees of seriousness in intergroup contact and conflict between Hindus and Muslims. Frequently, the situations were those that were commonly reported in the newspapers of Hindu–Muslim conflict. Data were collected on thirty Hindu and thirty Muslim respondents representing educated students, semi-literate, and unskilled workers. The data generated as free responses were content analysed and formed the basis for constructing response alternatives; they were later used as reactions to norm violations in the main study.

In the second pilot study 60 situations were selected from the first pilot study. The ten situations dropped from the first pilot study were those which had failed to elicit free responses readily. The second pilot study had the following objectives: firstly, to establish whether a norm violation has been perceived in the situation presented; secondly, to ascertain whether the incident was perceived as an intentional norm violation engaged in by the actor. To facilitate administration, the sixty situations were divided into sets of thirty situations each. Each set was presented to forty Hindu and forty Muslim respondents representing diverse professional groups and students. The respondents gave answers to three questions: (i) to what extent the act would be considered as norm violation; (ii) how 'bad' was the act considered; (iii) whether the act was considered intentional. On the basis of the results of the second pilot study, 21 situations were selected for the main study, which both Hindus and Muslims generally considered as norm violating and intentional, and which evoked negative feelings. In Appendix 4.1 the situations selected are presented along with the inappropriateness ratings.

Sample

In the main study the norm violation inventory was individually administered to a total sample of 75 Hindu and 75 Muslim subjects. The subjects represented different levels of occupations, income, education, and social class background. Approximately equal numbers of subjects representing these social categories were selected. The general demographic characteristics of the sample are given in Table 4.1. Both Hindu and Muslim respondents had a mean age around 30 years. The occupational profiles of the two groups were similar in both groups; more than half of them were either in business or held a job. The Hindus had a higher mean level of income and they were also slightly better educated than the Muslims.

Instruments

Norm violation inventory The norm violation inventory (NVI) developed consisted of 21 situations drawn from domains of social contacts, institutional contacts and social responsibility (see Chapter 2).

Table 4.1 Characteristics of Hindu and Muslim sample

Characteristics	Hindus ($n = 75$)	Muslims ($n = 75$)
Mean age	30.7 years	28.3 years
Place of residence		
urban	48.1%	64.4%
rural	51.4%	35.6%
Occupation		
service	33.3%	32.0%
business	21.3%	34.7%
semi-skilled worker	1.4%	–
any other	42.7%	24.0%
no response	1.3%	9.3%
Mean monthly income	Rs3020.62	Rs1746.61
Education		
less than high school	4.0%	9.6%
secondary school	5.3%	29.0%
B.A., B.Sc., etc	20.0%	43.8%
M.A., M.Sc., etc.	44.0%	9.6%
any other	26.7%	8.2%

Each situation (e.g. a Hindu doctor makes obscene gestures to a Muslim nurse) was followed by five possible reactions:

(1) a positive or constructive reaction (R+), e.g. request the doctor to apologise to the nurse;

(2) no reaction (R0), e.g. pay no attention to this incident;

(3) reaction milder than the original norm violation (R−), e.g. demand transfer of the doctor;

(4) reaction equally negative or as strong as the original norm violation (R=), e.g. insult Hindu doctors;

(5) reaction stronger than the original norm violation (R≡), e.g. beat up the doctor.

The order of these five reaction alternatives across different situations was randomized. Each situation was presented to both Hindu and Muslim respondents twice: (a) the Muslim is the actor and the Hindu is the victim; (b) the Hindu is the actor and the Muslim is the victim.

It should be noted that in the present study norm violations do not only occur in a dyadic context, but also the actor or the victim may frequently constitute a collective of group members, e.g. 'Some Hindus make fun of Muslim prophets, standing in front of a mosque. How will the Muslims react?' The variation from dyadic to collective interactions in intergroup norm violation behaviour was considered equally probable in real life and thus included in the inventory. The situations actually used are given in Appendix 4.1.

The respondents were required to indicate what the most likely reaction of the victim or the victim's ethnic group members would be. Thus, for each situation the scores for own group and anticipated other group reaction to norm violation were obtained ranging from 1 (positive reaction) to 5 (reaction stronger than the original norm violation). These reactions were summed up over the 21 situations and divided by 21 to obtain the mean own group reaction and mean anticipated other group reaction. The reliability coefficients α for own group reactions were 0.82 for Hindus and 0.80 for Muslims and 0.91 for both groups for anticipated other group reactions.

Measures of own group identification and attitudes The Hindu and Muslim own group identification and attitudes were measured following the format described in Chapter 2. Ten positive and ten negative adjectives were used on the basis of pilot interviews conducted with Hindu and Muslim respondents and earlier studies (Wish *et al.* 1976; Tripathi and Srivastava 1981). These were as follows:

lazy	dirty	trustworthy	narrow-minded
selfish	responsible	honest	quarrelsome
friendly	corrupt	proud	impulsive
mild-mannered	intelligent	fighter[2]	tolerant
liar	kind	helpful	courageous

A five-point scale ranging from 'most applicable' (5) to 'not at all applicable' (1) was used. Three sets of ratings were collected from the respondents. Ratings of self, ratings for own group and ratings for the other group. In addition, the respondents were also required to rate each adjective for its perceived desirability on a five-point scale, ranging from very desirable (5) to least desirable (1). An own group identification score was obtained by calculating the absolute difference between ratings of self and own group for each of the nineteen adjectives. Thus, a larger mean difference score for own group identification indicated a lesser degree of own group identification while a smaller score indicated greater own group identification.

For measuring attitudes towards the own group and the other group, adjective ratings were multiplied by their perceived positive or negative desirability ratings. The mean scores obtained could range between −10 to +10. The α coefficients for own group identification were 0.85 for Hindus and 0.73 for Muslims. For the other group attitude, they were 0.64 for Hindus and 0.46 for Muslims (which was less than satisfactory), and for own group attitude 0.82 and 0.80 for Hindus and Muslims respectively.

Perceived power The perceived power measure required the respondents to rate the degree of own group power in relation to the other group power. Three areas of political, economic, and social power were included. A five-point scale was used, ranging from very much (5) to very little (1). A *resource power* score was calculated for the own group by taking the mean ratings for perceived political, economic, and social power in comparison with the other group. The α coefficients were 0.86 and 0.76 for the Hindu and Muslim groups respectively.

In addition, two supplementary questions pertaining to *retaliatory power* of the own group were included: (i) 'to what extent can your own group members harm the other group members' and (ii) 'to what extent can your own group members influence the day to day life of other group members'. The mean of these two items provided an index of own group retaliatory power. The α coefficients were 0.70 for Hindus and 0.38 for the Muslims, which was not satisfactory.

It should, however, be noted that in contrast to the study on Turks and Dutchmen (Chapter 3), no measures of other group power ratings were obtained. Details of the rationale for the scale are outlined in Chapter 2. The correlations for the two indices of power were found to be 0.48 ($p < 0.01$) for the Hindus and 0.23 ($p < 0.05$) for the Muslims.

Fraternal relative deprivation Similar to the conceptualization as outlined in Chapter 2, fraternal relative deprivation (FRD) was measured in political, social, and economic spheres. The measure used was similar to that of the study reported in Chapter 3. Three summary indices were created: FRD-present, FRD-future, and FRD-satisfaction.

The index of FRD-present indicated the relative position of the own group with respect to the progress made in recent years in economic, political, and social spheres compared with the other group. The index of FRD-future measured the relative position with respect to the maximum progress own group members were likely to make in the future relative to the other group members in the three spheres. The index of FRD-satisfaction indicated the overall satisfaction of the own group members with their current economic, political, and social positions. The three indices were created by computing the mean of the responses in the three spheres for the respective set of items. The α coefficients for FRD-present were low for Hindus (0.48) and Muslims (0.44) and also for FRD-satisfaction for Hindus (0.37). They were satisfactory for FRD-future: 0.66 for Hindus and 0.82 for Muslims respectively. The α coefficient for FRD-satisfaction for Muslims was 0.60.

Results

Reactions to norm violation

To understand the nature of the reactions to a norm violation, mean percentages of Hindu and Muslim own group and anticipated other

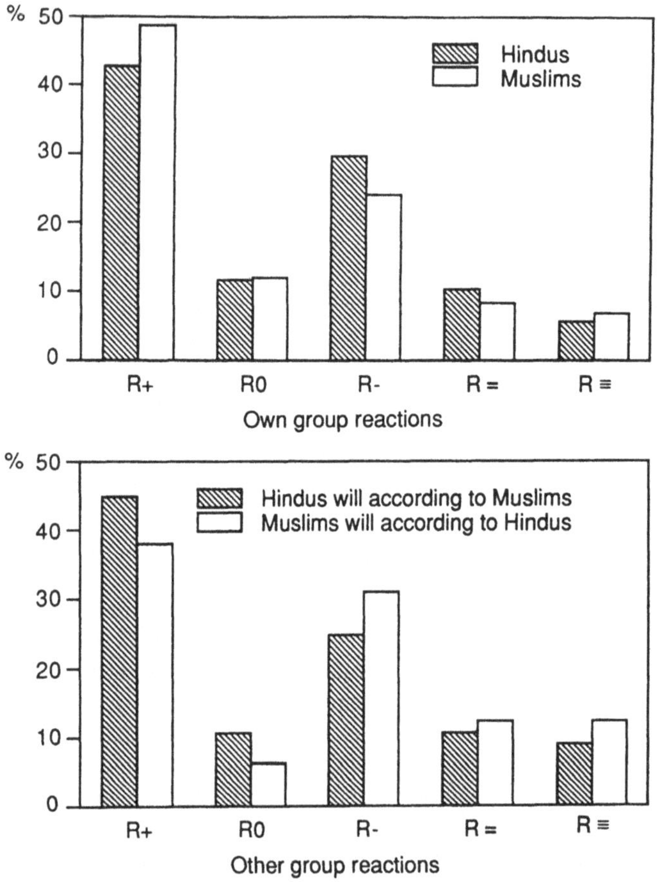

Figure 4.1 Reactions to norm violation by Hindus and Muslims

group reactions for the five reaction alternatives were calculated (Fig. 4.1).

An inspection of the mean percentages shows that on the whole positive reactions were more frequent, followed by weaker retaliation (R−). Extremely strong reactions (R≡) or 'tit for tat' reactions (R=) were generally less frequent. In comparison, anticipated other group reactions were found to be less positive for both the groups. Also, Muslims compared with Hindus gave somewhat more 'do nothing' (R0) type reactions for the anticipated other group reaction. Both groups gave similar mild reactions for own group victims. However, the Hindu respondents anticipated stronger reactions from the other group than did the Muslim respondents.

In Table 4.2 are presented the means, and standard deviations of reactions to norm violations. A 2 (groups) × 2 (own versus other group

Table 4.2 Own group and anticipated other group reactions to norm violations by Hindus and Muslims

Reaction	Hindus	Muslims	*t*
Own group			
mean	2.24	2.13	1.28
SD	0.57	0.56	
Anticipated other group			
mean	2.54	2.28	2.01*
SD	0.82	0.77	
t	−3.88**	−1.86	

* $p<0.05$, ** $p<0.01$.

reaction) ANOVA yielded a significant main effect for groups only. An inspection of the means of reactions shows that while there was a significant difference between Hindus and Muslims in the intensity of anticipated other group reactions ($t_{148} = 2.01$, $p < 0.05$), no such difference was obtained for own group reactions between the two groups. Results thus suggest that the Hindus in comparison with the Muslims anticipated more intense reactions to norm violation from the other group. When own group reactions of Hindu and Muslim respondents to norm violation and the anticipated reactions of the other group are compared, it is found that while the Hindus differentiated between the reactions of the own group and the anticipated reactions of other group members to norm violations ($t_{148} = 3.88$, $p < 0.01$), the Muslims did not. In other words, the Hindus tended to anticipate more severe other group reactions to norm violation, while the Muslims tended to predict equally strong (or equally weak) reactions to norm violations regardless of the victim's group membership.

An analysis of the twenty-one situations indicated a similar trend (Table 4.3). For the own group, differences in reactions were obtained for only five situations between Hindus and Muslims. On three situations (10, X blows cigarette smoke on Y passenger; 18, X refuses to offer seat to crippled Y; 21, X doctor refuses to attend to Y patient) Hindus predicted a more negative own group reaction than Muslims. On two situations (1, X teacher does not give attention to Y student; 17, X youth ridicules Y gods) Muslims predicted a more negative own group reaction. For anticipated other group reactions differences in reactions were obtained for four situations between Hindus and Muslims (3, X seduces and prostitutes Y girls; 7, X trying to convert Y's religion; 10, X blows cigarette smoke on Y passenger; 19, X doctor refuses to treat Y riot victim). In all these situations, Hindus anticipated more negative other group reactions than Muslims.

The Hindus' anticipation of more severe other group reactions from Muslims is further revealed by an analysis of own group reactions for

Table 4.3 Reactions to 21 norm violations of Hindus and Muslims (see Appendix 4.1 for full details)

Situation	Anticipated reactions			
	Own group		Other group	
	Hindus	Muslims	Hindus	Muslims
1 teacher	2.19^{a}	2.59^{b}	2.55^{ab}	2.63^{b}
2 rape complaint	2.67^{a}	2.76^{a}	2.71^{a}	2.81^{a}
3 seduction	2.79^{ab}	2.67^{ab}	3.08^{a}	2.73^{b}
4 teasing	2.56^{a}	2.09^{a}	2.59^{a}	2.51^{a}
5 selling injections	2.47^{a}	2.71^{a}	2.73^{a}	2.70^{a}
6 music	2.05^{a}	1.96^{a}	2.39^{a}	1.99^{a}
7 conversion	1.97^{ab}	1.65^{b}	2.33^{a}	1.79^{b}
8 not attend farewell	2.55^{a}	2.64^{a}	2.87^{a}	2.69^{a}
9 drunk at work	1.95^{ab}	1.71^{a}	2.52^{b}	2.01^{ab}
10 cigarette smoke	1.93^{bc}	1.52^{a}	2.24^{ac}	1.64^{ab}
11 sacred book	2.05^{ab}	1.84^{b}	2.43^{a}	2.01^{ab}
12 obscene gesture	2.25^{ab}	2.03^{b}	2.41^{a}	2.24^{ab}
13 heart attack	2.47^{a}	2.31^{a}	2.68^{a}	2.40^{a}
14 appointment	2.32^{a}	2.28^{a}	2.64^{a}	2.29^{a}
15 collapse of building	2.72^{ab}	2.33^{a}	2.92^{b}	2.51^{ab}
16 adulterated food	2.28^{a}	2.48^{a}	2.89^{a}	2.65^{a}
17 ridicule gods	2.05^{a}	2.80^{b}	2.61^{ab}	2.77^{b}
18 offer seat	2.05^{b}	1.52^{a}	2.26^{b}	1.96^{ab}
19 riot victim	1.81^{ab}	1.57^{b}	2.15^{a}	1.69^{b}
20 no relation with colleague	2.11^{ab}	1.87^{a}	2.41^{b}	2.17^{ab}
21 refuse patient	1.69^{a}	1.39^{b}	2.03^{a}	1.74^{ab}

Means for reactions not sharing common superscripts differ significantly ($p < 0.01$).

each situation and comparison with their anticipation by the other group (Table 4.3). Significant differences were obtained between Muslims' own group reactions and their anticipation as other group reactions by Hindus on as many as 11 situations out of 21 (numbers 3, 7, 9, 10, 11, 12, 15, 18, 19, 20, and 21). The Hindus' own group reactions and their anticipation by Muslims were, however, significantly different for only 2 out of 21 situations (numbers 1 and 17). Only in these two situations did the Muslims anticipate more negative reactions than those predicted as own group reactions by the Hindus.

Thus it appeared that, in particular, the Hindus' anticipation of Muslims' reactions in a considerable number of situations was more negative than the reactions given by the Muslims themselves.

Context variables

Own group identification As mentioned above, the own group identification was measured in terms of the discrepancy between self and own group ratings on a number of adjectives. Table 4.4 gives the mean scores for the two ethnic groups. The results indicated that Hindu subjects had a significantly higher discrepancy between self and own group ratings (mean 1.11) than Muslim respondents (mean 0.84) ($t_{148} = 3.12$, $p < 0.01$). Muslims, in other words, showed a higher own group identification in comparison with the Hindu respondents.

Attitudes towards the own group and the other group Two measures of intergroup attitudes were computed, namely own group attitudes and other group attitudes. Table 4.4 gives the mean scores of the ethnic groups for intergroup attitudes. Results indicated that Muslims had more positive attitudes towards their own group than Hindu respondents ($t_{148} = -4.54$, $p < 0.01$). However, no significant mean difference was obtained for other group attitude. In fact, both groups indicated similar low positive or neutral attitudes towards the other group and significantly more positive attitudes towards their own groups.

Table 4.4 Own group identification and attitudes of Hindus and Muslims

	Hindus	Muslims	*t*
Own group identification			
mean	1.11	0.84	3.12**
SD	0.60	0.46	
Own group attitude			
mean	0.93	2.03	−4.54**
SD	1.23	1.71	
Other group attitude			
mean	0.23	0.19	0.18
SD	1.18	1.45	

A lower score on own group identification is indicative of higher own group identification. Intergroup attitude scores range from −10 to +10.
** $p < 0.01$.

We also asked our respondents about their desire to maintain contact with the other group along Bogardus' social distance scale. It was found that 8 per cent of Hindus reported no desire for contact with the Muslims compared with 1 per cent of the Muslims. More Muslims desired Hindus as their neighbors (31 per cent) compared with the Hindus (11 per cent). Similarly, 24 per cent of the Muslim respondents said that they would like family or marital relations with the Hindus compared with only 14 per cent of the Hindus. In short, Muslims expressed a stronger liking for contact with Hindus than vice versa.

Perceived power Hindus and Muslims were expected to differ on various indicators of perceived power. Table 4.5 gives the means and standard deviations for resource power and retaliatory power of Hindu and Muslim respondents. A 2×2 ANOVA was performed with two levels of ethnic groups and two types of power. Only the main effect of

Table 4.5 Resource and retaliatory power of Hindus and Muslims

	Hindus	Muslims	*t*
Resource power			
mean	3.26	2.40	5.22**
SD	0.91	1.09	
Retaliatory power			
mean	3.27	2.70	3.24**
SD	1.15	1.08	

Scales employed: 1 very little, 2 little, 3 neither less nor more, 4 much, 5 very much.
** $p < 0.01$.

ethnic groups was found to be significant ($F_{1,148} = 45.87$, $p < 0.001$).

The results indicated that for resource power (power in political, social, and economic spheres) Hindu respondents perceived significantly higher own group power than did the Muslim respondents ($t_{148} = 5.22$, $p < 0.01$). Further, with respect to retaliatory power (power to influence day to day life and cause harm to the other group), the Hindu subjects again perceived higher own group power in comparison with Muslim respondents ($t_{148} = 3.24$, $p < 0.01$).

Fraternal relative deprivation Table 4.6 gives the means and standard deviations of the three indicators of fraternal relative deprivation for Hindu and Muslim respondents. A 2 (groups) × 3 (fraternal relative deprivation indicators) ANOVA was performed. It yielded a significant interaction effect ($F_{2,148} = 11.02$, $p < 0.001$) as well as main effects for groups and fraternal relative deprivation indicators. Results indicated that with respect to FRD-present, Muslims expressed higher fraternal relative deprivation in comparison with Hindu subjects ($t_{148} = 8.28$, $p < 0.01$). In relation to FRD-future, similar results were obtained, i.e.

Table 4.6 Fraternal relative deprivation (FRD) of Hindus and Muslims

	Hindus	Muslims	*t*
FRD-present			
mean	3.21	2.09	8.28**
SD	0.81	0.84	
FRD-satisfaction			
mean	2.61	2.01	4.44**
SD	0.77	0.87	
FRD-future			
mean	3.35	2.99	2.07*
SD	0.98	1.15	

A lower score on FRD-present and FRD-future is indicative of a greater amount of fraternal relative deprivation. A high score for FRD-satisfaction indicates high satisfaction.
* $p < 0.05$, ** $p < 0.01$.

Muslims were relatively less optimistic of doing well in comparison with Hindu respondents ($t_{148} = 2.07$, $p < 0.05$). Finally, with respect to FRD-satisfaction, the Muslim subjects again expressed less satisfaction in comparison with Hindu respondents ($t_{148} = 4.44$, $p < 0.01$). An inspection of the table of means showed that whereas Muslims felt presently more relatively deprived, they viewed their future with greater hope. The discrepancy of the means of FRD-present was consequently much larger for the two groups than the discrepancy found in the case of FRD-future.

Relationship between social context factors and norm violation

Appendix 4.2 shows the relationship between social context variables and reactions to norm violation. For both groups a significant correlation was found between own group reaction and anticipated other group reaction. That is, the stronger the own group reaction, the stronger was the anticipated other group reaction for both groups ($r = 0.59$ for the Hindus; $r = 0.43$ for the Muslims). For Hindus, higher own group identification was related to a more positive ingroup attitude ($r = -0.59$), and conversely, a lower own group identification was correlated with a more positive outgroup attitude ($r = 0.27$). The own group identification was also positively correlated with resource power ($r = 0.23$) for Hindus. In addition, Hindus who had a more positive own group attitude also expressed greater satisfaction with the current state of economic, political, and social conditions, i.e. with FRD-satisfaction.

Prediction of reaction to norm violation from context factors Reactions to norm violations, i.e. own group reaction and anticipated other group reaction were predicted on the basis of the own group identification, other group attitude, power, and fraternal relative deprivation. Besides the own group identification and other group attitude, the two measures of power retaliatory and resource power, and three measures of fraternal relative deprivation (FRD-present, FRD-future, and FRD-satisfaction) were also entered using a forced entry procedure in the order listed above. Separate regression equations were formed for the Hindu and Muslim subgroups.

The predictions obtained for the Muslim subgroup were generally non-significant. In the case of Hindus, while the overall *F*-value obtained for the regression for own group reaction was found to be non-significant, the prediction of anticipated other group reactions to norm violation was found to be significant ($F_{6,143} = 3.13$, $p < 0.01$). The seven predictors altogether explained approximately 25 per cent of the total variance in anticipated other group reaction to norm violation ($R = 0.50$, $p < 0.01$). It was found that the higher the own group identification ($\beta = -0.28$) the greater the satisfaction with the present conditions ($\beta = -0.23$), and the lower the hope of doing well in the future ($\beta = -0.23$)

the more negative were the Hindus' anticipated other group reactions. The first five predictors, without FRD-satisfaction and FRD-future, explained 15.4 per cent of variance, of which approximately 12 per cent was accounted for by own group identification. For this five-variable equation, the β coefficients were −0.28 for own group identification, 0.24 for FRD-satisfaction and −0.23 for FRD-future.

Thus, relationships between social context variables and norm violations showed that there is some evidence of context factors predicting anticipated other group reaction to norm violation in case of the Hindus. By comparison, the Muslim respondents' reactions to norm violation are not predicted by the context factors.

Discussion

The focus of the present study was to investigate reactions to norm violations in the context of Hindu–Muslim relations. It was predicted that the degree and strength of these reactions will be a function of the context variables, namely intergroup attitudes, own group identification, perceived power and fraternal relative deprivation.

More specifically, it was hypothesized that while both Hindus and Muslims will react negatively to norm violations, the anticipated other group reactions would be more negative compared with the own group reactions. The findings of this study lend considerable support to the hypothesis formulated (Table 4.2). Both Hindus and Muslims gave similar mildly negative mean own group reactions to norm violations (Hindu means 2.24, Muslim mean 2.13). However, in the case of anticipated other group reactions to norm violations, Hindus gave significantly more negative reactions than Muslims ($t = 2.01$, $p < 0.05$).

It should be noted that in both cases, regardless of ethnic group membership, reactions to norm violations were generally slightly negative. In addition, it was also noticed that irrespective of group membership of the respondent, own group and anticipated other group reactions to norm violations were found to be correlated (Hindu $r = 0.59$, Muslim $r = 0.43$). It thus appears that similarity in the process of reactions to norm violations is indicated regardless of ethnic group membership. It is only in the intensity or strength of reactions that the two contrast groups differed, and this only with respect to anticipated other group reactions.

An analysis of the percentage of different categories of responses to norm violation (R+, R0, R−, R=, R≡) also showed considerable similarity in the two contrast groups (Fig. 4.1), indicating further similarity in the processes underlying reactions to norm violations. Similar patterns of reactions for the own and other groups were obtained for both Hindus and Muslims.

A major finding of the present study was that the Hindus' anticipated other group reactions to norm violations were found to be more negative than the own group reactions to norm violations ($t = -3.88$, $p < 0.01$). No significant difference between own group reactions and anticipated other group reactions to norm violation were obtained for the Muslims. The Hindus in comparison with Muslims, thus anticipated stronger reactions to norm violations from the other group.

It may be observed further that although Muslims predicted that the reaction of their own group to norm violation would be weak (mean 2.10), the Hindus did not concur and anticipated a much stronger reaction by a Muslim victim (mean 2.54). There was, however, greater congruence of perception between Hindu own group reactions (mean 2.24) and the anticipation of these reactions by Muslims (mean 2.28). In other words, while Hindus displayed a somewhat exaggerated anticipation of stronger other group reactions, the Muslims tended to show a more consensual, shared, and valid appraisal of other group reactions.

A situation-wise analysis of own group reactions and comparison with their anticipation by the other group is also supportive of the general pattern of results for the overall means of the 21 situations as stated above (Table 4.3). Significant differences were obtained between Muslims' own group reactions and their anticipated other group reaction by Hindus on 11 situations. In all these situations the Hindus anticipated more negative other group reactions than own group reactions to norm violation by Muslims themselves. However, Hindus' own group reactions to norm violations were only significantly different from anticipated other group reaction on two situations. In these two situations the Muslims anticipated the other group reaction to be more negative than that predicted by the Hindus as their own group reactions.

Thus, in general terms it may be summarized that while both Hindus and Muslims show similarity in patterns of reactions to norm violations, in the context of their respective own groups, differences are noted between Hindus and Muslims in the anticipation of reactions of the other group. The Hindus, it appears, show a greater apprehension in their anticipation of Muslim reaction, while the Muslims displayed a less differentiated own versus other group reaction to norm violation. Clearly these modes of reactions are closely linked to the context of intergroup relations prevailing between the two contrast groups.

We were expecting differences in the responses of the two groups in the light of their sociohistorical relationships but in most cases these were found missing, In retrospect, however, expecting this may have been a mistake. It is quite likely that for groups which have a long history of ethnic violence, as in the case of the Hindus and Muslims, the initial response to norm violation by the interacting members may be conciliatory with the express purpose of de-escalating the conflict. Just because two groups have been locked up in conflict, one should not expect that they will take up the first opportunity to strike back. They also know the cost involved in it. This logic is supported by the results obtained in another study done by us (Tripathi and Ansari 1980). In this study, the modes of resolution of communal conflict employed by the Hindus and Muslims were investigated. We presented seven situations involving communal intergroup conflicts and asked them for their preferences for the manner in which they should be resolved. The modes of resolutions suggested were along the lines of Blake and Mouton (1964). Both Hindus and Muslims overwhelmingly opted for compromise as the preferred mode for the resolution of such conflicts. The second most preferred mode was withdrawal. Forcing came out as the third preferred mode. It, therefore appears that for groups like the Hindus and Muslims with a history of conflict, deliberate attempts may be made to maintain peace and also to avoid being blamed for the conflict. This, however, does not explain how such groups repeatedly become locked up in conflict. At this stage we can only propose a hypothesis. It appears to us that the crucial reaction which may explain how groups are locked into conflict is not the first but the second reaction (or call it norm violation) of the norm violator to the victim reaction. This may be explained better with an example. Suppose a Muslim teases a Hindu girl. Now suppose that the girl (or other Hindus) slaps the boy, the boy (or his group members) may apologize or may hit back. In case of the former reaction the conflict would dissipate, whereas in the second case escalation of conflict is more likely. Felson (1984) also found results which can be interpreted as supportive of this hypothesis at the interpersonal level. He analysed descriptions given by persons involved in incidents of varying intensity, such as involving guns, slapping or hitting, screaming and shouting, and incidents in which individuals became angry but did nothing. Felson analysed the order of actions involving the four types of incidents and found that in all cases social control tended to occur early. The action becomes more severe as the incident progresses.

The rather cautious reactions of the Muslims in this study may have another explanation. While the data for this study were being collected, an incident involving the two communities took place which led to considerable tension between them. The District Administration had to impose restrictions on the movement of the people in certain areas of the town. Although we allowed considerable time to pass before starting our data collection, it is not inconceivable that this may have influenced the reactions of both communities, especially those of the minority community of Muslims. As noted earlier, in almost all communal riots, Muslims have suffered greater loss of life and property. Any communal incident is likely to make respondents less open to talking about it.

It may be suggested that considering the Islamic history of conquest in India, the Muslims are stereotypically viewed as more cruel, barbaric, and violent by the Hindus. Support for such stereotypical views can be sought in the history of forced conversions to Islam, destruction of Hindu temples, and pillage for more than five hundred years by different Muslim rulers. Combined with the recent Hindu revivalism in the form of Vishwa Hindu Parishad (World Hindu Council), there could be a projection of such Hindu fears to threats by the Muslims. Doctrines of revivalism require 'slogans' and 'enemies' who can be easily identified and attributed hostile intent. It is therefore plausible to suggest that the Hindu apprehension of a Muslim 'backlash' is a result of anticipation of chain reactions to a series of reciprocal norm violation sequences in their intergroup relations. It may also be pointed out that both Hindu and Muslim precepts provide a differential structure of society. The Hindu social structure is homohierarchically arranged whereas the Islamic social structure is based on brotherhood and the equality of all. It is therefore suggested that an ethnocentric bias for Hindus is more in line with hierarchical structuring and characterizations of social groups, whereas the Muslim prediction of similar reactions to norm violation regardless of the victim's group membership may represent the Islamic values of equality in sociostructural relations.

What about the role of social contextual factors played in this study? Except for own group identification and fraternal relative deprivation indicators in the case of anticipated other group reactions by Hindus, none of the context variables predicted reactions. The relationships among the context variables themselves, however, were found to follow expected lines. For almost all the variables, except other group attitude, differences between Hindus and Muslims were obtained. Among the context variables, differences between the Hindus and Muslims were obtained for own group identification (that of the Muslims being greater), own group attitude (Muslims regarded their group more positively), resource and retaliatory power (Muslims were lower), and the three indicators of fraternal relative deprivation (Muslims had higher levels of FRD-present and FRD-future and were less satisfied with their current position). Only the variance of anticipated other group reaction of the Hindus was significantly explained by social context factors ($R = 0.393$, $p < 0.05$). Of the predictors only own group identification was found to be significant. It alone exlained 12 per cent of the variance ($R = 0.343$, $p < 0.01$). Two fraternal relative deprivation indicators, FRD-future and FRD-satisfaction, improved the prediction when added (from $R^2 = 0.154$ to $R^2 = 0.246$). The intensity of the Hindus' anticipated other group reaction was thus associated with greater own group identification, greater satisfaction with their current conditions and negative apprehensions about the future of their group.

These results were very similar to results obtained in other research. For example, the greater own group identification found for the Muslims may be seen as an effort to achieve a greater degree of positive group distinctiveness (Tajfel 1982). In fact, we computed the discrepancy for both the positive and negative traits attributed to self and own group for the two groups. It was only with respect to the positive traits that the differences between the two groups were found to be significant ($F_{1,73} = 11.71$, $p < 0.01$). The findings on intergroup attitudes also supported the above results. Muslims held a much more positive attitude of their own group, as has been reported previously (Majeed and Ghosh 1981; Tripathi and Srivastava 1981; Mohsin 1984; Ghosh and Huq 1985). However, no differences in other group attitudes were found, as was expected. Nevertheless, when one considers the ratings given by the respondents to the outgroup and the ingroup on negative and positive traits separately, it was found that the Muslims did rate the Hindus less positively relative to their own group ($F_{1,73} = 26.51$, $p < 0.001$). It should also be mentioned that both Hindus and Muslims expressed more positive attitudes for their own group than for the other group. Such a finding is supportive of a general ethnocentric own group preference in the context of studies related to intergroup attitudes. What is relevant, however, is that a similar own group bias was not evident in the results pertaining to reactions to norm violations by the two contrast groups. It is plausible to suggest that since reactions to norm violation refer to behavioural situations, the attitudinal own group bias is considerably moderated by the social contextual dynamics of Hindu–Muslim intergroup relations. Thus the Muslims predicted similar reactions to norm violation for both own group victim and other group victim. The Hindus, however, displayed an own group bias and anticipated a more negative other group reaction to norm violations.

The difference between the two groups with respect to power perhaps also reflects the objective conditions of the Muslim minority, although our measures were perceptual. Not only are Muslims numerically small, they are generally poor as a group and politically less powerful. These objective conditions also feed into their feelings of fraternal relative deprivation. They reported greater fraternal relative deprivation relative to the Hindus for all the three domains and for all the three indicators. These findings corroborated what was found in other studies by Naqvi (1980) and Ansari (1983). The interesting result was the interaction effect between the groups and the three indicators of fraternal relative deprivation. Muslims relative to the Hindus showed a greater degree of rising expectations and had a rosier picture of their future, although the expectations they had were still below the expectations of the Hindus. We computed the discrepancies in the mean ratings between FRD-present and FRD-future for the three domains for both groups. For the Muslims, these were found to be 0.81 for the economic, 0.97 for the social, and 1.02 for the political domains. The comparable discrepancies for the Hindus in economic, social and political domains were found to be 0.21, 0.03, and 0.11 respectively. For the Muslims fraternal relative deprivation was greater in the economic domain, followed by the political and social domains. Folger (1986) considers that resentment from relative deprivation is a function of (i) one's perception that one's present condition is due to unjust procedures, and (ii) poor expectations about one's future. Could this be the reason that fraternal relative deprivation did not act in the manner in which it was expected to in the case of the Muslims? Also can one explain the stronger anticipated other group reactions of the Hindus because of their apprehensions about the future and feelings that the Muslims are getting more than they deserve. These are possibilities one could test in future studies.

One may ask why our model is only partially supported. There appear to be several reasons for this. We have already alluded to a theoretical reason, i.e. the first reactions – to the extent that they are conflict free – may not be explained by the social contextual variables. In any case, most of the reactions obtained by us were positive reactions. One could not expect variance of such reactions to be explained in terms of the social contextual variables which appear to be most useful in explaining behaviour in situations of conflict. Only when, as a result of norm violation, groups are locked in conflict and conflict attains a social texture, can social contextual factors explain the action of group members involved in conflict. Another plausible reason for the context variables not explaining adequately the variance in Muslim reactions may be the large measurement error associated with measures of other group attitude, retaliatory power, FRD-present, and FRD-satisfaction. In all these cases, reliability values of the scales were less than satisfactory.

Finally, some implications of the results obtained in this study may be drawn. They will necessarily have to be tentative in the light of the results obtained and the theoretical and methodological problems mentioned above. As far as the reactions to norm violation are concerned it appears that the Hindus' anticipation of stronger reactions from the Muslims may lead them to become involved in conflicts which are avoidable, particularly in view of the fact that they enjoy greater resource and retaliatory power. What also appears critical here is that the Hindus are not as optimistic abot their future as the Muslims are. Part of the reason for this may be that the Muslims feel that they cannot be ignored by any political party because of their numbers. Most political parties, therefore, symbolically at least use rhetoric of secularism. This is resented by a large number of Hindus. Even the slightest concession to Muslims or assertion by the Muslims of their identity moves the Hindus a step towards fundamentalism. The conditions do not yet seem ripe for better intergroup relations between the two communities.

Notes

[1] The term 'communal' is used as the opposite of 'secular'. A communal person is credited with the belief 'my group – right or wrong' and berates other groups in society. Communal riots are riots involving Hindu and Muslim communities.
[2] The adjective 'fighter' was later dropped from the analysis as it was rated as 'desirable' by the Muslims and 'undesirable' by the Hindus. Thus, nineteen adjectives (ten positive and nine negative) were used in the scales.

5 The darker side of the worker–manager relationship in a coal area in India[1]

Ravi B. P. Singh and Jai B. P. Sinha

Introduction

Within the theoretical framework outlined in Chapter 1, we intend to examine how managers are likely to react to norm violations by their workers and how workers are likely to react if their managers violate norms. The strength of the reactions is postulated to be influenced by a number of factors, some of which are spelled out as own group identification, attitudes to own and other group, power, and fraternal relative deprivation of managers and workers (Chapter 1). These proximate factors may themselves be rooted in the broader socioeconomic and political milieu which in India is characterized by rapid expansion of industrial activities, politicized and fragmented trade unions, increasing intervention of the government in the functioning of work organizations, and the steeply hierarchical social system which renders the manager–worker contrast quite salient.

The milieu

At the time of Independence, around 80 per cent of the industrial activities in India were confined to cotton, jute, coal, and one small and one large steel mill. The remaining activities were accounted for by small and medium size private enterprises. The public sector domain was limited to railways, post and telegraph, and ordnance factories. In 1951 there were only five units in the public sector with a total investment of Rs 290 million[2]. By 1980 the number of centrally established units increased to 179 with Rs 225 000 million investment. If the local and state units are included, the number may exceed 600 with net assets of over Rs 250 000 million. The total number of registered factories was more than 18 000 with a capital investment of over Rs 350 000 million (Statistical Abstracts 1984). With the base line of industrial production at 100 in 1951, the index has climbed to 608.80 in 1985 (Agrawal *et al.* 1988, p. 114). India is considered to be one of the ten most industrialized countries in the world. The total employment in the industrial sector in 1986 was of the order of 25 million; of which about 71 per cent was located in the public sector, accounting for about two thirds of industrial activities. The employment in the industrial sector, however, constituted only about 13.50 per cent of the total employment in the country (Centre for Monitoring Indian Economy 1985).

The increasing size of the work-force had a direct bearing on trade unionism in the country. The number of trade unions increased from 3.77 thousand in 1950–51 to about 34.5 thousand in 1979. All major political parties maintain a trade union wing which is fragmented as soon as the parent party breaks into two or more factions. They compete for the workers' allegiance by being increasingly more militant. Hence, the number of industrial disputes increased by about 23 per cent from 1961 to 1985, the number of workers involved increased by 52 per cent, and the man days lost climbed to about 83 per cent. Not only the number of strikes (8 per cent) but also the instances of lockout[3] increased (70 per cent) during the period. In fact the increase in the number of workers involved in strikes and the resultant increase in man days loss (51 per cent and 74 per cent respectively) were smaller than the increases caused by lockouts (60 per cent and 89 per cent respectively, Agrawal *et al.* 1988, p. 146).

Industrial relations, thus, remain conflict ridden despite the elaborate procedures designed for the formation and recognition of trade unions, and prevention and settlements of disputes (Industrial Dispute Act 1947). The Constitution of India (1949) subscribed to the principle of workers' and managers' partnership in running a work organization. The Industrial Policy Resolution (1956) reiterated that 'labour is a partner', and the Scheme of Workers Participation in Industry (1975) was implemented by an executive order of the Government of India in all manufacturing and mining industries employing more than 500 workers. The draft of the 7th Five Year Plan (1977–83) spelled out the philosophy behind such a persistent effort to introduce a participative scheme: 'Planned economic growth can be ensured only with the workmen leading the maintenance and promotion of industrial harmony' (p. 274). Despite such persistent efforts, industrial relations seemed to be far from harmonious. Because managers are expected to represent the management, the problems of industrial relations often spill over the manager–worker relationship. Managers and workers are formally defined as distinct and non-overlapping groups. Managers are those who are designated as managers, are put on the officer's pay roll, delegated with authority over non-managers, and have at least one assistant working under them. Workers are wage board employees, they are entitled to be unionized, and are so defined in the Industrial Dispute Act (1947). Not only do the roles and positions of workers and managers differ, their backgrounds are different too.

Indian managers are reported to be college educated, they are socialized in English medium schools, are urbanized, the sons of white collar workers, and generally cherish the values of elitism (Jain 1971; Subramaniam 1971; Dhingra and Pathak 1972; Saiyadain and Manappa 1977). They are highly status conscious (Sinha 1980) and probably tend to maintain greater power distance from their workers. They are used to give orders to their workers who are expected to follow them without questions.

The workers as a group are relatively less educated, are paid less, are drawn from the lower castes and lower socioeconomic strata, and are treated as 'hands' which must be made to work by their managers. They are not a part of the management, and hence are not obliged to share the organizational goals. They have to work as directed. However, many of them are now conscious of their rights and do not subscribe to the restricted role boundaries. They resist their managers and even pressurize them to let them get away with the least possible amount of work. Managers in many organizations yield to them. Those who resist invite hostilities and conflicts, particularly from the unionized workers. Instances of disobedience, defiance, abuse, assaults, and riotous behaviour by workers, particularly in the public sector, have been reported by Sharma (1979), S. Singh (1988) and Sinha (in press). Managers' reactions vary from lying low and saving their own face, through charge sheeting,[4] to strong retaliations.

The coal industry does not seem to be an exception. It is one of the core sectors which preceded the industrial growth of the country. The first coal mine was opened in 1815 (Seth 1940). By 1951 there were 893 mines producing about 35 million tons with a work-force of 352 thousand (Agrawal *et al.* 1988, p. 84). Most of the mines were privately owned, open and shallow, unscientifically operated with hand labour, and naturally gave a very poor yield. The Government of India nationalized them (barring a few) by 1973 and reorganized them into a number of zones for rapid development and modernization. The unproductive mines were closed down. In 1983 the number of mines was reported to be 493 (Statistical Abstracts 1984, p. 81). By 1986–7 the production climbed to 175.4 million tons (p. 115) and the employment (in 1985) to 550 thousand. The number of trade unions in coal and quarrying was 143 (Agrawal *et al.* 1988, p. 143).

Research setting

The coal zones were further demarcated into areas. One of the 17 areas of a zone in the eastern part of the country was selected for the study. The area had nine collieries, three workshops, one regional store, and an area office. Production varies from 943 thousand to 1777 thousand tons (1982–86). There were 141 managers who were differentiated into nine levels with the general manager at the head of the area. The collieries were headed by managers, also called agents, who had three tiers of managers under them. The workers too belonged to a number of categories which differed in the nature of work, service conditions, and benefits. Some were daily rated workers, others were monthly rated. Some were clerical and support staff working in the offices of the collieries. The bulk were the miners who were by and large uneducated and manual workers. There were six unions and three more craftmen's unions. During January 1985 to July 1986 (the period of the study), the area experienced 11 strikes causing the loss of 1988 man days and 21 159 tons of production. The monthly absenteeism rate from December 1984 to August 1986 was as high as 36.95 per cent, of which 21.71 per cent was illegal.

We collected a number of instances of unauthorized absenteeism, disobedience, undiscipline, abuse and threats to officers, and drunkenness of workers for which charges were formally framed for disciplinary action. There were many more cases which were not recorded either because the managers concerned did not feel comfortable reporting or because the workers apologized and were excused. Similarly, workers narrated a number of instances of managers using abusive language, pressurizing the workers to do their personal errands, and exploiting them in many different ways. These were, however, beyond the reach of the normal procedures of censure or punishment, or even recording by either the management or the unions. Thus, the nature of the manager–worker relationship in this coal area seemed to share many of the features reported elsewhere (Sharma 1979; S. Singh 1988; Sinha, in press) and, therefore, was selected as an appropriate setting for examining reactions to norm violations by managers and workers.

Hypotheses

As stated earlier, managers and workers constitute distinctly separate groups in terms of the conceptualization of a group by Sherif (1967). They are labelled separately with identifiably different positions and roles. The boundaries are not permeable, i.e. managers cannot be downgraded to workers' levels and significant numbers of workers are unlikely to be promoted to the managers' levels. At best they aspire to become supervisors. The groups are in transaction in the sense that the managers and their workers work together and are in regular contact with each other. Although their goals may be incompatible, their roles render them interdependent in work-related activities; despite the fact that their backgrounds, education, skills, etc. are quite different. Hence in the light of the discussions in Chapter 1, the following hypothesis may be postulated.

Hypothesis 1. Both managers and workers will have a strong own group identification and a positive attitude to their own group. By the same token, both groups will have relatively less positive attitudes to the other group.

Managers and workers as groups are not only different but are differentiated hierarchically. Managers have higher positions than workers on the organizational rungs. Their positions are vested with greater legal and formal power which allows them to order and direct their workers, and to apply sanctions against them if workers do not follow their directions. Managers are more privileged in terms of their social background, economic status, and pay and perks. They are in a better position to cultivate political linkages or to establish networks with those who matter in other spheres of society (cf. Sinha 1982, 1986). Because the groups of managers and workers interact regularly, they are likely to compare their own group with the other group. The comparison is likely to create the following situation.

Hypothesis 2. Managers will perceive themselves as more privileged and powerful than workers who, in turn, will perceive themselves as relatively more deprived and less powerful than managers.

Following the norm violation theory (Chapter 1) and the manager–worker contrast as described above, the following may be expected.

Hypothesis 3. Norm violations by either managers or workers will lead to negative reactions on the part of the other group.

It is further expected that managers and workers will differ in the intensity of their reactions to norm violations by the other group. The superiority of managers in terms of their privileged positions and power and the workers' fraternal relative deprivation and lack of power are likely to moderate the perception of the seriousness of norm violations. Managers may expect greater conformity to the norms from their workers than workers expect from the managers. Hence, norm violations by workers may be perceived as more serious by managers who are, therefore, likely to react more negatively than they would anticipate the workers to react if the managers violated a norm.

Hypothesis 4. Managers will react more negatively to norm violations by their workers than the workers will if their managers violate norms.

Hypothesis 4 may not hold true in those situations where a relatively deprived group of workers, which has tolerated fraternal relative deprivation for a long time, has started to confront the managers by developing a capacity to retaliate. The evidence in the preceding section indicates that the workers in the coal area where the study was conducted did indulge in acts of disobedience, undiscipline, and abuse of their managers. Sharma (1979), S. Singh (1988), and Sinha (in press) reported similar situations in other organizations. This suggests the following hypothesis.

Hypothesis 5. The workers' perception of their own retaliatory power will be positively related to the strength of their negative reactions to norm violations by managers.

A positive correlation between retaliatory power and negative reactions to norm violations is likely to be found in any contrast group. Ng (1982, p. 202) pointed out that power makes latent negative reactions manifest. If this is so, then hypothesis 5 will also hold true for managers. In fact, because they perceive greater retaliatory power in their managers, the workers may apprehend stronger negative reactions by managers.

Hypothesis 6. The workers will expect stronger negative reactions by managers to norm violations by workers than they expect their own group's reaction to be to norm violation by managers.

Method

Sample

The sample consisted of 78 managers and 80 workers who were interviewed with the help of a questionnaire. One worker and one manager were dropped because the information in their questionnaire was found to be incomplete. Hence, the final sample consisted of 77 managers and 79 workers. The supervisory staff were excluded in order to maintain a clear contrast between managers and workers. The average age of managers was 38.03 years (SD = 8.32), and that of the workers was 32.57 years (SD = 5.93). The age difference was significant ($t_{154} = 4.75$, $p < 0.01$). Most of the managers had college education while the majority of workers were illiterate. A small percentage of them had junior or high school education.

Before starting the interviews, the first author approached the top executive of the area for permission to conduct the research. He carried a letter of introduction from the second author who described the purpose, the procedure, and the implications of the research. The top executive granted permission and gave to the second author a letter of permission with copies to all departments and collieries. The first author spent one month in the area, met managers, workers, and trade union leaders, and interacted with them freely in order to explain the purpose of the research, to establish rapport, and to collect secondary source data. Thereafter, he interviewed all managers individually with the help of a questionnaire. Interviews were conducted either in their office or at their residence according to their convenience. Workers were sampled in the day shift. Those who were available were contacted individually. As the majority of them were illiterate, items were read out to them. Their responses were recorded by the first author. All were assured that their responses would be kept confidential. Some busy managers took the questionnaire to their home and returned it the next day. The secondary source data were collected from the offices. Altogether the data collection took a little more than six months.

Instruments

As discussed in Chapter 2, a pool of common measures was jointly developed by the three research teams. They were (i) situations of norm violations and reactions to them, (ii) own group identification, (iii) attitudes to own group and other group, (iv) power of own group and other group, and (v) fraternal relative deprivation. The measures were subjected to pilot-studies in India and The Netherlands. Our pilot run led to a number of revisions. The revised measures for the present study were as follows.

The norm violation inventory Thirty pairs of situations describing norm violations by either manager(s) or worker(s) were drawn from the common pool (see Chapter 2). Wordings of some of the situations were changed to suit the Indian condition. For example, the matching item for 'workers threw garbage in front of manager's house' was formulated as 'the servants of managers threw garbage in front of worker's house'. Another item 'during a strike, workers broke some machines in order to implicate the managers' was paired with 'during a strike, managers got some machines broken in order to implicate the workers'. Both examples depict situations where a group of workers or managers violated norms. In other situations, norm violations occurred in a dyadic context, for example 'a worker abused a manager' or 'a manager abused a worker'. Both types of situations, of course, pertain to intergroup behaviour.

The situations were given to a panel of seven judges who had a master's degree in one of the social sciences. They were asked to judge if the situations involved any norm violation and were realistic in the Indian setting. Three situations which did not meet the criterion of 70 per cent agreement among the judges were dropped.

Twenty-seven situations were given to a sample of 20 managers and 20 workers drawn from a public sector oil refinery in the eastern part of India. Each situation was followed by five alternative reactions to norm violation. The reactions ranged from mildly positive (1) to strongly negative (5). An example of a pair of situations with the five alternative reactions is the following.

> A manager beats up a worker's son for roughing up his own son. How will the worker react? He will

(1) try to please the manager in order to avoid conflict in the future, R+ (mildly positive);
(2) do nothing, R0;
(3) quarrel with the manager seriously, R− (mildly negative);
(4) beat up the manager's son at the first opportunity, R= (negative reaction as strong as the preceding violation);
(5) harass the manager in the work situation, R≡ (strongly negative).

> A worker beats up a manager's son for roughing up his own son. How will the manager react? He will

(1) try to be friendly in order to avoid any such event in the future, R+ (mildly positive);

(2) do nothing, R0;

(3) warn the worker seriously, R− (mildly negative);

(4) beat up worker's son at the first opportunity, R= (negative reaction as strong as the preceding violation);

(5) harass the worker in the work situation, R≡ (strongly negative).

The alternatives were randomized in order to avoid any response set effect. Whether an alternative was coded R+, R0, R−, R=, or R≡ depended partly on the seriousness of a norm violation. For example, if a worker abuses a manager, the workers' assault of the manager may constitute R≡, while giving warning may be R−. But a warning to a worker who 'while coming to work on his scooter did not give a lift to his manager' is R≡ and even implausible. In other words, a sliding scale was employed with due precaution to keep the strength of alternatives as comparable across the situations as feasible. Because most of the situations involved serious violations, the alternatives were more or less comparable.

On the basis of the pilot study, seven situations which did not elicit negative reactions (R−, R=, R≡) or failed to have at least 25 per cent variations in reactions of the combined groups of managers and workers of the main study (n = 156) were dropped. Finally, 20 pairs of norm-violating situations were retained. The mean reaction scores with standard deviations are given in Appendix 5.1. The α coefficients for own group reactions were 0.63 for managers and 0.65 for workers. For the anticipated other group's reactions the respective α coefficients were 0.75 and 0.84. Thus, the reliability coefficients of anticipated reactions of the other group were higher and satisfactory while those for the own group reaction were just acceptable.

Measures of attitudes and own group identification Fifteen positive and 15 negative adjectives of the common pool were retained in the present study (Table 5.1).

The respondents (n = 40) in the pilot-study rated their applicability three times: first for themselves, then for managers, and finally for workers. A five-point scale of 'most applicable' (5) to 'not applicable at all' (1) was employed. The respondents commented during the interviews, and later on the data substantiated, that it was difficult to differentiate between 'most applicable' and 'applicable' or between 'not applicable' and 'not at all applicable'. The conceptual frame of the respondents seemed to consist of a binary response mode of either applicable or not applicable. Hence, 77 managers and 79 workers in the main study were asked to check 15 positive and 15 negative adjectives as either applicable or not applicable to (i) self, (ii) managers, and (iii) workers. The endorsements of 'applicable' for a positive adjective and 'not applicable' for a negative adjective were scored 2; while 'not applicable' for a positive adjective and 'applicable' for a negative adjective were scored 1. Thus, if

Table 5.1 Adjectives used for the measurement of attitudes and own group identification

Positive	Negative
1 Laborious	16 Lazy
2 Gentle	17 Coward
3 Grateful	18 Ungrateful
4 Generous	19 Cunning
5 Stalwart	20 Emotional
6 Helpful	21 Corrupt
7 Useful	22 Harmful
8 Strong	23 Hostile
9 Bold	24 Militant
10 Productive	25 Jealous
11 Intelligent	26 Dull
12 Clever	27 Manipulative
13 Polite	28 Liar
14 Trustworthy	29 Selfish
15 Soft	30 Cruel

The order of positive and negative adjectives was randomized.

a respondent endorsed 10 positive and 5 negative adjectives for, say, the self, his score amounted to (10 positive endorsed $\times 2$) + (5 positive not endorsed $\times 1$) + (5 negative endorsed $\times 1$) + (10 negative not endorsed $\times 2$), i.e. 50, which was divided by 30 to obtain his mean score of, for example, 1.67. The scores were analysed in different combinations to yield three attitude measures and two indices of group identification as discussed below.

The attitude towards the *self* was manifested by the average of the sum of all adjective (scores) endorsed by the managers and the workers for themselves. The scores were computed separately for managers and workers. The α coefficients for managers and workers were 0.60 and 0.59 which were just acceptable.

The attitude towards the *own group* was the average of the mean scores of all adjective (scores) endorsed by the managers for the manager's group and by the workers for the worker's group. The α levels for managers and workers were high (0.82) and satisfactory (0.73) respectively.

The attitude towards the *other group* was derived by computing the average of the mean adjective scores of the managers for workers and of the workers for managers. The α coefficients were high for both managers (0.79) and workers (0.88).

Own group identification indices were computed separately for the managers and the workers by subtracting the average of the own group score from the average of the self score for each of the 30 adjectives irrespective of their being positive or negative. For example, if the mean score of the managers for self for the adjective 'laborious' was 1.80 and the mean score of the managers for managers was 1.55, the own group identification score of the managers for the adjective 'laborious' is 0.25. For the same adjective, the workers mean score for self might be 1.90 and their mean score for the workers might be 1.79, thus yielding a workers' score of 0.11. Because the scores were derived by subtracting the group scores from their corresponding self scores, smaller scores indicated greater own group identification. For example, the workers in this example showed a greater own group identification than the managers for this adjective. The scores were averaged across 30 adjectives to provide an average own group identification score separately for managers and workers. The α coefficient for the managers was satisfactory (0.75), while for the workers it was just acceptable (0.60).

Power The power of the managers and workers was measured differently from that of the other studies (See Chapters 2–4). In the other studies, the political, economic, and social power of the own group over the other group and that of the other group over the own group were rated on five-point scales. In addition, two items of retaliatory power of the own group and the other group were rated on five-point scales. Retaliatory power was assessed as the extent to which one group can (i) harm the other group and (ii) influence the day to day life of the other group. Our own pilot-study showed that the respondents, particularly the workers, did not differentiate between economic, social, and political power. They did place managers and workers at different positions on a ladder of social, economic, and political privileges, but failed to connect them cognitively. Instead, they seemed to have a global picture of the extent to which the own and other groups could (i) help and/or (ii) harm and harass each other. Hence, managers and workers were asked six straightforward questions.

How much power:

(1) managers have over workers;

(2) workers have over managers?

To what extent, workers, if they so wish can:

(3) harass;

(4) harm managers?

To what extent, managers, if they so wish, can:

(5) harass;

(6) harm workers?

The ratings were obtained on a five-point scale ranging from 'not at all' (1) to 'very great extent' (5) with 'some extent' (3) in the middle. The scores on the six items were so rearranged as to provide four indices of power.

1. The resource power of the own group was the power of managers to influence workers and the power of workers to influence managers. The scores were the ratings on items (1) and (2) for managers and workers respectively. The scores varied from 1 to 5. The α coefficients were quite high for managers (0.91) and for workers (0.88).

2. The retaliatory power of the own group of the managers was the mean power score of managers to harm and to harass workers (items (5) and (6)). Similarly, the retaliatory power of workers was the mean power score of workers to harm and harass managers (items (3) and (4)). The scores again ranged from 1 to 5. The α coefficients were satisfactory for both managers (0.75) and workers (0.76).

3. The other group's resource power of the managers was their rating of the capacity of workers to influence them (items (1) and (2)). Similarly, the other group's resource power of the workers was their rating of the managers' capacity to influence them. That is, the other group's resource power was the extent of their expectation to be influenced by the other group. The scores ranged from 1 to 5. While the α coefficient for the managers was very high (0.98), it was acceptable (0.68) for the workers.

4. The other group's retaliatory power was the managers' perception of the workers' mean power to harm and harass the managers (items (3) and (4)). Similarly, the other group's retaliatory power of the workers was the managers' mean power to harm and harass the workers (items (5) and (6)). The scores again ranged from 1 to 5 with an acceptable α coefficient for the managers (0.73) and unsatisfactory coefficient for the workers (0.43).

Fraternal relative deprivation The measure of fraternal relative deprivation was similar to the other studies in this book. However, our pilot study necessitated a different format. Other studies (see Chapters 2–4), required the respondents to rate their own group's position on a five-point scale (much lower to much higher position) compared with that of the other group for social, political, and economic dimensions. Our pilot study, as stated in the measure of power, revealed that the managers and the workers were capable of comparing each other on social, economic, and political dimensions. However, they felt uncomfortable with the format of the items of fraternal relative deprivation. After checking with our respondents we used a simpler measure, the ladder test, which provided a familiar visual display of the dimensions and thereby rendered the comparisons rather easy. We added a fourth dimension of education. We tried the ladder test with 20 coal workers. They seemed much more comfortable with the ladder test. So four ladders were presented to the managers and the workers, one for each of four areas: social, economic, educational, and political. Each ladder had ten rungs with zero as the lowest point and ten as the highest position of privileges. The lower the score, the relatively more deprived the group was considered to be. The samples of managers and workers were asked to locate managers and workers on each of the ladders. The responses generated the following indices.

1. The relative position of the own group signified (i) the managers' perception of the managers' positions and (ii) the workers' perception of workers' positions on social, economic, educational, and political ladders. The scores were averaged across four ladders to yield a score of relative position ranging from 1 to 10.
2. The relative position of the other group meant (i) the managers' perception of the workers' positions on four ladders and (ii) the workers' perception of the managers' positions on four ladders. The scores were again averaged across the four ladders to provide a score of relative position of the other group.

The α coefficients of own and other group ratings by managers were acceptable (0.61 and 0.69 respectively). However, the corresponding coefficients for workers' own and other group ratings (0.54 and 0.57 respectively) were unsatisfactory.

Results

The design for the analyses of reactions to norm violations, attitudes, group identification, power, and fraternal relative deprivation was common. It involved a 2×2 ANOVA in which the groups (managers/workers) constituted a between-subjects factor own group (managers' reactions about managers and workers' reactions about workers) versus anticipated other group reactions (managers anticipation of workers' reactions and workers' anticipation of managers' reactions) which were within-subjects effects. Furthermore, the mean comparisons for the group effects separately between own group and anticipated other group reaction were made by t-tests.

Reactions to norm violations

Before the results of the ANOVA are examined, it may be worthwhile to look at the pattern of reactions to norm violations. The mean percentage of managers' and workers' own group and anticipated other group reactions to the five alternatives (R+, R0, R−, R=, R≡) are presented in Fig. 5.1.

It appears that sizeable percentages of managers reported that their own group is likely either to take a positive view or to react mildly negatively to norm violations by workers. They also anticipated that the modal reaction of workers would also be mildly negative. However, a relatively greater number of managers (15.19 per cent) expected their

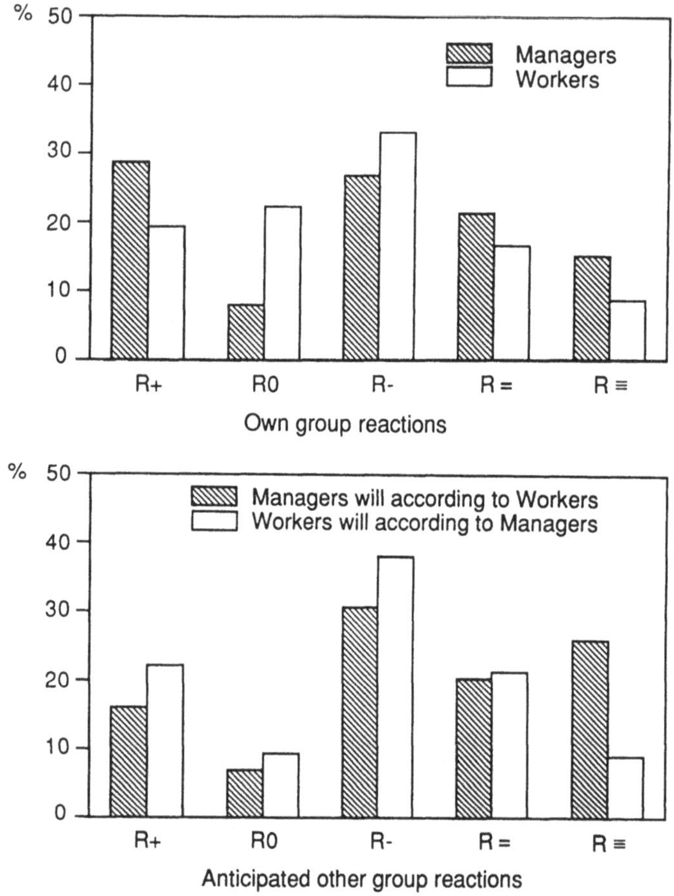

Figure 5.1 Reactions to norm violation by managers and workers

own group to react more strongly than they anticipated the workers to react (9.09 per cent). The workers too perceived that their own group as well as the managers would react negatively but mildly (R−) to norm violation. However, a large percentage of them anticipated more strongly negative reactions from the managers (R≡) than from their own group. About 22 per cent of the workers felt that their own group would do nothing (R0) as a result of norm violations by managers. In fact, larger percentages of workers anticipated equally negative (R=) or strongly negative reactions by managers (R≡) than by their own group.

Managers' and workers' perceptions of their own group and anticipated other group reactions were averaged across five alternatives and are reported in Table 5.2.

Table 5.2 shows that managers on the whole did not report any difference in their own group reactions and the anticipated reactions of

Table 5.2 Reactions to norm violation: means and standard deviations of managers and workers

Reaction	Managers	Workers	*t*
Own group			
mean	2.86	2.73	1.89
SD	0.45	0.41	
Other group			
Mean	2.86	3.33	−5.04**
SD	0.48	0.67	

Scale employed: 1 positive reaction, 2 no reaction, 3 minor reaction, 4 equal violation, 5 stronger violation.
** $p<0.01$.

workers. Their own group reactions did not differ from that of workers own group reactions either. However, the interaction effect was highly significant ($F_{1,154} = 34.72$, $p < 0.001$). That is, the workers' anticipation of managers' reactions was more negative than either their own group reactions ($t_{78} = 5.70$, $p < 0.001$), managers' own group reactions ($t_{154} = 5.46$, $p < 0.001$), or the managers' anticipation of workers' negative reactions ($p < 0.001$). Thus, hypothesis 6 was substantiated.

Results for context variables

Workers' and managers' attitudes The managers' and workers' attitudes towards self, own group, and other group are given in Table 5.3. Workers were more positive about themselves and their own group than were the managers. Furthermore, workers had relatively more unfavourable opinions of managers than the managers had of the workers or of their own group ($t_{154} = 7.74$, $p < 0.001$). Similarly, the managers were less favourable to workers than the workers were to their own group ($t_{154} = 8.17$, $p < 0.001$). Both managers and workers reported higher mean scores for self than for own group. The means for own group, in turn, were higher than for the other group ($F_{2,308} = 193.24$, $p < 0.001$). Thus hypothesis 1 was confirmed.

Own group identification Own group identification was calculated by the degree of similarity between self and own group for the adjectives (irrespective of their being positive or negative). Thus, the extent of own group identification of the managers and the workers was ascertained for each of the 30 adjectives by subtracting the own group score from the score for self. Zero indicated complete identification and a score of 1 a total absence of identification, i.e. the smaller the score, the greater the own group identification. The results did not show any significant

Table 5.3 Attitudes of managers and workers to self, own group and other group: means and standard deviations

Reaction	Managers	Workers	t
Self			
mean	1.76	1.97	−14.13***
SD	0.10	0.10	
Own group			
mean	1.67	1.76	− 3.84**
SD	0.16	0.13	
Other group			
mean	1.58	1.45	4.68***
SD	0.15	0.20	

The higher the score, the more positive the attitude, the score range is 1–2.
*** $p<0.001$, ** $p<0.01$.

difference ($t_{154} = 0.77$, $p = 0.44$) for the managers (mean 0.19, SD = 0.13) and workers (mean 0.18, SD = 0.10).

Power of managers and workers The mean scores of resource and retaliation power of managers and workers over each other are reported in Table 5.4.

Table 5.4 shows that managers' own group resource and retaliation power scores were greater than that of the workers' own group power ratings. The finding was further substantiated by the workers' perception of managers as having greater resource and retaliatory power than the

Table 5.4 Resource and retaliation power of managers and workers: means and standard deviations

Power	Managers	Workers	t
Resource power of own group			
mean	3.75	2.03	12.11***
SD	0.91	0.88	
Retaliation power of own group			
mean	3.05	2.27	4.67***
SD	1.06	1.02	
Resource power of other group			
mean	2.52	4.46	−14.38***
SD	0.98	0.68	
Retaliation power of other group			
mean	2.95	4.18	− 8.72***
SD	1.05	0.68	

Scale employed: 1 not at all, 2 very small extent, 3 some extent, 4 great extent, 5 very great extent.
*** $p<0.001$.

managers perceived the workers to have. Perceptions of resource and retaliation power by managers and workers did not differ significantly ($F_{1,154} = 1.27$, $p = 0.26$). However, managers did differ significantly ($F_{1,154} = 242.95$, $p < 0.001$) in their perception of own group and other group power. Furthermore, the triple interaction of managers' and workers' ratings of own versus other group's resource and retaliation power was highly significant ($F_{1,154} = 43.66$, $p < 0.001$). Mean comparisons revealed that workers perceived managers as having greater resource and retaliation power than the managers perceived their own group to have ($t_{154} = 5.51$, $p < 0.001$ and ($t_{154} = 7.95$, $p < 0.001$ respectively). Managers also perceived workers as having a greater power to influence and to retaliate than the workers perceived their own group to have ($t_{154} = 3.27$, $p < 0.01$ and $t_{154} = 4.11$, $p < 0.001$). A visual display of the triple interaction is given in Fig. 5.2.

Figure 5.2 indicates that the workers contrasted their own and the other group's power much more than the managers did. The difference between resource and retaliation power obtained for managers was not as striking as the perception of own group and other group power by the workers. In sum, hypothesis 2 was confirmed in that managers were indeed perceived to be more powerful, particularly by the workers.

Fraternal relative deprivation of managers and workers As stated earlier, the fraternal relative deprivation scores were based on managers' and workers' perceptions of the own group and other group

Figure 5.2 Resource and retaliation power of own group and other group (managers and workers)

Table 5.5 Fraternal relative deprivation of managers and workers: means and standard deviations

Variables	Managers	Workers	*t*
Own group			
mean	6.47	3.74	11.64***
SD	1.54	1.38	
Other group			
mean	4.90	8.00	−12.79***
SD	1.55	1.47	

Scale employed: 0 lowest possible position (most deprived), 10 highest possible position (least deprived).
*** $p < 0.001$.

positions on a ten-rungs ladder test. Four ladders were employed to examine the relative positions in social, economic, educational, and political areas. Managers' and workers' positions were averaged across four areas. The mean scores are reported in Table 5.5.

Table 5.5 discloses that the managers' own group position was much better than the workers' judgments of their own group position. The finding was validated by the workers' ratings of the managers' position being higher than the managers' ratings of the workers' position. The interaction effect of managers' versus workers' relative positions of own versus other group was highly significant ($F_{1,154} = 311.18$, $p < 0.001$). In fact, workers located managers at a much higher position on the ladder than the position at which managers placed themselves ($t_{154} = 6.36$, $p < 0.001$). Managers too placed workers at a significantly higher position on the ladders than the workers placed themselves ($t_{154} = 4.93$, $p < 0.01$). The interaction effect is displayed in Fig. 5.3.

Similar to the pattern shown in Fig. 5.2, the workers again made a greater differentiation between their own and the managers' positions in social, economic, educational, and political matters. They considered managers as much higher and themselves as much lower on the various privileges than the managers perceived, thus confirming a part of hypothesis 2.

In summary, a general trend which runs through all the findings discussed so far is that the workers maintained a much sharper contrast between their own and the other group than the managers did. Both perceived managers as relatively more highly placed on the social, economic, educational, and political ladders. They also reported that managers had more power to influence as well as to retaliate than workers. In fact, the workers believed that they were poorer in privileges and less powerful than the managers thought they were. Furthermore, they saw managers as more powerful and privileged than the managers reported themselves to be. Thus, hypothesis 2 was confirmed.

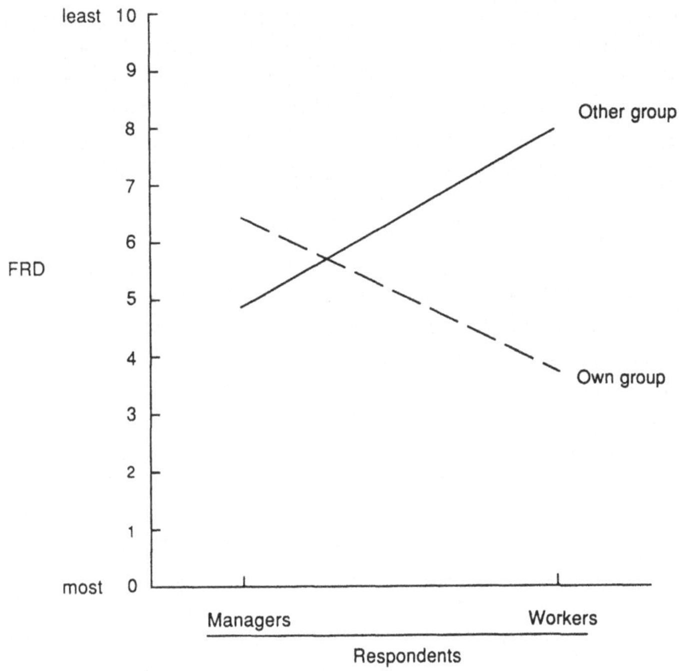

Figure 5.3 Fraternal relative deprivation (managers and workers)

Despite their lesser power and more deprived position, workers maintained more positive attitudes towards self and their own group than towards the managers. Furthermore, they had a less favourable attitude towards managers than the managers had had towards their own group. The workers' group identification was not weaker than that of the managers.

Prediction of reactions to norm violation

Managers' and workers' own group and anticipated reactions of the other group to norm violations were predicted by eight contextual factors: own group identification, other group attitude, resource power of own group, retaliation power of own group, resource pwer of other group, retaliation power of other group, relative position of own group, and relative position of other group. Separate stepwise regression equations were obtained for managers' own group reactions and anticipated other group reactions, and workers' own group and anticipated other group reactions.

The managers' own group reactions could not be predicted by any factor. The zero-order correlations between managers' own group reactions with anticipated other group's reactions ($r = 0.37$, $p < 0.001$), resource power of managers ($r = 0.20$, $p < 0.05$), and the relatively lower position of workers ($r = 0.18$, $p < 0.05$) were significant (see Appendix 5.2). The managers' anticipation of workers' reaction was predicted significantly ($F_{1,75} = 5.33$, $p < 0.02$). Multiple R (0.258) explained 6.64 per cent of the variance. The power of the own group (managers) to retaliate was the single significant deterrent ($\beta = -0.117$, $t = 2.30$, $p < 0.02$) for the workers' negative reactions.

Eight predictors altogether explained 14.86 per cent of the variance ($R = 0.385$) of workers' own group reactions ($F_{1,77} = 13.44$, $p < 0.001$) of these the power of the workers (own group) to retaliate was again the single significant predictor ($\beta = 0.155$, $t = 3.67$, $p < 0.001$). The power of the managers (other group) to retaliate approximated a statistical level of significance ($\beta = -0.199$, $p = 0.058$) indicating that the other group's retaliatory power was a deterrent. The workers' anticipated reactions of the other group (managers) was explained by the managers' (other group's) negative attitude ($\beta = -0.857$, $t = 2.38$, $p < 0.03$). That is, the more unfavourable the managers were perceived to be, the more negative their reactions were anticipated to be. The relatively lower position of their own group (workers) on the ladders of privileges seemed to facilitate the other group's negative reactions ($\beta = 0.207$, $p < 0.06$). In sum, retaliatory power seems to be the most significant predictor of negative reactions to norm violations. In one instance, unfavourable attitudes towards the other group were found to facilitate an apprehension of negative reactions from the other group. Altogether the predictors explained 6.83 per cent of the variance with $R = 0.261$ ($F_{1,77} = 5.64$, $p < 0.05$).

Discussion

Managers on the whole did not report any difference in own group reactions and the anticipated reactions of workers to norm violations. The average score in both cases was negative, but slightly milder than the preceding norm violation. On the other hand, the workers on average anticipated the reactions of the managers to be more negative than either their own group reactions, the managers' own group reactions, or the managers' anticipation of workers' reactions. Thus hypothesis 6 was confirmed.

Both managers and workers differed in the frequency of their choice of five alternative reactions. About 29 per cent of managers thought that their own group would take a positive view of norm violations by workers; but about 27 per cent reported that their own group would react mildly negatively, whereas about 15 per cent believed that managers would react more strongly than the preceding norm violation. It is only this group of managers who seem to support hypothesis 4. About 38 per cent of managers anticipated that the workers would also react negatively, but rather mildly, and only 9 per cent of workers were anticipated to react very negatively. On the other hand, 26 per cent of the workers apprehended that managers would react very negatively, compared with about 9 per cent of workers who predicted that their own group would react in a strongly negative fashion. A large percentage of workers (33 per cent) reported their own group as giving a mildly negative reaction, as was their anticipation of the managers' reactions (31 per cent).

Comparisons for each situation (Table 5.6) disclosed that in 18 out of 20 situations, the workers anticipated more negative reactions from the managers than from their own group. In fact in 11 situations they anticipated the managers' reactions to be significantly ($p < 0.05$) more negative than the managers anticipated the reactions of the workers to be. Some of the situations where the difference was highly significant ($p < 0.001$) were as follows: 'X had his tea served first', 'X claims that Y comes dead drunk to work', 'X did not give lift to Y', 'X did not report or ignored the report of Y that the machine was out of order'.

In 10 situations the managers predicted more negative reactions from their own group than the workers anticipated from the managers. In the remaining 10 situations, they anticipated more negative reactions from the workers than from their own group. However, in some situations, the managers' own group reactions were more negative than either the anticipated other group's (workers') reactions, the workers' own group reactions, or the workers' anticipation of the managers' reactions. For example, for the situations in which 'a worker did not complete his work but shifted the blame to his manager', where 'he was found sleeping during the night shift', 'always came late to work', and 'spent a lot of time in canteen' (mean 3.69), the managers' own group reactions were more negative than the workers' own group reactions to similar violations by the managers. The workers also anticipated the managers to react rather strongly ($p < 0.001$) in situations where 'a worker held his manager responsible for his own incomplete work', 'kept sitting while his manager was standing', and 'did not give him a ride on his motorcycle'. The workers' own group reactions were predicted to be more negative than those of the managers' own group reactions in situations where 'X disconnected or had disconnected the water and electricity connection in the residential colony of Y' ($p < 0.001$), 'X did not give lift to Y' ($p < 0.01$), 'X or his servant threw garbage in front of Y's house' ($p < 0.01$), and 'X had his tea served first' ($p < 0.01$). It may be noted that all these norm violations which caused stronger own group reactions by the managers pertained to the work setting. Managers are believed to be the custodians of work-related norms. Hence, violations of these norms are expected to evoke 'tit for tat' reactions or even a more negative retribution. On the other hand, the workers own group negative reactions and anticipated strongly negative reactions from the managers pertained to social norms reflecting the differential status of the two groups.

Table 5.6 Reactions to 20 norm violations: means (standard deviations), and *t*-ratios

Situations		Managers	Workers	*t*
1 tea served first	Own	1.90 (0.80)	2.30 (0.86)	−3.03**
	Other	2.35 (1.15)	3.27 (1.34)	−4.67***
2 accusation	Own	2.76 (1.35)	2.99 (1.01)	1.21
	Other	2.25 (1.29)	3.30 (1.27)	−5.17***
3 small mistake	Own	3.28 (1.27)	2.50 (1.38)	3.83***
	Other	2.73 (1.28)	3.21 (1.28)	−2.36*
4 no uniform	Own	2.72 (1.73)	2.16 (0.83)	2.55*
	Other	2.60 (0.96)	3.36 (1.64)	−3.56***
5 shift blame	Own	4.23 (1.03)	3.47 (0.81)	5.11***
	Other	3.49 (0.95)	3.92 (1.20)	−2.55*
6 not fulfil duty	Own	3.74 (1.14)	3.20 (1.20)	2.89**
	Other	3.23 (1.14)	3.49 (1.22)	−1.35
7 chair	Own	2.82 (1.28)	2.20 (1.29)	3.04**
	Other	2.95 (1.49)	3.52 (1.35)	2.56*
8 machine broken	Own	2.53 (1.26)	2.06 (1.24)	2.33*
	Other	1.95 (1.30)	2.84 (1.24)	−4.40***
9 refuse give lift	Own	2.06 (1.10)	2.59 (1.01)	−3.09**
	Other	2.22 (1.08)	3.77 (1.36)	−7.98***
10 garbage	Own	2.56 (0.98)	2.96 (0.58)	−3.11**
	Other	2.94 (0.69)	3.24 (1.25)	−1.88
11 school admission	Own	2.44 (1.39)	2.97 (1.30)	−2.52*
	Other	3.51 (1.24)	3.22 (1.56)	1.28
12 disconnect water	Own	2.36 (1.22)	3.29 (1.23)	−4.80***
	Other	3.44 (1.34)	3.34 (1.18)	0.49
13 beat up son	Own	2.19 (1.29)	2.27 (1.08)	−0.44
	Other	2.42 (1.31)	3.31 (1.51)	−3.95***
14 tease daughter	Own	2.20 (1.57)	2.27 (1.39)	−2.97*
	Other	2.50 (1.34)	3.25 (1.58)	−3.22**
15 petrol	Own	3.35 (1.23)	2.49 (0.99)	4.82***
	Other	2.74 (1.05)	3.41 (1.25)	−3.63***
16 forsake work	Own	3.49 (1.34)	2.97 (1.39)	2.35*
	Other	2.97 (1.17)	3.32 (1.26)	−1.81
17 implicate others	Own	2.49 (1.63)	2.98 (1.11)	−2.22*
	Other	3.03 (1.08)	3.05 (1.71)	−0.10
18 fail to clean	Own	2.68 (1.85)	2.86 (1.39)	−0.70
	Other	2.46 (0.86)	2.82 (1.60)	−1.79
19 canteen	Own	3.69 (0.52)	3.20 (0.96)	4.03***
	Other	3.37 (0.87)	3.19 (0.75)	1.43
20 come late	Own	4.00 (0.62)	2.99 (1.18)	6.75***
	Other	3.74 (0.87)	3.69 (0.79)	0.39

* $p<0.05$, ** $p<0.01$, *** $p<0.001$.

The managers' and workers' perceptions of their own and of the other group showed significant interaction effects for almost all measures ($p < 0.001$). Comparisons of mean scores further disclosed that the workers made greater differentiation between the perception of their own group and that of the managers than the managers did. The difference between own and other group mean ratings by the workers, compared with the managers, was 3.44 times greater for attitudes, 1.98 times for resource power, 19.10 times for power to retaliate, and 2.72 times for relative positions of managers and workers with respect to economic, social, educational, and political privileges. On the whole, the workers perceived their own group as having less resource and retaliatory power than their managers had, and even than the managers thought their own group had. Thus hypothesis 2 received a strong confirmation. The managers also reported the workers as having greater resource and retaliation power than the workers perceived their own group to have. The same pattern held true for managers' and workers' relative positions in social, economic, educational, and political matters. The managers' own group position was much better than the workers' own group position. In fact, the workers placed managers at a higher position than the managers placed their own group. The higher position of managers was further validated by their higher scores for own group position than for the other group position.

Nevertheless, the workers were no less embedded in their own group. The mean own group identification scores of managers and workers did not differ significantly. In fact, the workers' attitude to their own group was significantly more positive than that of the managers to their own group ($p < 0.01$). In line with the findings of other research, the workers had a relatively more unfavourable attitude towards the managers than the managers had towards the workers or themselves ($p < 0.001$). The findings thus supported hypothesis 1.

It was probably the configuration of these contextual factors which led workers to apprehend stronger reactions by managers, if they violated norms. The contextual factors were meaningfully correlated (Appendix 5.2). Resource and retaliatory powers were highly correlated for the own as well as for the other group in the case of both managers and workers ($p < 0.01$). For workers there was an inverse relationship between the resource and retaliatory powers of their own group with the other group's power ($r = -0.26$, $p < 0.01$, and -0.22, $p < 0.05$ respectively). The more workers perceived managers as having resource and retaliatory power, the more negatively they felt about the managers ($r = -0.18$, for both variables, $p < 0.05$). However, the better the position of the other group (i.e. managers), the more positive workers were towards them ($r = 0.25$, $p < 0.01$). The workers' own group identification was strongly related to their power to retaliate ($r = 0.24$, $p < 0.01$). That is, the more retaliatory power they attributed to their own group the more they identified with it. For managers, the own group identification was also positively related to their power to retaliate ($r = 0.19$, $p < 0.05$) and negatively to their attitude towards the workers. Surprisingly, the more resource power managers perceived their own group to have, the more positive their attitude was towards the workers ($r = 0.21$, $p < 0.05$) and the higher was their rating of the workers' position ($r = 0.27$, $p < 0.01$). The managers' perception of the workers' resource power was positively related to the workers' relative positions ($r = 0.23$, $p < 0.05$). It seems that the managers' perception of their own group's resource and retaliatory power, the relative position of the workers, and their attitude towards them, did not create such a sharp contrast between managers and workers as the workers seem to maintain. Hence, the managers' other group reactions and anticipated reactions of workers were found to be positively correlated ($r = 0.37$, $p < 0.001$).

Stepwise regression analyses indicated that the power of the own group to retaliate is the single significant predictor of the managers' anticipation of workers' negative reactions (adjusted $R^2 = 0.054$) and of the workers' own group reactions (adjusted $R^2 = 0.138$) to norm violations. Workers also felt that the power of the managers to retaliate would be a deterrent to their own group's negative reactions ($\beta = -0.199$, $p < 0.06$). In other words, both managers and workers reported that if the managers had retaliatory power, the workers would react less negatively. Similarly, the workers felt that if they had retaliatory power, they too would react more negatively. Thus hypothesis 5 was confirmed. The workers' anticipation of managers' reactions was predicted by the workers' attitude towards managers (adjusted $R^2 = 0.056$). Furthermore, the higher the position of the workers, the less negative were the anticipated reactions of the managers ($\beta = -0.207$, $p < 0.06$).

Although hypothesis 3, which states that managers and workers will react negatively to norm violations, was confirmed, the strength of their reactions probably reflected a conciliatory rather than an aggravating stance (see Fig. 5.1). Jha *et al.* (1985) identified interpenetrating processes of conflict and cooperation in interclaste (class and caste) relationships in an eastern state of India. There it appeared that situations of conflict have built-in ingredients of cooperation to contain the conflict and to help the conflicting groups to accommodate to each other (cf. Chapter 8). This is not to say that a conflict never materializes in manager–worker relationships. We recorded a number of instances of disobedience, defiance, abuse, and assaults of managers by their workers in the coal area. Similarly, numerous stories of managers abusing, assaulting, or exploiting the workers were narrated to us. Such acts of norm violations were also reacted to. Chargesheets[5] were issued to workers, letters of warning were given, some workers were suspended, some were fined, and occasionally a few workers were fired too. Similarly, in many instances, the unions took up the complaints of workers against managers and resorted to protests, demonstrations, sit-ins, and even wild cat strikes. Occasionally, conflicts persisted for a while too.

However, more often than not, actions and reactions were short lived and sporadic; and compromises were made by both sides. A typical scene looks somewhat like this: suppose a worker abuses a manager who lodges a complaint to the management. The worker comes to his house or office the next day and brings a coworker or a union leader along who apologizes on behalf of the worker. The worker, he explains, was drunk or afflicted with family problems and was 'out of his mind'. The manager pardons him and as a token punishment asks him to run some personal errands which establishes his power and authority and soothes his bruised ego. The complaint is withdrawn and the matter ends. In a similar instance suppose a manager abuses a worker. The union takes up the matter. A higher level officer brings the manager, the union leader, and the worker together in his office. The manager would dwell at length on how much he cares for his workers (including the victim), how much he has helped him in the past, etc. He contends that what he did the other was a paternal reprimand either for the good of the worker himself or for the sake of the organization. He might even be induced to say 'sorry' for his misunderstood but 'well intentioned' behaviour. The worker returns to his work happy that his manager said 'sorry'.

These observations, however, do not negate the fact that norm violations are negatively reacted to. Our findings at least partially validated norm violation theory as presented in Chapter 1. Norm violations in work-related matters were more strongly reacted to by managers than incidents pertaining to other spheres of life. Workers also anticipated negative retributions from managers in these instances. But managers were believed also to be concerned with social norms (e.g. taking tea first, giving a ride, etc.), and were expected to react strongly if workers violated these social norms. The power to retaliate (i.e. harm and harass) was found to be associated with negative reactions. Because the managers had and were perceived by workers to have greater power to retaliate, they were anticipated to react more negatively. However, the negative reactions were unlikely to be accelerated into full-blown violence or riotous behaviour because of a number of factors.

Two of these factors were a common task system and continued interactions over a period of time which had resulted in personalized relationships between managers and workers who used to help each other even in non-job matters. The group contrast was no doubt still salient because of the role differences and the differences in their status and power. The grievances to each others were also inbuilt in such a relationship. Yet the outgroups were never viewed as 'the faceless and nameless others' who might be strongly reacted to at the first instance of norm violation. In some large organizations, such as in the neighboring public sector steel company (Sinha, in press) with a workforce of 45 000 (including 4000 managers) the intergroup relationship was reported to have deteriorated to such an extent that the workers and the managers reacted to each other as unacquainted antagonists. If the management of such a large organization fails to cultivate the norms of interdependence and/or discipline, the groups bully and domineer each other. The workers, because of their being unionized and having the numerical strength, use coercive power and put the managers on the defensive. The managers in such cases keep a low profile and gloss over instances of norm violations even of a major nature. In contrast, the organizations (such as a private steel company which also employs a unionized workforce of about 42 000 and 1500 managers and is located not far from the public steel company) which have effectively established norms for peaceful industrial relations also have an excellent harmonious relationship (Sinha, in press; see also Chapter 8).

The coal area we studied did not experience the extremes of either the public steel or the private steel companies. It had nine collieries which were separately located and were identifiable units under the administrative control of the area office. In each colliery, because of its smaller size and the nature of the work, managers and workers interacted daily, and rather closely. They knew each other personally and therefore probably did not always attribute a negative motive to norm violations. Hence, the reactions were negative but only mildly so.

Furthermore, none of the two groups was as monolithic as they appeared to us in the beginning. The miners who worked underground were very hard workers. They were generally uneducated, poor, but believed to be sincere by the managers. On the other hand, the workers in the offices of the collieries were relatively more educated, much more clever, and tended to shirk their work. They exploited and abused the underground miners perhaps more than the managers did. Both types of workers were exploited by the mafia leaders who controlled the labour unions. The mafia leaders had criminal records. They employed muscle men to coerce workers and to extract money (in the name of membership fees and subscriptions). The workers seemed to dislike them even more than they disliked their managers. Hence, by comparison, their attitude towards the managers might have been softened, although it was still unfavourable.

Similarly, the managers in the collieries had many grievances against those managers who were posted in the area office who had a quite negative attitude towards the colliery managers. Both charged each other with being thoroughly corrupt. In other words, the manager–worker contrast was salient, but managers and workers cold hardly be viewed as pitched against each other to the extent that norm violations by one group would necessarily initiate chain reactions. However, the darker side of the worker–manager relationship in the present study was not as dark as we found elsewhere (Sharma 1979; S. Singh 1988; Sinha, in press).

Notes

[1] The chapter is based on half of the Ph.D thesis of the first author who conducted his research under the guidance of the second author (Singh 1988). The other half examined the reactions to pro-social behaviour of managers and workers. The authors are thankful to A.N.S. Institute of Social Studies for providing facilities for research and to Tilburg University for computer analyses of the data.

[2] At the current rate Rs 15.00 = US$ 1.00 (approximately).

[3] Closure of a factory by the management which no longer remains responsible for giving wages to the employees during the closure period.

[4] Framing charges against a worker and communicating them to him for a reply before taking disciplinary action.

[5] A recent new item: Coal India Limited has embarked on a package of security measures to stop the incidence of physical assaults on its officers in the different coal fields (*Times of India*, Patna, March 3, 1989, p. 10).

6 Dutch employee relations: supervisors' and subordinates' perspectives

Richard DeRidder

Introduction

The present chapter focuses on relations between employees in The Netherlands. We report a study on subordinates' and supervisors' reactions to norm violations or rule breaking behaviour.

As spelled out in Chapter 1, reactions to norm violations are expected to be determined by a number of context factors, such as supervisors' and subordinates' identification with their own group, their attitudes towards one another and existent differences in power. The strength of these factors, in turn, is the result of a historically grown social-economic, ideological, and political relationship between supervisors and subordinates. Therefore, before reporting the actual study, we will provide a brief overview of the Dutch employment situation.

Employment in a social welfare state

In social-economic terms The Netherlands can be characterized as an industrialized social welfare state. In 1987 approximately 26 per cent of the total Dutch population of 14.6 million received their income through the government's social security agencies (Tweede Kamer 1988, p. 8). In the same year, the official unemployment reached 6.5 per cent of the available work-force.

About 58 per cent of the population between 15 and 64 years of age earned a living with paid labour (Ministerie van Sociale Zaken en Werkgelegenheid 1988, p. 38). Thirty-four per cent of the work force was employed in public services, such as in hospitals, social welfare institutions, and in education. Other important work settings included industry (21 per cent), trading and catering industries (17 per cent) and banking and insurance companies (12 per cent) (Ministerie van Sociale Zaken en Werkgelegenheid 1988, p. 85).

Value of work and workers' ideology

The Dutch value work highly, as the results of a survey on work values in different Western countries indicate (MOW International Research

Team 1987, pp. 274–5). A representative sample of the population rated work as rather central to their lives. Over 90 per cent considered work as being of medium to utmost importance. Next only to 'having a family', work was rated as the most central activity in life. Dutch employees showed a strong preference for good pay and intrinsically interesting work. In comparison with India, The Netherlands scores relatively low on Hofstede's power distance index (Hofstede 1980, pp. 104–6, 120–2).[1] This score suggests that relations between subordinates and their bosses in The Netherlands are characterized by values like 'all people should have equal rights', 'superiors are people like me' and 'subordinates are people like me' (Hofstede 1980, pp. 120–2).

Labour unions and work councils

Politically, relations in industry and the public services in The Netherlands can be described as rather peaceful. The role of Dutch labour unions and the laws of the so-called work councils are relevant to understand this state of affairs.

In contrast to other European countries and the USA, labour unions have done little to polarize industrial relations in The Netherlands over the past 40 years. It was only between 1962 and 1979 that unions demanded higher wages, better working conditions for shop-floor workers, and claimed a say for workers in the production process and organizational structure of their companies. Apart from that period, labour unions have fully cooperated with employers. After the Second World War, until the beginning of the sixties, the unions focused on national development and in 1982 the labour unions officially agreed to refrain from strikes and demands for more pay in order to reduce unemployment. Labour unions felt a shared responsibility with the employers to overcome the economic crisis (Harmsen and Reinalda 1975).

In legal terms, the 1971 and 1981 revisions of the law on enterprises of 1950 had an enormous effect on Dutch labour relations. Since 1971, every organization employing more than 100 persons is obliged by law to have a work council. Since the 1981 revision, work councils also exist in smaller organizations. These councils are autonomous and have far-reaching rights, such as the hiring of outside experts to solve organizational conflicts. In the councils, representatives of the employees from different organizational levels meet, at least twice a year, to discuss important organizational matters. Changes in the hierarchical structure of the organization, improvement of working conditions, and organizational conflicts are frequently recurring topics in the meetings of the work councils (cf. Teulings 1981, pp. 151–2, p. 211).

Because of the position of the labour unions and the legal means available to the work councils, organizational conflicts in The Netherlands tend to be contained within an organization and do not lead to more general social or political unrest.

Predictions

Given the preceding social-economic, ideological and, legal-political context, two kinds of qualifications can be made with respect to the hypotheses about reactions to norm violations formulated in Chapter 1. On the one hand, power differences between supervisors and subordinates in organizational settings are clearly defined. Therefore, it can be expected that supervisors will react more negatively to their subordinates' norm infractions than subordinates.

On the other hand, it is expected that only small differences in reactions to norm violation will be found between Dutch supervisors and subordinates and that neither of the two groups involved will react very negatively. This prediction is based on the relative unclarity of the supervisor/subordinate intergroup contrast and on the existence of institutional means of conflict resolution through work councils. The first part of this argument is derived from the Dutch employees' adherence to 'egalitarian' values which should also lead subordinates and supervisors to de-emphasize their group membership and to emphasize intergroup similarities rather than differences. In Tajfel's terms 'intergroup differentiation' is reduced and the probability of engaging in negative intergroup behaviour will be low (Tajfel 1978*b*). The second part of our reasoning stems from Deutsch (1973, p. 101) who argues that the institutionalization and regulation of conflicts decrease 'the likelihood that conflict will take a destructive course'.

Method

Pilot studies

Two pilot studies were conducted before the main investigation took place.

In the first study, semi-structured interviews were held with 30 key informants (23 belonged to industrial companies, seven to public service institutions). All respondents had extensive experience with employee supervision at the lowest level of the organization. They provided information about the relevant dimensions along which low level workers (the shop-floor workers in industry) compared themselves with their direct superiors. The important dimensions mentioned were: sense of duty or responsibility, trustworthiness, (in)formality, and authority. Furthermore, the informants also suggested a number of concrete situations which frequently led to conflict and how problems were solved in their organization. This pilot study enabled us to construct a questionnaire to assess intergroup attitudes and a provisional version of the norm violation inventory consisting of 50 items.

In the second pilot study, 24 employees belonging to the middle and lower levels of different organizations rated these provisional items. They indicated to what extent they considered the actor's behaviour as inappropriate, e.g. if a worker 'interrupts a conversation with a supervisor for a chat with a colleague'. They also rated whether the actor was, in their view, aware of his norm-breaking behaviour, and whether the situation and the possible reactions presented for the situation were realistic and plausible (see Chapter 2 for more information about the criteria for situation selection). This study resulted in the final version of the norm violation inventory with 24 situations. In this final version two situations, pertaining to the infringement of safety regulations and to the disposal of poisonous waste (see Appendix 6.1, situations 19 and 20), were retained although higher level employees judged them as unrealistic. In contrast, the lower level judges rated these situations as highly realistic and relevant. Except for these two situations, all other items in the norm violation inventory fulfilled the criteria specified in Chapter 2.[2]

Sample

In the main study we preferred not to limit ourselves to employees of a single or a few organizations. Therefore, a sample of subordinates and supervisors from different companies and public services was taken.

Eighty-six employees (male and female) living in a medium large city in the south of The Netherlands answered our questionnaire on employee relations. They were randomly selected from a large pool of volunteers for research. The data of 61 respondents were retained for further analyses. The other 25 were excluded from the analysis for two reasons. Some of them (14) had too many missing data. The other 11 were dropped because respondents could not unequivocally be classified as either subordinate or supervisor.

The general demographic characteristics of the subordinates and supervisors and the organizations for which they worked are summarized in Table 6.1. Inspection of this table reveals that subordinates and supervisors were similar in age and education. On some other variables the two groups differed. In comparison with supervisors, subordinates in our sample were employed in smaller sized organizations, worked part-time and most of them were in the public service. Moreover, about two thirds of the subordinates were females, while the opposite was true of the group of supervisors.

The differences mentioned between subordinates and supervisors can be related to the general characteristics of Dutch subordinates and supervisors. In the general population, females are more likely than males to work part-time in subordinate positions and in public service organizations, such as hospitals, education, and social work. It should also be acknowledged that, compared with the general Dutch population, public service subordinates are over-represented in our sample and

Table 6.1 Characteristics of subordinates and supervisors

	Subordinates ($n = 34$)	Supervisors ($n = 27$)
Mean age	35 years	36.5 years
Gender		
female	68%	31%
male	32%	69%
Completed education		
lower professional	20%	16%
secondary & high school	30%	28%
high professional	33%	28%
college & university	10%	16%
missing	7%	12%
Number of years in present organization/company	3.5 years	6.2 years
full-time	35%	96%
part-time	65%	4%
Kind organization/company		
industry	15%	38%
trading and catering	15%	8%
transportation/communication	9%	27%
public services	61%	27%
Size organization/company		
< 100 employees	62%	31%
> 100 employees	38%	69%
Mean hierarchical level*	3.6	6.9

* Hierarchical level varies between 1 (low) and 9 (high).

those in industry are under-represented. Similarly, far more supervisors came from transportation and communication companies than from the trading companies.

Instruments

The initial questions in the questionnaire concerned the kind and size of the organization in which the respondent was employed, a description of his[3] function, some questions related to demographic characteristics and a question about the hierarchical level at which he perceived himself to work (see Table 6.1).

Next, the subordinate and/or supervisory status of the respondent was assessed. For this purpose he indicated (i) how many subordinates and superiors he had and (ii) whether he perceived himself as subordinate or supervisor. A respondent was classified as *subordinate* if he stated himself as having no subordinates to supervise and when he did not perceive himself as supervisor. A respondent was classified as *supervisor* if he stated himself as having subordinates, no matter how many superiors he himself had and no matter whether he felt himself to be a superior or a subordinate (in fact all the supervisors in the present study had superiors themselves).

Subsequent separate parts of the questionnaire measured the main variables of the theoretical model. All scales were phrased with 'subordinate(s)' and 'direct supervisor(s)' as reference points.

Norm violation inventory Supervisors' and subordinates' reactions to norm violations were measured by the norm violation inventory. The final version of this scale consisted of 24 situations, sampled from the domains social contacts, institutional contacts, and social responsibility (see Chapter 2). Each situation, e.g. 'A supervisor breaks a promise he made to his subordinate', was accompanied by five possible reactions from which the respondents had to choose the most likely one:

(1) a positive or constructive reaction (R+) 'ask the supervisor whether he will be able to do what he promised';
(2) no reaction (R0) 'shrug his shoulders';
(3) mildly negative retaliation (R−) 'complain about the supervisor's behaviour at the personnel department';
(4) 'tit for tat' retaliation, i.e. retaliation as strong as the preceding violation (R=) 'not keeping promises made to the supervisor on future occasions';
(5) strongly negative retaliation (R≡) 'disobey from then on the supervisor's orders'.

As explained in Chapter 2 the seriousness of the three norm-violating reactions (R−, R=, and R≡) for each item was matched to the inappropriateness of the norm violation depicted in the item stem.

Each situation was presented to the respondents in two versions. In one of them a supervisor committed the norm violation and the respondents indicated the 'most probable' reaction of a subordinate. In the other, a subordinate committed the norm violation and the respondents indicated the 'most probable' reaction of a supervisor. Because the respondents were either supervisor or subordinate, for each group an own group and an anticipated other group reaction score were obtained for every situation, ranging from 1 (positive reaction) to 5 (strongly negative retaliation).

Own group identification and other group attitudes Supervisors' and subordinates' own group identification and other group attitudes were measured following the general format described in Chapter 2. The respondents judged themselves, the group of supervisors, and the group of subordinates on the following 25 adjectives:

impulsive	helpful	impertinent
not careful	aggressive	tolerant
intelligent	dutiful	egotistic
trustworthy	friendly	lazy
authoritarian	sociable	arrogant
profiteering	honest	polite
informal	quarrelsome	loyal
self-conceited	corrupt	narrow-minded
boring		

All adjectives were rated on five-point scales ranging from 'completely applicable' to 'completely inapplicable'. They also indicated to what extent they considered a particular adjective 'desirable' on a five-point scale.

An own group identification score was obtained for each individual by taking the absolute difference between the ratings of self and own group. The other group attitude was defined as the sum of the adjective ratings for the other group multiplied by their perceived desirability. Similarly, an own group attitude was calculated. The own group identification and attitude scales were reliable for both subordinates (α between 0.84 and 0.91); and for supervisors (α between 0.77 and 0.86).

Perceived power The respondents judged to what degree supervisors and subordinates had political, economic, and social power over each other (see Chapter 2 for more detailed information). A resource power score for own group and other group was calculated by taking the mean of the ratings for the perceived political, economic, and social power.

The mean of the responses to two additional questions ('To what extent can subordinates make life miserable for their supervisors if they wish to do so?' and 'To what extent are subordinates prepared to stand up for their rights if these are threatened by their supervisors?') provided an index of the individual's perception of own and other group's retaliatory power.

It must be noted that the reliability of these different power scales was rather low, particularly for the group of supervisors (α between 0.30 and 0.57). The α coefficients for subordinates' resource power were 0.74 for the own group's power and 0.66 for the perceived other group's power. For retaliation power they were 0.64 and 0.43 respectively for own group and other group. For supervisors the α values were even lower (0.30 and 0.32 for own and other group's resource power; 0.57 and 0.56 for own and other group's retaliation power).

Fraternal relative deprivation Judgments of subordinates' and supervisors' fraternal relative deprivation were obtained by requesting the respondents to make a direct comparison between their own and the other group's position in political, economic, and social matters. Their (dis)satisfaction with their relative position in these spheres was also assessed. For both measures five-point scales were employed (see Chapter 2 for details). The reliability of the scale for measuring relative position was somewhat lower (0.43 for supervisors and 0.53 for subordinates) than that by which satisfaction was assessed (0.80 for supervisors and 0.83 for subordinates).

Results

Reactions to norm violation

A comparison of the mean reactions to norm violations of subordinates and supervisors, presented in Table 6.2, reveals that on average neither the subordinates nor supervisors reacted very negatively. All mean reactions were somewhere between 'doing nothing' (R0) and a 'mildly negative retaliation' (R−).

Table 6.2 Reactions to norm violation: means and standard deviations of supervisors and subordinates

Reaction	Supervisors	Subordinates	*t*
Own group			
mean	2.43	2.38	0.41
SD	0.42	0.42	
Anticipated other group			
mean	2.27	2.55	−3.06*
SD	0.36	0.35	

Scores range from 1 (positive reaction) to 5 (strongly negative reaction).
* $p < 0.01$.

An ANOVA performed on the average reaction to norm violation showed a significant interaction of employee status (supervisors versus subordinates) and own versus anticipated other group reactions ($F_{1,58} = 15.08$, $p < 0.001$). The subordinates expected their own group to react more positively to a supervisor's norm infringement than they anticipated the supervisors to act when a subordinate violated a norm. Supervisors expected their own group to react more negatively to a subordinate's norm violation than they anticipated subordinates to react to their norm violation. Thus, in the perception of both groups, supervisors will react more negatively to a subordinate than subordinates will to a supervisor. Additional *t*-tests showed that this discrepancy between supervisors' and subordinates' reactions to norm violation was only significant when respondents had to anticipate the other group's reaction ($t = 3.06$, $p < 0.01$, see Table 6.2).

In order to obtain an idea of the nature of the overall differences found between subordinates and supervisors, the percentages for each response category (R0, R+, R−, R=, and R≡) were calculated for all situations. The mean percentages of all situations for each category for own group reaction and anticipated other group reaction are presented in Fig. 6.1.

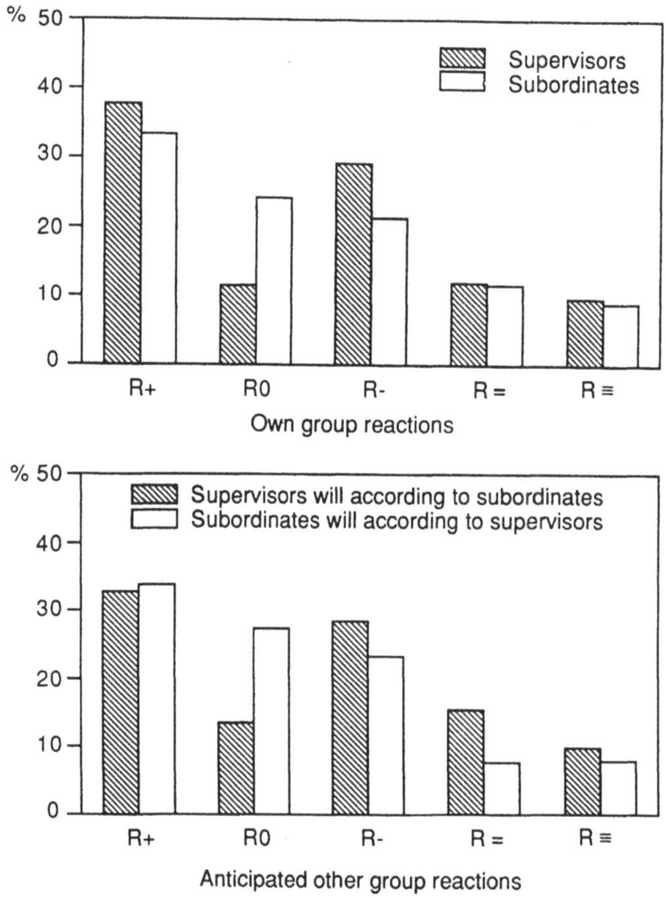

Figure 6.1 Reactions to norm violation by supervisors and subordinates

Inspection of these percentages shows that the majority of reactions, of subordinates as well as of supervisors, fell in the first three response categories ('positive', 'no reaction', and 'mildly negative retaliation'). Moreover, both subordinates' and supervisors' own group reactions were similar to what their respective other groups anticipated them to be for each of the five response categories separately. For instance, subordinates indicated that in 24.2 per cent of the instances that their supervisor violated a rule, their own group would 'not react'. The supervisors shared this opinion. In the supervisors' view, subordinates would show 'no reaction' in 27.3 per cent of the cases of a supervisor's norm infraction. The same type of agreement subordinates and supervisors was found for the other reaction alternatives.

A comparison of the own group reaction percentages, for each separate category, between subordinates and supervisors revealed that supervisors are more likely than subordinates to react with R− (weaker retaliation) and less likely to show R0 (no reaction). The percentages obtained for the anticipated other group reactions suggest that supervisors were less likely than subordinates to give R0 and slightly more likely to retaliate with R= ('tit for tat' retaliation).

The results of the two preceding analyses can be summarized as follows. In terms of the average seriousness of reactions, no differences could be found between supervisors and subordinates when they indicated how their own groups would react. Only when anticipated other group reactions were compared, were supervisors found to react more negatively than subordinates. Our frequency analysis showed that both supervisors' and subordinates' most frequent and most frequently anticipated reaction was R+ (try to solve the problem in a constructive fashion). Subordinates 'shrugged their shoulders' or expressed their indifference to a supervisor's norm violation in other ways (R0) more often than supervisors. Supervisors, in contrast, retaliated negatively with R− and R= and were anticipated to do so more often than subordinates. With respect to the two negative reaction alternatives, supervisors expected that their own group would predominantly use R−, whereas subordinates anticipated that supervisors would retaliate both with R− and R=.

Taken together, these results lend suport for our prediction that neither supervisors nor subordinates would react very negatively to a norm violation by the other group. Furthermore, these results seem to show that supervisors, generally, react and are anticipated to react more negatively than subordinates. Viewed from a different perspective, however, the patterns of frequencies obtained for supervisors and subordinates indicate the following. Subordinates employed the reaction alternatives R+, R0, and R− with a decreasing frequency, whereas supervisors used either R+ or R− and abstained from R0. A comparison of these two patterns suggests that, in general, supervisors did not react more negatively than subordinates, but that they reacted sometimes more negatively, and sometimes more positively, than subordinates. In which situations each of these reactions occurred can be seen in the results for the 24 situations separately, presented in Table 6.3.

From these results it can be learned that in eight out of 24 situations there were no differences in reactions of supervisors and subordinates. In two of them, both groups reacted and were anticipated to react with a minor retaliation (items 1 and 6); in the other 6 situations (items 3, 12, 13,

Table 6.3 Reactions to 24 norm violations of subordinates and supervisors (see Appendix 6.1 for full details)

Item	Description	Subordinates		Supervisors	
		own group	other group	own group	other group
1	often drunk at work	3.12^{a}	3.18^{a}	3.22^{a}	3.11^{a}
2	laughs at Y's mistake	1.85^{a}	2.85^{b}	2.85^{b}	1.56^{a}
3	parks car in Y's parking space	2.06^{a}	2.12^{a}	1.63^{a}	2.48^{a}
4	ignores request not to smoke	2.35^{ab}	2.47^{a}	1.78^{b}	2.04^{ab}
5	too late at work	2.59^{a}	3.24^{b}	2.63^{a}	2.22^{a}
6	Y blamed and fired	3.03^{a}	2.91^{a}	3.00^{a}	3.07^{a}
7	employ rude language	1.91^{ab}	1.62^{a}	1.67^{a}	2.48^{b}
8	stop conversation for a chat	2.27^{a}	3.68^{b}	3.85^{b}	2.48^{a}
9	break a promise	1.91^{a}	1.09^{b}	1.00^{b}	1.33^{b}
10	not react to Y's greeting	2.09^{ab}	2.41^{a}	2.63^{a}	1.74^{b}
11	no appreciation for gift	1.71^{ab}	3.12^{a}	3.33^{a}	1.67^{b}
12	take Y's seat	1.79^{a}	1.77^{a}	1.59^{a}	2.11^{a}
13	obtrude on Y's wife	2.32^{a}	1.91^{a}	2.22^{a}	2.37^{a}
14	ignore Y's advice	2.74^{a}	1.27^{b}	1.11^{b}	2.07^{c}
15	interrupt Y's work	2.47^{a}	2.77^{a}	2.30^{a}	2.15^{a}
16	machine becomes out of order	2.00^{a}	3.09^{b}	3.11^{b}	1.89^{a}
17	steal tools	1.97^{a}	3.03^{b}	3.04^{b}	2.04^{a}
18	report sick but healthy	2.00^{a}	2.79^{b}	2.89^{b}	2.22^{a}
19	throw poisonous waste away	2.21^{a}	2.91^{a}	2.82^{a}	2.41^{a}
20	neglect safety regulations	2.38^{a}	2.15^{a}	2.26^{a}	2.52^{a}
21	not wearing protection cap	3.03^{a}	1.65^{b}	2.11^{c}	2.96^{a}
22	ignores Y's accident	3.29^{a}	3.94^{b}	3.07^{a}	3.00^{a}
23	Y's bad moods	2.47^{a}	2.35^{a}	1.70^{b}	2.22^{a}
24	make private phone calls	3.73^{a}	3.18^{a}	2.81^{b}	3.73^{a}

Means in each row which do not share a common superscript are significantly different by *t*-test ($p < 0.05$).

15, 19, 20) the average was 'no reaction'. For own group reaction it was found for five situations, in line with our hypothesis, that supervisors reacted more negatively than subordinates (items 2, 8, 16, 17, 18). For five other situations, however, the opposite was found: subordinates reacted more negatively than supervisors (items 9, 14, 21, 23, 24). Interestingly, for the anticipated other group reaction, parallel differences were found for the first five situations mentioned. In the majority of situations in which subordinates' own group reactions were more negative than those given by the supervisors, different results were obtained when anticipated other group reactions are considered. For situations 9, 23, and 24 no significant differences for anticipated other group reaction were found between subordinates and supervisors.

In summary, although in one third of the situations in our norm violation inventory no differences in reactions between subordinates and supervisors emerged, supervisors reacted more negatively than subordinates in five situations and more positively in five other situations. Moreover, it appeared that parallel results were obtained for anticipated other group reactions for those situations in which supervisors reacted more negatively than subordinates. In other words, supervisors and subordinates only had the same view of their different reactions when the differences went in one direction, that is, when supervisors reacted more negatively than subordinates.

Context variables

Own group identification On the own group identification index, which could vary between zero and four, subordinates and supervisors had almost identical mean scores. These were 0.88 for the subordinates and 0.84 for the supervisors. This difference was non-significant. The overall mean scores indicated that the absolute difference between respondents' rating of themselves and that of their own group were rather small, less than one point on a five-point scale. Thus, both groups identified with their groups equally.

Intergroup attitudes The attitudes of subordinates and supervisors towards one another varied from neutral to slightly positive (see Table 6.4).

A 2 × 2 ANOVA performed with employee status and own versus other group as attitude object, showed that the respondents rated their own group significantly more positively than the other group ($F_{1,57}$ = 38.61, $p < 0.001$). No significant differences were obtained for employee status. Thus, subordinates and supervisors had similar attitudes towards each other and were similarly mildly positive about their own groups.

It must, however, be emphasized that none of the ratings of either group can be considered extremely positive when one takes into account that the means varied between −0.05 and +1.11 on a scale of −10 to

Table 6.4 Attitudes of subordinates and supervisors towards their own group and the other group

Attitude	Supervisors	Subordinates	t
Towards other group			
mean	0.36	−0.05	1.05
SD	1.19	1.67	
Towards own group			
mean	1.11	0.69	1.35
SD	0.69	1.38	

The attitude score can vary between −10 and +10.

+10. The only adjectives on which more substantial differences between supervisors and subordinates were found were the other group judgements for 'dutiful' and 'authoritarian'. Superiors considered their subordinates to be less dutiful ($t_{57} = -2.09$, $p < 0.05$) and they themselves were viewed as being much more authoritarian ($t_{56} = 2.96$, $p < 0.01$).

Power On all separate questions related to power, supervisors were perceived as significantly ($p < 0.01$) more powerful than subordinates. That is, they were rated as superior to subordinates in economic, political, and social power, as well as in their capacity for retaliation. Reliability analyses, performed to find out whether the questions for the two types of power (resource power and retaliation power) could be meaningfully combined, showed satisfactory results. The results on power perception are presented in Table 6.5.

Table 6.5 Resource and retaliation power of supervisors and subordinates

Power		Supervisors	Subordinates	*t*
Resource power				
own group	mean	3.19	1.64	10.08*
	SD	0.65	0.54	
other group	mean	1.79	3.42	−9.78*
	SD	0.41	0.77	
Retaliation power				
own group	mean	4.12	2.96	5.47*
	SD	0.64	0.92	
other group	mean	3.19	4.15	−4.99*
	SD	0.85	0.63	

Scale employed: 1 very little, 2 little, 3 a fair amount, 4 much, 5 very much.
* $p < 0.001$.

A 2 (subordinates/supervisors) × 2 (resource versus retaliation power) × 2 (own group/other group) ANOVA was performed to find out whether perceived power differences between supervisors and subordinates varied with the type of power, the perceiving group or with the reference point taken (own versus other group). The analysis shows that the perceptions of power differences of the own group generally matched with those of the other group. Supervisors perceived their own group as having more power than the other group and subordinates rated their own group power as inferior to that of the other group, the supervisors. In brief, there was consensus between supervisors and subordinates about their power differential.

An additional finding of this analysis was that the perceived power differences between supervisors and subordinates were smaller for retaliation power than for resource power (the second-order interaction involving employee status × type of power × own/other group was highly significant, $F_{1,58} = 16.37$, $p < 0.001$).

In sum, there was a common perception of the supervisors' superior resource and retaliation power, although the difference in retaliatory power was smaller compared with that of resource power.

Fraternal relative deprivation As the judgments of relative position and of satisfaction correlated highly for the economic, political, and social domains, overall indices for relative position and satisfaction were calculated (see Table 6.6).

Table 6.6 Feelings of fraternal relative deprivation: means and standard deviations for supervisors' and subordinates' perceived relative position and (dis)satisfaction

		Supervisors	Subordinates	*t*
Relative position	mean	1.87	4.42	−19.26*
	SD	0.53	0.49	
Satisfaction	mean	2.69	3.63	−4.11*
	SD	0.86	0.88	

Scale employed for position: 1 much higher, 2 somewhat higher, 3 equal, 4 somewhat lower, 5 much lower. Scale for satisfaction: 1 very high, 2 rather high, 3 moderate, 4 rather low, 5 very low.
* $p<0.001$.

The results presented in Table 6.6 show that supervisors rated their hierarchical position higher than the subordinates did. They also expressed less dissatisfaction than the subordinates. The subordinates' dissatisfaction with their relatively low position indicated that they felt deprived relative to supervisors.

In sum, the preceding analyses of the various measures showed the following similarities and differences between subordinates and supervisors with respect to the context factors.

1. Own group identification: supervisors and subordinates had an equally high own group identification and no differences between the two groups were found.
2. Other group attitudes: supervisors and subordinates had equally positive other group attitudes; no differences between the two groups existed.
3. Power: Supervisors had more resource and retaliation power than subordinates.
4. Fraternal relative deprivation: subordinates felt more relatively deprived than supervisors.

Relationship between context factors and reactions to norm violation

According to the theoretical framework presented in Chapter 1, a group's reaction to a norm violation by another group will be influenced by the group members' own group identification, their attitudes towards the other group, their perceived power, and feelings of fraternal relative deprivation. In order to check the plausibility of these presumed effects for the groups involved in the present study, regression analyses were performed on the own group reactions and on anticipated reactions on the part of the other group.

Although it could be argued that the variables which influence reactions by supervisors might be different from those affecting the subordinates' reactions, the number of respondents in each group was too low to yield stable results in a regression analysis (Draper and Smith 1981). Therefore, we combined the data of the two groups for this analysis to answer the more general question—which of the context factors predicted reactions of *employees* to norm violation?

Two stepwise regression analyses were executed with each employee's average reaction to the 24 items of the norm violation inventory taken as the dependent variable (see Table 6.2). In the first analysis, employees' feelings of relative deprivation and power to retaliate came out as significant predictors of their own group reactions ($R^2 = 0.22$, $p < 0.01$). More precisely, it was found that the higher their dissatisfaction with the other group's position ($\beta = 0.35$, p 0.01) and the greater the own group's power to retaliate ($\beta = 0.31$, $p < 0.01$), the more negative employees thought their own group's reaction would be. In the second analysis, with the expected other group reaction as the dependent variable, only the other group's resource power turned out to be significant ($R^2 = 0.10$, $p < 0.02$, $\beta = 0.31$, $p < 0.02$). That is, the more resource power the other group was perceived to have, the more the other group's reactions were anticipated to be negative.

Thus, dissatisfaction with the other group's status and perceived differences in power appeared to be reasonable predictors of employees' reactions to norm violations.

Discussion

The results of the subordinates and supervisors in the present study showed that both groups identified with their own group to the same extent. They had a neutral to mildly positive attitude towards one another. Subordinates had, in their own view and in that of the supervisors, less power than their direct superiors. The difference was larger for power in political, economic, and social matters (resource power) than in retaliatory power. Furthermore, subordinates perceived their organizational position as lower than that of their supervisors and they were more dissatisfied with it than the supervisors were with their superior position.

The observed similarities in group identification and the neutral to mildly positive attitudes, along with differences in perceived power and relative deprivation, furnish the background for understanding the supervisors' and subordinates' reactions to norm violations. The results of the regression analyses particularly attest to the plausibility that perceived relative power and feelings of fraternal relative deprivation influence the reactions of employees in general. With respect to the variables power and relative deprivation, it should be noted that the reliabilities of the sub-scales distinguished were rather low. Moreover, all indices of the scales – resource power, retaliatory power, relative position, and satisfaction with the position of one's own and the other group – were highly related, for subordinates as well as for supervisors (see Appendix 6.2). This means that we cannot be sure which context factor explains the employees' reactions to norm violation: purely the perception of power differences, feelings of relative deprivation or a combination of both.

In line with our prediction, the results for our main dependent variable, reactions to norm violation of own group, were weak. The predominant employees' reactions were: (i) 'try to react in a constructive or positive way', (ii) 'not react at all', and (iii) 'mildly negative retaliation'. On a scale from 1 to 5 the overall mean for all respondents was 2.40. Contrary to our prediction, based on expected power differences, the supervisors did not react in a significantly more negative fashion than the subordinates when own group reactions were compared. It was only when anticipated other group reactions of the two groups were tested that supervisors reacted more negatively than subordinates. In other words, when each group expressed how they would react in the case where an other group member broke a rule or violated a norm, no significant differences between supervisors and subordinates emerged. However, when they stated their anticipation of the other group's reaction to their own norm violation subordinates expected supervisors to react much more negatively than the supervisors expected the subordinates to react. Could this mean that subordinates and supervisors only *think* that they react differently, but that in reality no differences exist?

The results of the analysis of the raw frequencies of the own group reaction for subordinates, and supervisors and those of the analyses of the 24 situations separately, suggest otherwise.

Let us first consider the frequencies for the five reaction alternatives for all 24 situations lumped together. They showed that both supervisors and subordinates most often reacted to norm violation in a constructive manner (R+), for instance 'try to discuss the problem', 'ask the other to change his mind', 'try to convince the other'. Subordinates reacted, and were anticipated to react by the supervisors, more often than supervisors with not showing any reaction to a supervisor's rule braking (R0), for instance 'ignore what happened', 'just continue working', 'don't pay any attention', 'shrug their shoulders'. When all negative reactions are combined (R−, R=, and R≡), the supervisors reacted more often than subordinates in a negative manner to norm violation. This pattern of reactions is obtained for the own group as well as for expected other group reactions.

Thus, in terms of general strategies for solving problems, supervisors tended less often than subordinates to ignore the problem or withdraw from it, but they were more likely to resort to negative reactions. Subordinates and supervisors did react differently and anticipated that each group would react differently. By and large, supervisors and subordinates did what the other party expected them to do.

It can be concluded from the frequencies of the reaction alternatives used by the supervisors and subordinates that their reactions were similar, in the sense that both reacted most often in a constructive manner to the other party's norm violation. Their reactions did differ, however, in the sense that the supervisors had a stronger tendency to abstain from letting a norm violation pass without any reaction on their part. Therefore, the main difference between supervisors' and subordinates' reactions appeared to be one of *reacting* versus *not reacting*.

Let us now consider subordinates' and supervisors' own group reactions for the 24 situations analysed separately, because it appears that whether and how subordinates and supervisors react to the other group's norm violation is dependent not only on existing differences in power and/or feelings of relative deprivation, but also on specific situational features.

It was found that in 10 out of 24 situations the own group reactions of supervisors and subordinates were significantly different. A closer look at the content of these situations suggests the following.

Subordinates did not show any reaction when the situation was one in which power differences were very salient (e.g. 'a supervisor who interrupts a conversation for a chat with a colleague', or 'a supervisor who breaks his promise'). They simply lacked the power to do anything to change their superior's behaviour. They also preferred to shrug their shoulders when not they themselves but the company suffered from the consequences of supervisors' norm infractions (e.g. supervisors who stole tools). Subordinates did react, however, when they suffered themselves and thought they could change the situation or had the right to do so (e.g. 'a supervisor ignores subordinates' advice'). It also appeared that subordinates reacted negatively in situations in which supervisors were in the privileged position of being able to profit from the company's facilities, while subordinates themselves were unable to do so (e.g. 'a supervisor regularly phones abroad at the company's cost'). Supervisors did react much more (constructive or negative) than subordinates because they considered it their task to create acceptable working conditions and a good atmosphere. They would not let subordinates get away with rule infractions when they themselves could perhaps be held accountable by their superiors for damage done to the company.

The above reasoning assumes that reactions of both subordinates and supervisors are dependent on (i) the direct or indirect *costs* they incur when they do not react to a norm infringement and (ii) the *expected outcome* of the reaction. Both factors, in turn, are affected by perceived differences in power. Although the costs (negative consequences) are directly present for subordinates in most of the situations of the norm violation inventory, they react with less intensity than supervisors in identical situations because they do not expect any positive effect of their reactions, owing to existing differences in power. Supervisors react more or less strongly, depending on the expected outcome of each reaction and on the costs they would expect to incur if they did not react (e.g. negative sanctions applied by their own superiors).

The above reasoning presumes that own group reactions could be determined by a combination of situational and relational factors (power). It takes into account the findings of the regression analysis that satisfaction with the other group's relative position and own retaliatory power are predictive of the negativity of employee reactions. Moreover, the reasoning is consistent with earlier attempts to explain relations between organizational groups in terms of a cost-reward analysis (e.g. Vroom 1964; Brown 1983).

Although a vast amount of research has been conducted on supervisor–subordinate relations (see Jablin 1979; Dansereau and Markham 1987, for reviews), to our knowledge there only exist a few earlier field studies on conflicts between supervisors and subordinates. Most of these conflict studies were inspired by Blake and Mouton's strategies for conflict management (Blake and Mouton 1964). Burke (1970), for instance, reported that in the subordinates' view supervisors are most likely to use 'confrontation' for dealing with conflicts. This result is in line with our finding that subordinates anticipate mildly negative reactions from supervisors. Renwick (1975), however, did not find any differences between subordinates and supervisors when she compared the two parties on each of Blake and Mouton's strategies. In contrast to Renwick, however, we found that subordinates were in their own view and in that of the supervisors more likely to ignore what happened, i.e. to 'withdraw' in the terminology of Blake and Mouton. It may be that the high degree of convergence between subordinates and supervisors in conflict strategies found in Renwick's (1975) study are limited to the consultative type of organizational climate to which her employees belonged.

Emphasizing the similarities and mutually agreed differences between supervisors and subordinates is not sufficient when we are interested in the emergence of conflict. Particularly relevant are those situations in which one of the groups' most likely behaviour does not fit the other party's a priori expectations. In the present study we found that in some situations the own group reactions clearly differed from what the other group expected (items 4, 5, 9, 14, 21, 22, 23, and 24 of Table 6.3). The general deviation was that subordinates tended to overestimate the negativity of supervisors' reactions. Thus, supervisors themselves stated that they would react less negatively than the subordinates anticipated them to do. Supervisors' anticipation of subordinates' reactions that in most instances subordinates will do nothing, matched the reactions given by subordinates, except in two situations ('breaking a promise' and 'ignore advice'). Especially in the latter situation, subordinates reacted more negatively than the supervisors anticipated.

It can be concluded that supervisors are on unsafe grounds if they assume that subordinates will invariably not respond to their norm violations, because subordinates do not care or are too powerless to react. The subordinates' idea that supervisors will react negatively to their norm violations might be too pessimistic, at least if we are to believe supervisors' own statements about their most probable reactions.

Some of the limitations of the present study need to be emphasized. The sample studied was relatively small and, as was earlier acknowledged, there were considerable differences in the background characteristics of the subordinates and supervisors who participated in this study. Some of the most salient of these differences were that in the subordinates' group there were more female, part-time and public service employees than in the supervisors' group.

These differences imply, that the observed differences between subordinates and supervisors in the present study could in part be due to gender differences, the full-time or part-time function of the employees, and the kind of public service organization to which the subordinates belonged. That gender played an important role seems implausible as no signficant gender effects were found when gender was introduced in the analyses. With respect to the full-time or part-time status of the employees, it could be argued that full-time employees are more committed to the group to which they belong than part-timers. According to some authors (e.g. Deutsch 1973), commitment may lead to more destructive conflict strategies, i.e. in the present case to more negative reactions to norm violations. Separate analyses of subordinates' reactions do not support this idea. In the present study full-time subordinates did not react significantly differently from part-timers. (This analysis could not be done for supervisors because only one part-time supervisor participated in the present study.)

The preceding analyses rule out the possibility that the observed differences in reactions between supervisors and subordinates are due to gender effects or to the part-time status of a considerable number of the subordinates. What is left, of course, is that the results of the study cannot be considered as representative for employee relations in The Netherlands because most of the participants had a relatively high education and worked in public service institutions.

One of the main problems, which in part led to the exclusion from analysis of a considerable number of participants, was that some subordinates resisted the label 'subordinate' to such an extent that they called themselves 'supervisor' although they had no subordinates to supervise. Other respondents classified themselves explicitly neither as subordinate nor as supervisor. These are strong indications that respondents participating in the present study resisted classifying and perceiving themselves in hierarchical terms. Additionally, 38 per cent of the supervisors indicated that although they had subordinates to supervise, they felt like a subordinate themselves. Therefore, it comes as no surprise that no differences in own group identification and attitudes were found in the present study. This problem of self-categorization should not be taken to mean that the respondents retained for further analyses were indifferent about their group membership. The opposite is true: both subordinates and supervisors had a significantly more positive attitude towards their own group than towards the other.

The present chapter dealt with subordinates' and supervisors' perspectives on reactions to norm violations. It was suggested that a number of context factors, such as differences in power between hierarchical groups in an organization, would affect the reactions of subordinates and supervisors when confronted with the other party's norm violation in their day to day work setting. Although, in general, supervisors' and subordinates' opinions matched with respect to differences in their relative power and what each group's reaction would be, there also appeared to be some notable discrepancies in opinions. In some situations one group's statement of its most likely reaction clearly deviated from the other group's anticipations. In other words, what one group said they would do differed from the other group's expectation. It will be evident that the present study was not meant and is unable to check which party's views are wrong or incorrect. Therefore, additional research will be needed to find out to what extent, in reality, subordinates and supervisors in The Netherlands will react differently in behavioural terms to other group members' norm violations. Only when behavioural measures are taken in a number of different situations might it become clear under which circumstances the supervisors' assumption of 'careless and powerless' subordinates and the subordinates' assumption of 'negatively retributing or punishing' supervisors will and will not hold.

Notes

[1] Hofstede's power distance index varies between 0 and 100. For The Netherlands a mean score of 38 was found (for India it was 77). For Dutch employees, however, a large variation across occupations is reported. It was particularly high (83) for unskilled plant workers (Hofstede 1980, p. 106). Because unskilled

workers did not participate in the present study we refer to The Netherlands as a low power distance index nation.

[2] We are indebted to Diem Wolff for conducting the major part of the first two pilot studies. It is noteworthy that the target persons from industrial companies almost without exception emphasized the open and egalitarian relations between subordinates and supervisors. Employees from public services stressed the bureaucratic atmosphere and differences in power between subordinates and supervisors. Lower level workers from industry (labour union members) emphasized differences in power between supervisors and subordinates in the same way as employees from public services did.

[3] The masculine form is used only for convenience. He and his should be understood also as she and her.

7 Overall analysis

Ype H. Poortinga and Xander H. M. Jansen

After the presentation of the separate studies we can now address the two questions formulated in Chapter 2, namely whether the framework of Fig. 1.2 can help to explain the results of the four studies, and whether there are differences between contrasts and societies in the interrelationships of components in the framework. In the first section of this chapter we study the cross-cultural equivalence of the scores. In the second section the results for the separate measurements in the four main studies are summarized. In the third section we give both the gist of the hierarchical regression analysis that was chosen as the main statistical technique, and the results of this analysis.

Cross-cultural equivalence of the data

Equivalence issues arise at two levels: within a society when there are cultural differences between the groups within a contrast pair, and across societies in the case of comparisons between Indian and Dutch subjects. We have assumed that cultural differences between the groups within a society did not bias the results, except for the Dutch–Turkish-migrants contrast where this possibility was explicitly analysed. The results, to be discussed in Chapter 8, did not give reason to question the equivalence of overall scores on the norm violation inventory.

As mentioned in Chapter 2, the construction of scales that could be taken to show strictly comparable or equivalent scores was considered impossible for subjects in cultures as far apart as India and The Netherlands. In addition, variations in items and administration procedures compounded the problems. Therefore, no direct cross-cultural comparisons of scores were attempted and no data from the two countries were entered into any single analysis.

Still, we found little evidence of substantive shifts in the meaning of items. The translation of terms referring to general principles (e.g. political power, or social position of a group in society) and the translation of person/group descriptive adjectives created no serious problems. For the norm violation inventory about half of all items could be directly translated and applied in a meaningful way. In the research team we found that the moral and social values underlying any item were readily communicable and meaningful in both cultures. Only the expression of a value in a concrete action could easily convey a different meaning. For example, jumping a queue appears to be offensive far more often in The

Netherlands than in India. Similar difficulties arose with respect to the response alternatives. For example, we have the impression that verbal insults are more serious norm violations in India, but that the difference in seriousness between verbal insult and physical violence is smaller in India than in The Netherlands.

Results for the separate variables

An overview of the own group reaction to norm violation (NV-own) and the anticipated other group's reactions (NV-other) of the various groups is presented in Tables 7.1 and 7.2. The numbers of subjects in these and subsequent tables do not always correspond to those reported earlier because more stringent conditions on missing data for the hierarchical regression analyses were imposed than in previous chapters.

For the NV-own variable there is a significant difference in one contrast pair only: the Dutch subjects reported on average a stronger reaction to a norm violation by Turkish migrants than Turkish subjects reported for a norm violation by members of the Dutch autochthonous population. For the NV-other scores three of the four pairs show a significant difference, with the less powerful groups expecting stronger retaliation. For the Hindu–Muslim contrast pair, the *t*-statistic just fails to reach a significant value. In this pair the Muslim group has the lower mean score.

The results for the own group identification (OGI) scales are summarized in Table 7.3. The two ethnic contrasts show a significant difference, with the minority group subjects expressing a stronger sense of own

Table 7.1 Own group reactions to norm violation (NV-own): summary of results

	N_s	N_i	Mean	SD	α	t	p_t
The Netherlands							
Turkish migrants	102	36	2.31	0.32	0.71	−11.05	<0.001
Dutch autochthones	118	36	2.90	0.45	0.85		
India							
Muslims	63	21	2.15	0.58	0.83	−0.72	0.471
Hindus	71	21	2.22	0.56	0.81		
India							
workers	79	20	2.73	0.41	0.65	−1.89	0.060
managers	77	20	2.86	0.45	0.63		
The Netherlands							
subordinates	34	24	2.39	0.43	0.69	−0.43	0.669
supervisors	26	24	2.44	0.42	0.72		

N_s number of subjects; N_i number of items.

Table 7.2 Anticipated other group reactions to norm violation (NV-other): summary of results

	N_s	N_i	Mean	SD	α	t	p_t
The Netherlands							
Turkish migrants	102	36	2.73	0.37	0.75	4.02	<0.001
Dutch autochthones	118	36	2.52	0.41	0.83		
India							
Muslims	63	21	2.29	0.76	0.90	−1.90	0.060
Hindus	71	21	2.55	0.84	0.91		
India							
workers	79	20	3.33	0.67	0.84	5.06	<0.001
managers	77	20	2.86	0.48	0.75		
The Netherlands							
subordinates	34	24	2.57	0.35	0.59	3.08	0.003
supervisors	26	24	2.28	0.37	0.63		

group identification (mean score closer to zero). For the managers and workers in India and the Dutch supervisors and subordinates only small non-significant differences were found.

Attitudes towards the outgroup (ATT-out) can be positive or negative. A 'neutral' attitude would lead to a score of $E(x) = 1.5$ for the Indian managers and workers and a score $E(x) = 0.0$ for all other groups. The sample of Indian workers displays a (significant) negative attitude towards the managers. Also, the Dutch autochthones are negative about the Turkish migrants. Significantly positive attitudes towards the other group are found for the managers in India and for the supervisors in the Netherlands.

Table 7.3 Own group identification (OGI): summary of results

	N_s	N_i	Mean	SD	α	t	p_t
The Netherlands							
Turkish migrants	102	25	0.77	0.32	0.76	−6.63	<0.001
Dutch autochthones	118	25	1.08	0.37	0.79		
India							
Muslims	63	20	0.84	0.45	0.76	−3.31	<0.001
Hindus	71	20	1.14	0.59	0.86		
India							
workers	79	30*	0.18	0.10	0.60	−0.77	0.442
managers	77	30*	0.19	0.13	0.75		
The Netherlands							
subordinates	34	25	0.89	0.40	0.83	0.39	0.697
supervisors	26	25	0.84	0.51	0.90		

* Dichotomous item scales (values 0 and 1).

Table 7.4 Attitudes towards the other group (ATT-out): summary of results

	N_s	N_i	Mean	SD	α	t	p_t
The Netherlands							
Turkish migrants	102	25	0.11	0.72	0.74	−2.89	0.004
Dutch autochthones	118	25	−0.18	0.76	0.74		
India							
Muslims	63	20	−0.03	1.17	0.70	−0.23	0.816
Hindus	71	20	0.01	1.04	0.64		
India							
workers	79	30*	1.45	0.20	0.88	−4.52	<0.001
managers	77	30*	1.58	0.15	0.79		
The Netherlands							
subordinates	34	25	0.19	1.31	0.91	−1.17	0.245
supervisors	26	25	0.55	0.96	0.87		

* Dichotomous item scales (values 1 and 2).

An overview of the perceived power (POW) scores is given in Table 7.5. The two groups in a contrast pair agree on their relative positions when the two means are of the same magnitude, but differ in sign. The means of all samples differ significantly from zero ($p < 0.01$). The pattern of scores for each of the four pairs allows a clear answer to the question which of the two groups in a pair is seen as the more powerful. Despite the agreement in direction, differences in level, especially between the Indian managers and workers, are worth noting.

For the fraternal relative deprivation (FRD) scores (Table 7.6) the findings were similar to those for the POW variables. Agreement is most clear for the Turkish migrants and the Dutch. Workers and managers in

Table 7.5 Perceived power (POW): summary of results

	N_s	N_i	Mean	SD	α	t	p_t
The Netherlands							
Turkish migrants	102	4	−1.54	1.21	0.82	−19.65	<0.001
Dutch autochthones	118	4	1.65	1.19	0.80		
India							
Muslims	63	4	−0.69	1.02	0.72	−5.79	<0.001
Hindus	71	4	0.27	0.90	0.69		
India							
workers	79	3	−2.08	1.06	0.71	−13.47	<0.001
managers	77	3	0.48	1.30	0.70		
The Netherlands							
subordinates	34	5	−1.55	0.96	0.77	−11.77	<0.001
supervisors	26	5	1.21	0.82	0.74		

Table 7.6 Fraternal relative deprivation (FRD): summary of results

	N_s	N_i	Mean	SD	α	t	p_t
The Netherlands							
Turkish migrants	102	9	−0.93	0.63	0.87	−25.73	<0.001
Dutch autochthones	118	9	0.94	0.40	0.68		
India							
Muslims	63	9	−0.69	0.79	0.82	−6.28	<0.001
Hindus	71	9	0.07	0.59	0.62		
India							
workers	79	3	−4.25	2.16	0.47	−17.64	<0.001
managers	77	3	1.57	1.95	0.41		
The Netherlands							
subordinates	34	6	−1.52	0.54	0.38	−19.30	<0.001
supervisors	26	6	1.37	0.62	0.43		

India and subordinates and supervisors in The Netherlands agree on the direction of the differences in their positions, but the workers and subordinates report a larger intergroup difference than the managers and supervisors do. The data set on the Hindu–Muslim contrast forms an exception. The Hindu subjects hardly see the Muslims in a more deprived position, while the Muslim subjects see their group as significantly more deprived than the Hindus.

The correlations between the scores are given in Table 7.7 for the pooled data of each contrast pair.[1] Group identification (GROUPID) is a dummy variable reflecting mean differences between the samples of a pair. A clear relationship is found between POW and FRD. The correlations in some instances are so high that the two variables are almost interchangeable, especially when the attenutating effect of (or the lack of) reliability is taken into consideration. Also, the pattern of correlations of these two variables with the two norm violation scores is similar across contrasts. Finally, it should be noted that NV-own and NV-other with one exception show a positive and predominantly substantial correlation.

Hierarchical regression analysis

In terms of the framework in Fig. 1.2 the variables OGI, ATT-out, POW and FRD are supposed to be related to reactions to norm violations; we shall refer to these four variables as *context* variables. The question we want to answer is whether these context variables can help to explain differences in the dependent variable, i.e. differences between the two groups of a contrast in the expected reactions to norm violations.

Psychometrically this question can be analysed using a procedure

Table 7.7 Correlations between the main variables for all subjects in a pair of groups

	OGI	ATT-out	POW	FRD	NV-Own	GROUPID
Turks–Dutch pooled $N = 220$						
OGI	–					0.41**
ATT-out	−0.06	–				−0.19**
POW	0.35**	−0.09	–			0.80**
FRD	0.34**	−0.13*	0.85**	–		0.87**
NV-own	0.37**	−0.23**	0.57**	0.57**	–	0.60**
NV-other	−0.20**	−0.24**	−0.34**	−0.29**	0.00	−0.26**
Muslims–Hindus pooled $N = 134$						
OGI	–					0.27**
ATT-out	0.26**	–				0.02
POW	0.37**	0.18*	–			0.45**
FRD	0.15*	0.07	0.38**	–		0.49**
NV-own	−0.06	−0.07	0.10	0.14*	–	0.06
NV-other	−0.16*	−0.09	−0.01	−0.01	0.52**	0.16*
Workers–managers India pooled $N = 156$						
OGI	–					0.06
ATT-out	−0.20**	–				0.34**
POW	0.15*	0.34**	–			0.74**
FRD	0.14*	0.17*	0.65**	–		0.82**
NV-own	0.11	−0.01	0.31**	0.23**	–	0.15*
NV-other	−0.08	−0.35**	−0.33**	−0.36**	0.16*	−0.38**
Subordinates–supervisors The Netherlands pooled $N = 60$						
OGI	–					−0.05
ATT-out	−0.27*	–				0.15
POW	0.06	0.22*	–			0.84**
FRD	0.03	0.18	0.85**	–		0.93**
NV-own	0.13	−0.04	0.21	0.16	–	0.06*
NV-other	−0.01	−0.19	−0.27*	−0.28*	0.60**	−0.38**

* $p < 0.05$, ** $p < 0.01$.

analogous to that described by Poortinga and Van de Vijver (1987). This takes the form of a hierarchical regression analysis (Pedhazur 1982; Cohen and Cohen 1983). As used for the present study there are three stages. In the first stage it is established whether there exists a significant difference between the contrasting groups on the dependent variable. The intergroup difference is expressed as a squared correlation coefficient R_1^2. If a non-significant value is found for R_1^2, there appears to exist no difference and the analysis is terminated.

In the case of a significant difference, the second and third stages of the analysis are executed. In the second stage the context variables are entered into a stepwise regression procedure. This means that the context variable which explains most of the intergroup difference is entered first, then the variable which explains most of the remaining variance, etc. The analysis is stopped when the increment in explained variance ($R(c)_i^2$) after entering another context variable is no longer statistically significant.

Within this second stage a complication arises when a context variable is more closely related to the dependent variable in one group than in the other (cf. Pedhazur 1982, Chapter 12; Miller and Erickson 1981). To meet this possibility an alternative design of analysis is also used which does not only specify context variables and a dummy variable (coding for groups), but also a context × dummy effect which is called a product term and is similar to an interaction term. There are two ways to deal with significant product terms.

1. Such an effect points to psychometric inequivalence of the data (cf. Poortinga 1989). The analysis should be terminated and other factors should be searched for that can explain why the context variable behaves differently in the two groups.
2. Although the reason why more variance is explained in the one group than in the other remains open, the explanatory value of the context variable for the dependent variable remains essentially unaffected.

Here we shall follow the latter of these two interpretations, but take the presence of a significant product term as a warning that the results of the second stage of the analysis have to be interpreted with caution.

The third stage is the computation of the remaining intergroup difference on the dependent variable, after all the variance has been extracted that can be explained in terms of the context variables. This remaining difference is expressed as R_2^2. The value of R_2^2 will drop below a statistically significant value if the context variables can be used to explain the entire intergroup difference on the dependent variable. Of course, it is also possible that the context variables explain only part of the intergroup difference, or none at all. The possible outcomes of the analysis procedure with a single context variable (which is easy to generalize to more such variables) are summarized in Table 7.8. A technically more detailed description of the analysis procedure is given in Appendix 7.1.

There are two dependent variables for which the analyses will be reported, the own group reactions to norm violations (NV-own) and the anticipated other group's reactions (NV-other). In a separate paper (Poortinga and Jansen 1991) an analysis is presented based on a third variable which is defined in terms of differences in responses between the own group condition and the other group condition of the norm violation inventory.

Regression analyses of results

Hierarchical multiple regression analyses were carried out for the NV-own and the NV-other scores in each contrast pair. The results are

Table 7.8 Possible outcomes of the hierarchical regression analysis

R_1^2	$R(c)_i^2$	R_2^2	
=0			No intergroup difference is observed and no explanation is needed
>0	=0	>0	The context variable does not explain any part of the difference
>0	>0	>0	The context variable explains part of the difference on the dependent variable
>0	>0	=0	The difference can be explained entirely in terms of the context variables

presented in Tables 7.9 and 7.10. For three group contrasts there is no significant difference on the NV-own scores. With no variance to be explained these analyses were terminated. Only for the Turks–Dutch contrast was a significant difference found. In the second step of the analysis a large effect of the context variable POW emerged. ATT-out, OGI and FRD were also significant (the latter only at the 0.05 level), but these effects were small. The remaining variance after the extraction of the effects of the context variables is still significant, but so small as to be negligible.

Two points can be mentioned. First, in view of the high correlations between FRD and POW, a large overlap can be expected between the components of variance explained by these two variables. This means that only a low $R(c)^2$ will be found for FRD, once POW has entered the regression equation. When the analysis was repeated with a forced first entry of FRD, a value of $R(c)^2 = 0.32$ was found for the Turks–Dutch contrast.

The second point concerns the presence of product terms in addition to the effects listed in Table 7.9. In Appendix 7.2 a highly significant OGI × GROUPID term is reported. This has been taken to imply that the OGI variable does not behave the same way in the Turkish migrant group

Table 7.9 Effects of the four context variables on the NV-own score

Contrast	R_1^2	FRD	POW	ATT-out	OGI	R_2^2
Turkish–Dutch (The Netherlands)	0.359	(0.016)	0.326	0.030	0.035	(0.013)
Muslims–Hindus (India)	0.004 NS					—
Workers–managers (India)	0.023 NS		0.097			0.013 NS
Subordinates–supervisors (The Netherlands)	0.003 NS					—

Parentheses indicate $0.01 \leq p < 0.05$.

and in the Dutch group. However, in view of the low value of OGI in the main analysis ($R(c)^2 = 0.035$) this only marginally affects the interpretation of the regression analysis.

For the NV-other scores a non-significant value of R_1^2 is found in the Hindu–Muslim contrast. The other three pairs show a significant difference on this dependent variable. In Table 7.10 FRD emerged as the most important context variable in two cases, while in the third instance POW took the first position. A repetition of these three analyses with forced first entry of POW and FRD respectively, again showed that these two variables are almost interchangeable. For the workers and managers in India POW had a value $R(c)^2 = 0.110$, while this effect for the subordinates and supervisors in the Netherlands was $R(c)^2 = 0.074$. The Turks–Dutch pair showed an $R(c)^2 = 0.098$ for FRD when this variable was entered first into the regression equation.

Table 7.10 Effects of the four context variables on the NV-other score

Contrast	R_1^2	FRD	POW	ATT-out	OGI	R_2^2
Turkish–Dutch (The Netherlands)	0.069		0.117	0.076		0.002 NS
Muslims–Hindus (India)	0.027 NS					—
Workers–managers (India)	0.141	0.129		0.083		0.002 NS
Subordinates–supervisors (The Netherlands)	0.141	(0.077)				0.102

Of the other two context variables only ATT-out gave a significant effect, for the workers and managers in India and the Turks–Dutch contrast.

The product terms mentioned in Appendix 7.2 potentially affect the interpretation of the intergroup differences on the NV-other scores in two cases. One is the FRD variable in the workers–managers contrast in India. When POW was entered first virtually the same amount of variance was explained, but for this context variable no significant product term was found. Therefore, the overall interpretation need not be changed. The other case concerns the Turks–Dutch pair. When FRD was entered first in the regression analysis a significant product term was also found for this context variable. Correlations computed for each of the two groups separately indicated that they had the same sign for the variables POW, FRD and NV-other, but that they tended to differ in size for the two groups. Thus, it seems that the overall pattern of relationships is more or less invariant, but the significant product term indicates that the scores on the POW and FRD variables may not form strictly equivalent scales. Intergroup differences on these context variables have to be interpreted with caution.

For two contrast pairs (workers and managers in India, and Turks–Dutch) the differences in NV-scores that cannot be accounted for in terms of context variables are small and statistically insignificant. Only in the case of the Dutch subordinates and supervisors is there a significant and fairly substantial difference left unexplained.

Conclusion

It can be concluded that the context variables can help explain the differences in reactions to norm violations. Of the eight regression analyses in Tables 7.9 and 7.10 four were terminated because there was no significant intergroup variance to be interpreted. In two instances no significant intergroup difference remained after elimination of the proportion of variance that could be accounted for in terms of the context variables. In one instance a marginal amount of variance remained and in one instance a fairly substantial amount.

The most important finding of this chapter derived from the regression analyses and the correlation tables is that the differences in the social, economic, and political status of the two groups in a pair, assessed by the FRD and POW scales, appear to be the most important reasons for differences in reactions to norm violations in India as well as in The Netherlands.

Notes

[1] For reasons of space, correlations for the separate groups within a pair are not presented; they were taken into consideration during the analysis.

8 Norms of redress

Richard DeRidder, Rashmi Kumar, and Sandra G. L. Schruijer

The four studies reported in the previous five chapters show two types of results. First, it appears that fraternal relative deprivation and/or power are the most important predictors of negative intergroup behaviour (see Chapter 7). Second, inspection of the frequencies of the separate reaction alternatives chosen by the respondents shows the following. In general, members of the victim group indicated that a 'positive reaction' (R+), 'no reaction' (R0) and a 'mildly negative reaction' (R−) were the most likely reactions to another party's norm violation (see Chapters 3–6).

The issue we will address in this chapter is related to the second finding. Are the relatively positive reactions to the other group member's norm violation due to the respondents' desire to convey a positive impression of themselves on the investigator? This would mean that the reactions subjects gave in the questionnaires were biased by social desirability. It could also be, and this is the argument we will elaborate in this chapter, that their responses stemmed from shared opinions about the most appropriate reactions in instances where norm violation by one group may trigger a conflict. In other words, it will be argued, and studied empirically, that in groups, such as Hindus and Muslims, certain 'norms of redress' exist that stipulate how group members should react in situations in which another group starts a possible escalation of negative intergroup behaviour by violating a norm.

This chapter has the following structure. We will first discuss how plausible it is to assume that for the groups we investigated norms of redress exist. Next, three empirical studies will be reported in which we attempted to assess the normative character of different reactions to norm violation. The chapter concludes with a section in which the results of the three studies are compared and in which the validity is questioned of the notion of a universal 'norm of reciprocity' (Gouldner 1960) for exchanges of negative behaviour.

Anthropological evidence

It is commonly acknowledged in social psychology, sociology, and cultural anthropology that the establishment of group norms is an important feature of group formation (e.g. Turner and Killian 1972; Forsyth

1983) and a salient characteristic of existing communities (Beals *et al.* 1977).

Norms are neither formulated nor implicitly present for all types of behaviours group members may engage in. Usually their object is restricted to issues, persons, and situations that are important to the group (see e.g. Sherif and Sherif 1969, p. 141). As it may be assumed that for most of the groups we studied the other group constitutes a relevant outgroup (see Chapter 2), it follows that members of each of these groups will have opinions about appropriate behaviour towards their respective outgroups. Not only are norms to be followed under normal or peaceful circumstances likely to exist, but probably also some that apply in situations of tension or conflict. Moreover, we contend that in groups like Turkish immigrants, autochthonous Dutch, Hindus, Muslims, and groups in organizations, certain norms of redress are operating in situations of potential intergroup conflict.

Most of the supporting evidence comes from anthropological studies which deal with fighting and conflicts that occur in (tribal) societies or in small relatively closed communities (e.g. Radcliffe-Brown 1952, p. 215). One of the recurrent findings in these societies is that norms about conflict exist, but that their nature varies with the type of outgroup (see also Wright 1965, pp. 90, 737). An example of these differences can be found in Evans-Pritchard's study about the Nuer (Evans-Pritchard 1940). Gluckman summarizes them as follows. Among the Nuer 'there is no raiding within the tribe for cattle, and it is recognized that a man ought to pay cattle as compensation for killing a fellow-tribesman, though this is rarely done. Nuer tribes raid one another for cattle, but not for women and children; nor must granaries be destroyed. When raiding foreign people, women and children and even men can be captured, women and children can be killed, and granaries can be destroyed.' (Gluckman 1963, p. 9). It emerges from anthropological studies on fights, feud, and warfare that conflicts between *related groups* must be clearly distinguished from those between *foreigners*. Related groups have established a set of norms or customs, that regulate conflicts between them, whereas conflicts between foreign groups are 'lawless' or normless (see Fox 1975, pp. 137–9 for a more recent example of fights of the Irish on Tori Island).

The relatedness of different groups may have a number of origins, such as kinship, marriage ties, a common land or territory, or a common dependence on a larger political organization. Whatever the origin or type of a relationship between two different groups may be, the very existence of a relationship implies that customs and procedures will have been established that prevent an escalation of negative intergroup behaviour. If such norms did not operate, then at least one of the groups involved would have been driven out of existence in the past. Or to state it in a less extreme form: between closely related groups there is 'pressure towards the establishing of peaceful relations—or, rather, the re-establishing of peaceful relations after a breach. This pressure is exerted by common interest in a modicum of peace over a certain area, which is necessary if men are to live in any kind of security, and produce food, marry into another's families, or deal with one another' (Gluckman 1963, p. 19).

The point Gluckman makes can be illustrated by a study conducted by Bookman (1978) on Hindu–Muslim relations in a village called Gangapur in Saharanpur (Uttar Pradesh). He found that both communities shared certain 'over-arching values' which tied them together as members of a 'common culture'. The most important value which governed the relationship between the two communities was the idea of maintaining good relations and a harmonious village 'family'. Bookman cites the case of how, during the partition of India, one young Hindu advocated physical retaliation against the Muslim inhabitants of the village so as to avenge the killings of Hindus and Sikhs in Punjab. Muslims of the village fled to an all Muslim neighbouring village. Hindu elders desiring to maintain communal harmony, forced the young Hindu to leave the village and then invited the Muslim families to return to their homes. Bookman (1978) points out that common cultural traditions make it more possible to control conflicts between Hindus and Muslims in rural communities, where Hindus and Muslims identify strongly with their religious communities, than in urban areas.

Pospísil (1971) is one of the authors who emphasizes the importance of a more inclusive political organization to prevent conflicts between two groups to escalate. He states that 'Wherever feuds do occur, there exists a politically influential authority (a formal chief, an informal headman, a council of important men, or an individual of very limited power, such as a go-between) who is usually too weak or disinterested in controlling his constituents, with the result that prolonged fighting is not prevented. The weaker the political control, the longer feuds last and the harder it is to conclude them' (Pospísil 1971, p. 6).

In short, anthropological analyses of different kinds of communities demonstrate that people belonging to different groups have a set of norms to regulate their intergroup conflicts, provided that these groups are part of a larger unit or system. These studies additionally emphasize the functionality of these norms: an escalation of conflict is prevented and peace or the status quo of the intergroup relationship, as it existed before the incidents triggering the conflict occurred, is re-established. Since for co-existing groups we explicitly want to emphasize the latter function of these norms, we call them 'norms of redress'.

The relevance of these findings for our contention that norms of redress exist between the groups studied in this monograph, will be evident. Although these groups are much larger than the communities studied by anthropologists and although their members' identification with their groups is less strong, they share two important features with the communities analysed by anthropologists. On the one hand, they are part of a larger political or organizational system. On the other hand, all these groups have a history of co-existence with their outgroup and expect to continue to live with this outgroup in the future. Therefore, it seems plausible that norms of redress will exist among Turkish immigrants and autochthonous Dutch, among Hindus and Muslims in India and among groups within organizations.

In view of the anthropological studies discussed it comes as a surprise that a discussion of 'intergroup norms about conflict' is almost completely non-existent in the social-psychological literature on intergroup relations. The research of Rabbie and colleagues is perhaps the only exception. Rabbie and Lodewijkx (1987) applied Turner's 'emergent norm theory' (Turner and Killian 1972) to aggressive behaviour between interdependent groups and argued that dominant psychological orientations emerge in groups. These orientations lead to 'a shared understanding of what kind of causal attributions should be made about the intentions and actions of the opponent [. . .] and how the interdependent parties ought to behave toward one another' (Rabbie and Lodewijkx 1987, p. 93). In line with this argument Lodewijkx (1989) found that members of groups created in a laboratory reacted with aggression to another group's norm violation when such a negative reaction corresponded to the dominant ingroup norm.[1]

In summary, there appears to be sufficient anthropological evidence and some social psychological support to suggest that 'norms of redress' will operate in groups that are embedded in a larger political and/or organizational system. This makes it worthwhile to investigate these norms in the groups that we studied in this monograph.

Three empirical studies

The main purpose of these studies was to assess whether the groups' reactions reported in Chapter 3, 4 and 6 could be partly explained by the existence of certain norms of redress. Are these norms specific for a group in relation to a certain outgroup or are they relatively invariant across groups and/or outgroups?

To relate the results of the present studies on norms of redress to those obtained in the previous chapters, we employed the same situations and reaction alternatives as well as similar subjects as those employed in the main investigations. In the present studies, however, subjects were requested to indicate for each situation of the norm violation inventory the *appropriateness* of each of the five possible reactions employed in the main studies (a positive reaction, R+; no reaction, R0; a mildly negative reaction, R−; a tit for tat retaliation, R=; and, a strongly negative reaction, R≡).

Three empirical studies were conducted. In the first study autochthonous Dutchmen and Turkish immigrants participated, in the second

Dutch employees, and in the third Hindus and Muslims in India. The studies were slightly different in focus. The first two not only assessed respondents' judgements of inappropriateness of reactions to norm-violation, but also their evaluation of the initial norm violation. The group membership of the actor committing the initial norm violation was not specified, neither was that of the victim. This enabled us to ascertain whether variations in norms of redress are due to differences between these groups as such, i.e. uncontaminated by the actor's and/or victim's membership of the ingroup or of the outgroup. For instance, are norm violations—committed by someone—evaluated differently by a group of Turkish allochthones compared with a group of Dutch autochthones? In the last study, with Hindus and Muslims as respondents, the group membership of the actor of the original norm violation and of the suffering party was explicitly mentioned. This allowed us to find out whether different norms of redress apply to the ingroup and outgroup, according to Hindus and Muslims. More specifically, the following research questions guided the present studies.

1. Are norm violations evaluated differently by members of the different groups within a contrast pair (study 1)?
2. Are there differences between the groups in their evaluation of the five reactions to norm violations (studies 1, 2, and 3)?
3. Are judgments of reactions affected by the group membership of the initiator of the original norm violation and/or by the group membership of the victim group (study 3)?
4. Is a 'tit for tat' retaliation, from the different victim groups' perspective, an appropriate reaction to the suffering of an initial norm violation (studies 1, 2, and 3)?

Study 1: evaluation of norm violation and reactions by autochthonous Dutchmen and Turkish immigrants

The main objective of this study was to investigate whether Turkish immigrants and autochthonous Dutchmen had similar or different opinions about the (in)appropriateness of a norm violation committed by some person and about the reactions to such behaviour.

Subjects Fifteen male Dutch and 15 male Turkish subjects living in The Netherlands participated in this study. The age of the Turkish subjects varied from 19 to 49 years (mean age 30.7); the Dutch subjects were aged 20 to 59 years (mean age 28.3). The length of time the Turkish subjects had been living in The Netherlands ranged from 8 to 21 years (mean length 14.5 years). Seven of the 15 Turkish and one Dutch subject were unemployed. The remaining eight Turks held a job as factory-worker or mechanic. Of the Dutch subjects, eight were students, two had just finished their higher education, two were supervisors in industry and one was a teacher. Of one Dutch subject the profession was not known.

Method A Dutch research assistant distributed the norm violation inventory (see Appendix 3.1 for a summary of the items) to the Dutch respondents and a Turkish research assistant was present when the Turkish respondents completed the questionnaire.

The format of the inventory for this study was as follows. At the top of each of the 36 pages of the questionnaire a norm violation was presented. On a seven-point scale the respondents had to evaluate the norm violation in terms of appropriateness (1 inappropriate; 7 appropriate). Following this, five possible reactions by a victim were listed, labelled a, b, c, d, and e. The subjects were requested to indicate their judgement of the (in)appropriateness of each reaction alternative by placing a tick with a corresponding letter on a line 10 centimetres long with the endpoints 'inappropriate' and 'appropriate'.

For the 36 norm violations in the inventory the alternatives were presented in a random order and not according to the a priori underlying scale (R+, R0, R−, R=, and R≡).

Results We report the results for the ratings of the norm violations, of the reaction alternatives, and for the relationship between both sets of ratings.

Evaluation of norm violations. We first computed an overall inappropriateness score over the 36 situations per individual. This was done by adding 36 individual inappropriateness scores and consequently dividing it by 36. The difference between the means of the Turks (1.42) and the Dutch (1.92) was significant ($F_{1,23} = 8.68$, $p < 0.007$). In other words, the norm violations were considered more inappropriate by the Turks than by the Dutch.

Inspection of the (in)appropriateness ratings per situation indicated that the actor's behaviour in almost all situations was perceived as being inappropriate by both the Dutch and the Turks. In fact, in only one situation the actor's behaviour was not seen as norm infringing, namely the situation in which a girl tells her parents that she is going to marry a foreigner. Analyses performed on each of the 36 norm violations separately showed a significantly higher rating of inappropriateness for the Turks in 11 situations at a 0.05 level and in two situations at a 0.10 level (t-test, corrected for significant differences in variance).

In general, the appropriateness ratings were characterized by a small variance, which suggests that a high interindividual consensus existed about the inappropriateness of the behaviours included in the questionnaire. However, the variance of the Turkish subjects' ratings was still considerably smaller than that of the Dutch subjects.

Evaluation of reaction alternatives. The appropriateness ratings of the reaction alternatives were analysed as follows. Per subject, the mean score

Table 8.1 Means of 'appropriateness' ratings per reaction category for Turkish immigrants and Dutchmen

Reaction	Turkish ($n = 15$)	Dutch ($n = 15$)
R+	6.75_a	7.07_a
R0	5.97_{bc}	6.22_{bc}
R−	6.27_b	5.81_c
R=	5.66_c	4.73_d
R≡	4.47_d	2.83_e

R+ positive reaction, R0 no reaction, R− mildly negative reaction, R= tit for tat retaliation, and R≡ strongly negative retaliation. Column means with different subscripts differ significantly from one another (*t*-test for correlated data; $p < 0.05$). Scale employed: 1 inappropriate, 10 appropriate.

for each of the five reaction categories over 36 situations was computed. This implies that we had five scores for each subject, i.e. R+, R0, R−, R=, and R≡. The means for these scores are presented in Table 8.1. With these five scores as dependent variables and the cultural background (Turkish or Dutch) as the independent variable a multivariate analysis of variance was performed. This resulted in a significant effect for cultural background ($F_{5,16} = 4.82$, $p < 0.01$). Subsequent univariate analyses of variance showed an effect for R= ($F_{1,20} = 6.38$, $p < 0.05$) and R≡ ($F_{1,20} = 18.17$, $p < 0.001$). The Turkish subjects considered the equally strong reaction alternative and the stronger reaction alternative (R= and R≡) significantly more appropriate than the Dutch subjects.

Analyses of variance of the ratings for each of the 36 R= and R≡ reactions separately resulted in significant differences in 11 out of 36 situations for R=. In ten cases the Turks considered this reaction as more appropriate than the Dutch, and in one case the reverse was true. In 21 cases the Turks evaluated R≡ as more appropriate than the Dutch.

We also analysed whether, within each of the groups (Turks and Dutch), the means of the reaction category scores differed significantly (*t*-test for correlated data, see Table 8.1). It appeared that for both the Turks and the Dutch R+ was generally judged as significantly more appropriate than a reaction with norm violation (R−, R=, and R≡). Not showing any reaction (R0) was, on average, seen as less appropriate than R+. Absence of a reaction (R0), however, was not significantly different from R− or from R= in the case of the Turkish subjects. Moreover, it may be noted that the mean range of the ratings of the reaction categories of the Turkish subjects is smaller than that of the Dutchmen.

In sum, these data indicate that given a norm violation by another party, an attempt to solve the conflict in a positive way (R+) is generally considered to be more appropriate than doing nothing (R0) or reacting in a negative manner (R−, R=, and R≡). However, if members of the victim's party react with a 'tit for tat' retaliation (R=) or if they retaliate more strongly (R≡), the Turkish subjects consider such behaviour more appropriate (or less inappropriate) than the Dutch subjects do.

Relationship between norm violation suffered and reactions. Inspection of the Pearson-correlations between the appropriateness rating of each individual norm violation on the one hand and the appropriateness rating of each of the five reaction alternatives separately, on the other (Turkish and Dutch data combined), showed the following overall pattern. Negative correlations were generally obtained between the appropriateness of the initial norm violation and the appropriateness of R≡ (nine correlations are at a level of 0.005; three at a level of 0.10; only one positive correlation is found). That is, the more inappropriate the initial norm violation, the more appropriate it is to react with a stronger norm violation. Negative correlations were also found for R=. Here 16 negative correlations were significant at 0.05 level and three at 0.10 (two positive correlations were obtained as well). The more inappropriate the initial norm violation, the more appropriate it is to react in a 'tit for tat' fashion. For R− a similar pattern was found; 11 negative correlations at a level of 0.05 and six at 0.10 (no positive correlations).

The correlations between the appropriateness rating of the norm violation and the appropriateness rating of R0 were positive (eight at 0.05 level, three at 0.10). The more inappropriate the initial norm violation, the more inappropriate it was to do nothing. The results with respect to R+ were inconsistent. Four positive correlations are found ($p < 0.05$) and two negative ($p < 0.05$). Correlation analyses for the Turkish and the Dutch subjects separately, resulted in the same overall pattern of significant correlations, although less pronounced.

Overall, these results suggest that in the minds of the Turkish as well as the Dutch subjects, norm violation and reaction were related in terms of appropriateness. More precisely stated, the more they considered a norm violation on the part of another as being inappropriate the more it appeared to them as being appropriate to react with norm violation, either R−, R=, or R≡.

Discussion Violations of norms were perceived as more inappropriate by the Turkish than by the Dutch subjects. Moreover, although both cultural groups on average considered a positive reaction the most appropriate, the Turkish subjects tended to consider reciprocation of norm-infringing behaviour with a 'tit for tat' reaction or with a stronger retaliation as less inappropriate than the Dutch. Both groups consider a negative reaction as more appropriate the more they view the initial party's behaviour as inappropriate. Apparently, the two groups involved in the present study share a naïve evaluation of the appropriate reactions to norm violation suffered. The main differences between the two groups are that (i) the variation of responses of the Turkish respondents is smaller than that of the Dutch, (ii) they consider certain norm violations as being more inappropriate than the Dutch, and (iii) certain negative reactions are considered less inappropriate.

In order to understand these results, the differences between the two groups need to be specified. Not only do the groups investigated differ with respect to their cultural background, they differ on a host of other variables as well. Turkish allochthones in The Netherlands enjoy a much lower social and socio-economic status in comparison with the autochthonous Dutch, they have less power (be it social, economic or political), and in many ways they constitute a minority (cf. Hraba *et al.* 1989). Other differences worth mentioning are the following. The Turkish subjects completed the questionnaire in the presence of the research assistant, whereas the Dutch subjects filled it out alone at their homes. Also, the Turkish subjects were largely unemployed and their education level was lower than that of the Dutchmen.

Each of these factors or a combination may account for the differences in evaluations obtained. It may be, for instance, that a cultural difference is the cause of differences in appropriateness ratings. Turkey scores higher on the dimension of uncertainty avoidance than The Netherlands (Hofstede 1980). Hofstede argues that societies scoring high on this dimension are characterized by a need for written norms and regulations. From this it may follow that our Turkish subjects consider norm violations more inappropriate than the Dutch subjects. Another explanation could be that the Western norms have a greater positive salience for the Turks because they are undergoing acculturation in Dutch society.

In spite of the differences between the groups, we found many similarities. This may indicate that the norms covered in the questionnaire are relevant for groups with different cultural backgrounds living in The Netherlands. It is important to note that members of the different groups are part of the Dutch political and legal system. Norm violations were considered inappropriate and furthermore, the more inappropriate they were perceived to be, the more subjects judged negative reactions as appropriate (and vice versa). It should be emphasized, however, that overall such negative reactions were considered rather inappropriate. In fact, only a constructive or positive reaction to norm violation was generally approved of by both Turkish immigrants and autochthonous Dutchmen.

Study 2: evaluation of norm violation and reactions by employees in The Netherlands

This study intended to assess the norm-infringing character of the 24 situations of the norm violation inventory for employees used in Chapter 6 (see Appendix 6.1) and to ascertain the perceived appropriateness of the five alternatives of the response scale employed. The objectives were similar to those of the study discussed in the preceding section.

Subjects Thirty-one employees of different organizations (15 males and 16 females) participated in the study. Their ages ranged from 18 to 48 with a mean age of 35.8.[2]

Method The respondents evaluated the norm violations described in the 24 situations of the norm violation inventory and the five response alternatives offered. First, they judged the behaviour described in terms of (in)appropriateness on a five-point scale (1 completely correct, nothing to reproach; 5 completely unacceptable). Next, the five reaction alternatives were rated. Subjects were requested to give a *relative* rating of (in)appropriateness, i.e. they had to compare each of the five reactions presented (e.g. 'do nothing') in the light of the previous event (e.g. 'someone does not respect the safety regulations'). In other words, with these judgments the respondents considered to what extent each reaction constituted a correct or just punishment for what the other party previously did. The five-point scale employed ranged from 1 (completely adequate/correct) to 5 (completely unacceptable).[3]

Results

Evaluation of norm violation. For the 24 situations the average rating varied from 'rather inappropriate' to 'completely unacceptable' (2.68–4.97, see Appendix 6.1 for the means of each situation). The mean of the ratings over situations and subjects was 3.31.

Evaluation of reaction alternatives. The results for the ratings of the five reaction alternatives were as follows. Subjects showed consistent differences in their ratings of each reaction alternative for the 24 situations. The value for α was 0.49 for R+ and ranged between 0.81 and 0.89 for the other four reaction alternatives. Therefore, we considered it justified to calculate for each subject an individual score for the reactions R+, R0, R−, R=, and R≡ and to perform further analyses using these scores.

Inspection of Table 8.2, in which the means for the respondents' appropriateness ratings for the five reactions are presented, indicates

Table 8.2 Mean ratings of inappropriateness of the reaction alternatives of the norm violation inventory by employees ($n = 31$)

R+	R0	R−	R=	R≡
1.69[a]	2.60[b]	2.37[b]	1.33[c]	3.83[d]

Scale employed: 1 completely correct/appropriate, 5 completely unacceptable. Cells having no superscript in common are significantly different (*t*-test, paired observations; $p < 0.01$).

that the alternatives implying a negative reaction to a preceding norm infraction are considered increasingly inappropriate, and also less correct than a 'positive reaction'. The 'no reaction' alternative, however, is not significantly different from a 'mildly negative retaliation'.

Over situations the ratings on the five reaction alternatives were highly related. Positive correlations were found between the R+ and R0 reactions (0.57, $p < 0.01$) and between the three negative reactions (correlations between 0.66 and 0.91). The correlations between the R+ and R0 reactions on the one hand, and each of the three negative reactions on the other hand were *negative*. It seems that respondents, confronted with a situation in which another party infringes a norm, perceive the five-point scale as dichotomous, either react positively/do nothing or react in a negative way.

Relationship between evaluation of norm violation and the perceived acceptability of a negative reaction by a victim party. In order to assess this relationship various correlations were computed. On the basis of the previous study it was expected that employees would consider a negative retaliation more appropriate the more they considered the initial norm violation inappropriate. Only a few significant correlations were found. When the individual scores for ratings of norm infringements and for each of the five reactions were correlated, only the correlation between the initial norm infringement and R+ approached significance ($r = -0.33$, $p < 0.07$). That is, the more unacceptable the other's behaviour, the less appropriate it was perceived to react in a positive or constructive manner. However, the correlations between the first norm violation and the other reaction alternatives were not significant (0.09 for R0, 0.21 for R−, 0.04 for R=, and 0.11 for R≡).

Correlations computed between ratings of norm violations and reactions for the 24 individual items proved significant ($p < 0.05$) in a considerable number of situations for R+ and for R0. For R+, eight correlations out of 24 were significant, of which six were positive. For R0, ten significant positive correlations were found and no negative ones. For the other three alternatives R−, R=, and R≡, between three and seven out of 24 turned out to be significant (mostly negative).

These correlations provide some weak but suggestive evidence that the more employees perceive another person's behaviour as inappropriate, (i) the less acceptable it appears in their view to react in a positive way (R+), and (ii) the more acceptable they think it is 'not to react' (R0).

Discussion In general, norms of redress in an organizational context appear to be not as clear-cut as one might have expected on the basis of the contrast between Dutchmen and Turkish immigrants. Two findings emerge. First, it appears that a positive reaction to another employee's norm infraction is generally considered the most appropriate reaction. It is considered more correct than R0 or R− and definitely more correct than R= and R≡. Given that a score of two corresponded to the label that the reaction 'just barely passed muster', the findings for the respondents' judgement of the reaction alternatives indicate that only a positive or constructive reaction was generally considered acceptable. All other reactions were considered 'rather' to 'strongly' inappropriate (see Table 8.2).

The second but less clear finding concerns the relationships between perceived inappropriateness of the initial norm violation by the other party and the degree to which people found a 'positive reaction' and 'no reaction' correct ways to respond. Quite clearly, the more inappropriate the preceding norm violation was judged to be the less correct employees found it to react in a constructive fashion (R+). But what, one may wonder, will employees consider appropriate in the case of serious norm infractions? In some situations showing 'no reaction' was perceived as rather appropriate. In most of the situations, however, it was unclear what type of reaction is called for because the number of significant correlations between perceived inappropriateness of the other party's norm violation and the correctness of negative retaliation (R−, R=, and R≡) did not deviate significantly from zero.

Combining these two findings, the present study indicates that employees consider a constructive reaction as a generally appropriate reaction to norm violation. At the same time this 'constructive' reaction is considered to be less appropriate the more serious the preceding norm infraction. The more serious another's norm violation, the more correct it seems (in some cases) to ignore the incident.

In which situations the 'no reaction' norm applies and in which cases 'a constructive reaction' is called for cannot be determined on the basis of the present study because of the small number of respondents and the variety of organizations to which they belonged.

In summary, in organizational settings negative reactions to another employee's norm violation are unlikely to be regarded as appropriate. This may be due to several factors. It may be that such negative reactions are seen as too costly or risky, because they may result in losing one's job. It may also be, as suggested in Chapter 6, that in most organizations specific procedures and norms exist to prevent an escalation of conflicts. The so-called 'positive' or 'constructive' reaction employed in the present study and found to be perceived as most appropriate, may well be a kind of general formulation or summary label for a set of clearly specified norms or rules imposed by organizations to settle conflicts on their premises.

Study 3: norms of redress between Hindus and Muslims in India

Compared with the two studies reported thus far, the aim of the present study is in one respect more limited in another more elaborate. The focus is more limited as no attempt was made to measure the respondents' perceptions of the initial norm violation.[4] Instead it aimed at assessing more extensively possible differences in norms of redress which Hindus and Muslims apply not only to their own group but also to the other group. More specifically, the study measured the perception of the reaction alternatives employed in the norm violation inventory described in Chapter 4 in terms of 'appropriateness' and 'moral acceptability'. The latter question was included, because Gouldner (1960) asserts that the norm of reciprocity is a universally held moral norm and we wanted to find out whether judgments of appropriateness would be different from those of moral acceptability.

Subjects Twenty-five Hindu and 24 Muslim adult male respondents participated in the study. They had different levels of education and socio-economic background, similar to the subjects employed in the study reported in Chapter 4.

Method Respondents were individually presented with the 21 situations of the norm violation inventory (see Appendix 4.1 for the items employed) in two versions. In one a Muslim was the victim and in the other version the victim was a Hindu. Each person rated the five reaction alternatives belonging to a situation twice on eleven-point scales. First, they gave a judgement of 'appropriateness' (1 highly inappropriate; 11 highly appropriate). Next, they judged to what extent they felt that each reaction was 'good' or 'bad' in a moral sense (1 very good; 11 very bad).

Results For the two victim versions of the inventory (ingroup victim versus outgroup victim) the average ratings of 'inappropriateness' and 'goodness or badness' were calculated per reaction alternative. In this way the total number of 420 responses per person was reduced to 20. That is, for each reaction alternative (R+, R0, R−, R=, and R≡) there was one 'appropriateness' rating for the ingroup victim, one 'appropriateness' rating for the outgroup victim, one 'good/bad' rating for the ingroup victim, and one 'good/bad' rating for the outgroup victim.

The data were analysed with a MANOVA employing a 2 (religion, Hindu versus Muslim) × 2 (group membership, ingroup victim versus outgroup victim) × 5 (reaction alternatives) design.

Appropriateness of reactions to norm violation. For the 'appropriateness' variable significant between-group effects were obtained for group membership of the victim ($F_{1,74} = 13.60$, $p < 0.01$) and for the group membership × religion interaction ($F_{1,74} = 4.49$, $p < 0.05$). Hindus rated the reaction alternatives on average as more appropriate for the outgroup than for the ingroup (means for ingroup and outgroup respectively 6.28 and 6.51), whereas for Muslims' ratings no difference was obtained for the ingroup and outgroup (means respectively 5.97 and 6.04). In other words, the main effect of group membership can be attributed to the difference that Hindus make in their judgments between reactions by ingroup and outgroup members: when a Hindu violates a norm it is less inappropriate for Muslims to manifest a reaction than it is for Hindus when a Muslim violates a norm.

The preceding description of the between-subjects' effects obtained might have given the impression that Hindus have the idea that they should not show much of a reaction when their norms are violated. Such an idea may be expressed as a general norm of passive resistance. For Muslims in contrast, according to Hindus, such a norm is less applicable. Although this idea may well correspond to the dominant belief among Hindus that they are peaceful and non-violent, a more detailed analysis of the ratings of the separate reaction alternatives does not support it. Significant within-subjects' effects were obtained for the interactions group membership of the victim × reactions ($F_{4,188} = 5.91$, $p < 0.001$) and for religion × reactions ($F_{4,188} = 3.96$, $p < 0.01$) (see Table 8.3).

Table 8.3 Means of 'inappropriateness' ratings per reaction category for ingroup and outgroup by Hindus and Muslims

Reaction	Hindus ($n = 25$)		Muslims ($n = 24$)	
	ingroup	outgroup	ingroup	outgroup
R+	8.87_a	8.70_a	9.23_a	9.14_a
R0	4.71_b	5.65_b	5.13_b	5.49_b
R−	8.03_c	8.01_a	7.52_c	7.49_c
R=	4.81_b	5.11_b	4.20_d	4.24_d
R≡	4.99_b	5.10_b	3.78_e	3.83_d

Scale employed: 1 highly inappropriate, 11 highly appropriate. Column means with different subscripts differ significantly from one another (t-test for correlated data, $p < 0.05$).

In line with the argument we just made, inspection of the mean ratings relevant to the group membership × reactions interaction shows that the respondents had similar evaluations of all reaction alternatives except one, R0. In contrast to that argument, however, it is found—when a separate t-test for correlated data was applied to test for ingroup–outgroup differences for both groups—that *both* Hindus and Muslims feel that R0 is more appropriate for the outgroup than for the ingroup. For both groups ingroup and outgroup ratings of R0 were significantly different (Hindus, $t = 4.46$, $p < 0.01$; Muslims, $t = 2.50$, $p < 0.05$; see Table 8.3 for the means). When we take into account the meaning of the ratings obtained on the eleven-point scale for appropriateness (where a score lower than six means 'inappropriate'), the significant differences in evaluation obtained for ingroup and outgroup can be described as follows. Both Hindus and Muslims believe that showing no reaction when a norm violation against the other group is committed is rather inappropriate. However, it is less appropriate for members of the ingroup to let a norm violation pass over without a (proper) reaction than for members of the outgroup.

The data for the religion × reactions interaction provide some evidence for differences between Hindus and Muslims in their evaluation of the five reactions to norm violation. The general pattern of the different means suggests that Hindus rate negative reactions to norm violation (R−, R=, and R≡) as more appropriate than Muslims do, whereas for R+ and R0 the reverse is the case. Additional *t*-tests, comparing the ratings of each reaction alternative for the two groups, showed that Hindus only differed from Muslims in their appraisal of the most negative reaction (R≡, $t = 2.49$, $p<0.05$). That is, Hindus considered a strongly negative retaliation less inappropriate than the Muslims did.

In summary, although the MANOVA performed yielded some general differences between the Hindus and Muslims and between the ingroup and outgroup in terms of the appropriateness of reacting to norm violation, only two findings are upheld when the five specific reactions are taken into account. First, it is less appropriate for the ingroup *not to react* to a norm violation, and second, Hindus perceive a strongly negative reaction to norm violation as less inappropriate than Muslims.

However, both findings are relatively weak in comparison with the main effect obtained for reaction alternatives ($F_{4,188} = 151.45$, $p<0.001$). Inspection of the results in Table 8.3 shows that both Hindus and Muslims considered a positive or constructive reaction to a norm violation (R+) the most appropriate response, more appropriate than any of the other reaction alternatives. A mildly negative retaliation (R−) was perceived as being the next in terms of appropriateness. Although this reaction is rated by both Hindus and Muslims as being significantly less appropriate than R+, it is still judged as more appropriate than R0, R=, and R≡. Taking a score of six as the mid-point of the scale, for Hindus and Muslims R+ and R− are the only reactions that are viewed as appropriate reactions to norm violation. R0, R=, and R≡ are all rated at the inappropriate half of the scale.

Moral acceptability of reactions to norm violation. Results obtained for respondents' judgments of the moral acceptability of reactions to norm violations were less complicated than those for appropriateness. The results are summarized in Table 8.4, leaving out distinctions between respondents' religion and between ingroup and outgroup ratings.

For these ratings only a main effect for reaction alternatives attained significance ($F_{4,188} = 164.75$, $p < 0.001$). Main effects were not found for religion (Hindus versus Muslims) or for group membership of the victims (ingroup versus outgroup), neither were any significant interaction effects of these two factors with reaction alternatives found.

Inspection of Table 8.4 shows that respondents' ratings of the five reactions closely paralleled the findings obtained for appropriateness. A positive reaction was considered as morally better than any other. Next

Table 8.4 Means ratings of moral acceptability of the reaction alternatives of the norm violation inventory by Hindus and Muslims

R+	R0	R−	R=	R≡
3.01[a]	6.89[b]	4.40[c]	7.67[d]	7.78[d]

Scale employed: 1 very good, 11 very bad. Cells having no superscript in common are significantly different (t-test, paired observations; $p<0.01$).

in acceptability was a weakly negative retaliation. In fact, these two reactions (R+ and R−) were the only ones that were generally judged in the 'good' half of the response scale, while the others (R0, R=, and R≡) were rated in the 'bad' half. In search for possible differences between Hindus and Muslims we performed t-tests on the ratings of the separate reaction alternatives. It turned out that Muslim respondents rated a 'strongly negative retaliation' (R≡) as morally worse than Hindus did (means respectively 8.30 and 7.27, $t = 2.18$, $p < 0.05$). All other reaction alternatives were rated as equally good or bad by Hindus and Muslims.

Discussion Hindus and Muslims adhered to similar norms of redress. When confronted with a norm violation by a member of the other group Hindus and Muslims feel that responding either in a positive way or in a mildly negative fashion are the most appropriate and morally good reactions. Of these two reactions the positive one was rated as slightly more appropriate and better. The three other reaction alternatives offered (R0, R=, and R≡) were considered as rather inappropriate and morally 'bad' or 'wrong'. Hindus did not differentiate between the three negative reactions, whereas Muslim rated R= and R≡ as more inappropriate and 'bad' than R0.

With respect to these findings the following points should be noted. Firstly, the ratings of appropriateness and moral acceptability were highly related. All 20 correlations between inappropriateness and moral acceptability, calculated separately for Hindus versus Muslims, ingroup versus outgroup victim and the five reaction alternatives, were significant at $p < 0.05$ (correlations varied between 0.54 and 0.93). This means that the judgments of responses to norm violation in terms of 'inappropriateness' and 'good/bad' seem to refer to the same underlying dimension. To state it differently, the Hindu and Muslim respondents did not judge the reactions presented in terms of correctness or of a good/false response to a logical or intellectual problem. Neither did they search for an optimal solution to a problematic situation as an uninvolved observer. On the contrary, ratings of appropriateness of the reactions presented implied a moral judgement.

As a second point, the correlations between the five reaction alternatives should be mentioned. Significant positive correlations (pooled for Hindus and Muslims and the two group membership conditions) were found between the three negative reactions for the ratings of appropriateness (correlations between 0.41 and 0.86). The most negative of these (R= and R≡) were negatively related to R+. No significant correlations were found for R0 with any of the other reactions. This pattern of correlations suggests that the five alternatives presented to the respondents constituted four different options: 'a positive reaction', 'no reaction', 'a mildly negative reaction', and 'an equally negative or stronger retaliation'. Moreover, the less appropriate the respondents' judgement of the last option the more appropriate they evaluated a 'constructive solution' of the conflict to be (in Appendix 8.1 the complete correlation matrices are presented for the appropriateness ratings of the five reaction alternatives in the three studies reported in this chapter).

As the last and probably most significant point, the similarity of judgments across the two groups can be emphasized. For none of the reaction alternatives except one (R≡) were differences found between Hindus and Muslims in terms of appropriateness and moral acceptability. Both groups found the alternative reactions to norm violation offered similarly (in)appropriate and morally (un)acceptable.

The reason that Hindus judged a strongly negative retaliation less inappropriate than that Muslims did may be related to the past experience of these groups with the behaviours described in that reaction alternative. This response constituted the only escalation response of the norm violation inventory. In the majority of the situations (14 out of 21) this reaction was described as collective physical violence against the perpetrator(s). It could be that Hindus have less problems accepting this kind of reaction than Muslims, because they have experienced less suffering from riots that took place in the past than Muslims have (Engineer 1984; Krishna 1985).

Moreover, for neither Hindus nor Muslims were major differences found between ingroup and outgroup victim. The fact that both groups judged 'no reaction' as less inappropriate for the outgroup than for the ingroup can be interpreted in two different ways. On the one hand, it may be understood as an ingroup–outgroup effect. This would mean that people have less problems when a norm violation is left unanswered by outgroup members than when ingroup members are confronted with a norm violation. It could be argued, for instance, that such a tendency follows from people's higher involvement or identification with their own group than with the outgroup. On the other hand, the differences in evaluation of 'no reaction' could be due to different perceptions of the seriousness of the violation committed or suffered.

However, the difference in evaluation of R0 can also be explained by referring to differences in actor/victim position, because in the description of the incidents 'ingroup victim' implied 'outgroup actor' and 'outgroup victim' implied 'ingroup actor'. There is evidence that actors tend to perceive an identical norm violation as less norm-infringing and serious than victims (Mummendey *et al.* 1984*a*, *b*; DeRidder 1985).

Assuming that the seriousness of the norm violation is negatively correlated with R0 (see the first study in this chapter), differences in actor/victim position can explain the ingroup–outgroup effect obtained in the present study. That is, victims should react more than perpetrators to a norm violation because they perceive it as a more serious incident. Unfortunately, it cannot be determined which of the two interpretations is most valid, because in the present study actor/victim position and ingroup/outgroup membership were not independently varied.

We would like to emphasize the similarities in the judgments of inappropriateness and moral acceptability. In general, both groups applied the same norms of redress to members of their own group as to members of the other group. A similar finding is reported by Ansari (1983) in a study on preferred conflict resolution styles of Hindus and Muslims in intergroup tension situations. The overall pattern of preferred conflict resolution styles of Hindus and Muslims showed few differences.

To reiterate, Hindus and Muslims adhered to similar norms of redress and they assumed that their outgroup did too. The predominant norms, in the case where members of one of the parties violated a norm, turned out to be 'react in a positive fashion' or 'respond in a mildly negative way'.

General discussion

Group differences in evaluation of reactions to norm violation

The results of the three studies conducted provide the following answers to the four research questions raised. First, there may well exist differences between groups in their evaluation of the initial norm violation suffered. It appeared in the first study that Turkish immigrants evaluated a number of norm violations as more inappropriate than autochthonous Dutchmen did. This result is probably directly related to the importance Turkish immigrants attach to norms. A pilot study showed that they felt norms to be more important than Dutchmen did (Schruijer and DeRidder 1988). If the present data are valid, the vulnerable and threatened minority position these immigrants occupy in Dutch society (cf. Hraba *et al.* 1989) may partly explain their concern with norms and their relatively strong disapproval of norm violation.

The difference in majority/minority status between the two groups is a factor which may have influenced the appropriateness ratings of norm violations and reactions as well. First, minority members will have identified the actors in the situation descriptions as Dutch, since in daily life they are often confronted with majority group actors. For the Dutch, however, it appears to be farfetched to assume that they would identify the norm-violating actors as belonging to an outgroup, and to identify them as Turkish actors is even more unlikely. This assertion assumes that the Turkish subjects, members of a minority, judge the other's norm violation as more extreme than the Dutch do because the norm violation is in the Turkish subjects' view manifested by an outgroup member. Second, minority members can have differentiated little between reaction alternatives, since their past experience taught them that no reaction whatsoever to the majority's norm-infringing behaviour will prove to be effective. This line of reasoning may explain the smaller range of appropriateness ratings given by the Turkish subjects. Their concern with norms and disapproval of norm violation may have induced Turkish immigrants to be more lenient towards 'a negative' and 'a strongly negative' retaliation.

This point leads us to the second research question: are evaluations of reactions to norm violations different among groups? A finding similar to that just mentioned was obtained in study 3, where it appeared that Hindus evaluated 'a strongly negative retaliation' to be less inappropriate than Muslims did. As there is some empirical evidence that Hindus expect that their social, political, and economic situation will advance less in the future than that of Muslims (see Chapter 4), the similarity in findings for Turkish immigrants and Hindus suggests the following tentative hypothesis. Members of groups who feel their position in society is threatened are inclined to consider negative behaviour and violence as more appropriate means of conflict resolution than members of groups whose societal position is not threatened.

The answers given to the two preceding questions suggest that there may be some *group* differences in evaluation of norm violation and reaction. The third question focused on the appraisal of reactions in an *intergroup* situation. Do groups apply different norms of redress to members of the ingroup compared with members of the outgroup? Little evidence for a positive answer was found. The only relevant result found was for the reaction alternative 'doing nothing' in the Hindu–Muslim study and two interpretations of it were possible (see pp. 163–4).

Summarizing the (inter)group differences found, it can be stated that differences did occur in the evaluation of the first incident or norm violation, i.e. threatened groups are probably more apprehensive than non-threatened groups. Relatively few differences, however, appear to exist in evaluations of *reactions* to norm violations. Moreover, those that do exist are of minor importance; all the differences we found were for reaction alternatives that were generally considered as rather inappropriate. This leaves us with the most striking result of the three studies: the similarities in the evaluations obtained.

Similarities in evaluation of reactions to norm violation

Before summarizing the similarities found, we need to point out the differences in focus of the three studies. This difference can be best described as a variation along a dimension of 'interpersonal encounter' in the first study versus 'intergroup encounter' in the third study. That is, in study 1 the incidents in the questionnaire were described as situations in which 'someone' violated a norm against 'a person'. In study 3, the group membership of the actor and victim were spelled out: 'a Hindu (or Muslim)' committed a norm violation against 'a Muslim (or Hindu)'. The second study occupies an intermediate position. In that study the respondents knew that the situations described involved two employees belonging to the same organization. To state the issue differently, study 1 attempted to present the situations as interpersonal encounters, study 2 dealt with incidents among employees, and study 3 addressed intergroup contacts.

In spite of these different foci, surprisingly similar results were obtained with regard to the appraisal of reactions to norm violation. Turkish immigrants, autochthonous Dutch, employees in Dutch organizations, and Hindus and Muslims in India, agreed that *a positive or constructive reaction to another person's or party's norm violation was the most appropriate response*. Similarly all these groups, except maybe the Turkish immigrants, considered it inappropriate to opt for negative retaliation ('tit for tat' or strongly negative retaliation).

When we take into account the meaning of the scales employed in the studies, a distinction can be made between reactions judged as 'appropriate', and those rated as 'inappropriate' (see Table 8.5).

Table 8.5 Classification of reactions to norm violations in terms of perceived appropriateness for the groups that participated in the three studies

Group	Appropriate	Inappropriate
Turkish immigrants*	R+,R0,R−,R=	R≡
Dutchmen*	R+,R0,R−	R=,R≡
Employees**	R+,R0,R−	R=,R≡
Hindus***	R+,R−	R0,R=,R≡
Muslims***	R+,R−	R0,R=,R≡

For classification as 'appropriate' the scales were split at * less than 5.5, ** less than 3.0, and *** greater than 6.0; see Tables 8.1, 8.2, and 8.3.

Apart from the similarities just mentioned concerning R+, R=, and R≡, it can be seen in Table 8.5 that the different groups agreed on one additional point. All rated 'a mildly negative reaction' (R−) as rather appropriate although in almost all cases this reaction was viewed as less appropriate than R+.[5] The only reaction on which the groups clearly differed was: 'doing nothing'. Whereas the groups studied in The Netherlands rated R0 as appropriate, Hindus and Muslims in India evaluated it as definitely inappropriate. One can only speculate about the possible explanations for this difference. It may be, for instance, that people in The Netherlands, and especially employees occupying a low position in the organizational hierarchy, are taught or implicitly instructed to 'shrug their shoulders', to 'keep their mouths shut' or to take an 'I don't care' stand. In some types of organizations and/or for some types of employees these norms may be part of what Schein (1980, pp. 22–3) called a 'psychological contract' between employee and organization. Hindus and Muslims in India, in contrast, may have learned that 'things get worse' and 'problems aggravate' when you don't pay attention to them. We like to stress that this is just one of several interpretations possible. Further research should address this issue more carefully.

Three major norms of redress

Until now we have discussed the results in terms of the appropriateness of certain reactions in situations in which another person, employee or group violates a norm. Formulating the findings obtained as norms of redress, the following summary can be given. *If* another person, employee or group violates a norm, *then* one should:

(1) attempt to solve the conflict in a positive or constructive way;

(2) not aggravate the situation by showing a 'tit for tat' retaliation or by a 'strongly negative' reaction;

(3) react in a 'mildly negative' fashion.

The question can be raised whether we are justified in formulating the results of the studies in this way.

In an attempt to answer these questions, we first would like to point out some weaknesses in our studies. The number of respondents who participated is rather small (110 in total). Moreover, the data were gathered using questionnaires and were not the result of a study of behavioural patterns of conflict episodes. Another reason for caution is that some of our data are at variance with common-sense beliefs. For instance, in contrast to the opinion of Hindus that they are non-violent and that Muslims are 'fighters', we found that Muslims disapproved more strongly of a 'very negative (violent) reaction' than Hindus did. Finally, it may be argued that the second norm formulated above is opposite to the 'norm of negative reciprocity' proposed by Gouldner (1960; 1975), a norm for which some empirical evidence exists (e.g. Helm *et al.* 1971).

However, arguments can be put forward to consider the three norms proposed as a preliminarily valid statement. First, the characteristics of the respondents were highly varied and the focus of the studies differed from 'interpersonal' to 'intergroup' encounters. In spite of this, highly similar results were found. Second, the variances in rated appropriateness of the different reaction alternatives were small. A small variance can be considered as an indication that people belonging to a certain group have a shared understanding of a particular norm. For our third argument, the results of the ratings of appropriateness and moral acceptability obtained in study 3 are important. The similarity in judgments of each reaction with respect to these two ratings and the high correlations between them indicate that respondents did not simply perform a sort of intellectual matching task of initial norm violation with subsequent reaction. On the contrary, their evaluations entailed a moral judgement. Reacting in a positive way is not the 'best' or 'most correct' solution to preceding improper conduct. Rather, such a reaction is that which is morally prescribed; it has an obligatory or 'ought' character. For these reasons we think that the results of our studies demonstrate the existence of the three norms of redress formulated above.

We dismiss the idea that norms cannot be studied by means of questionnaires. Whereas a number of methods have been proposed to study communication rules, such as verbal and other reactions to rule braking (cf. Shimanoff 1980), the study of social norms using written questions about appropriateness is an accepted practice (e.g. Price and Bouffard 1974; see also Argyle *et al.* 1981, pp. 130–3). Moreover, the detection of sequential patterns in 'real life' conflicts may be suggestive of the existence of norms of redress, but this does not provide unequivocal proof. Collett (1977) correctly pointed out that *uniformity* in observed behaviour does not imply that it is norm governed.

The issue of the 'norm of negative reciprocity' deserves a more elaborate discussion. It will be addressed in the next and final section of this chapter.

The norm of negative reciprocity; a Western invention?

In 1960 Gouldner proposed that there exists a universal or 'general norm of negative reciprocity'. The prototypical example of the norm given by him is the *lex talionis* ('an eye for an eye'). Following Gouldner (1960, pp. 171–2) such a negative norm of reciprocity makes two minimal demands: (i) people should injure those who have injured them, and (ii) people should not help those who have injured them. Although Gouldner assumed this norm to be universal, he also emphasized that the conditions under which it exists in any given group is a matter of empirical investigation. Assuming that norm-infringing behaviour is experienced as unpleasant, negative or injurious, Gouldner's assertions would predict that in the studies we performed:

(1) all groups consider R+ as inappropriate and R= as appropriate, independently of the group membership of actor and victim of norm violation;

(2) the more people judge a norm violation suffered as inappropriate the more they consider a 'tit for tat' retaliation (R=) appropriate.

From our discussion in the previous section it will be recalled that the first prediction derived from Gouldner is clearly disconfirmed. In all three studies we found that R+ was generally considered appropriate and in studies 2 and 3 R= turned out to be evaluated as inappropriate. Only Turkish subjects rated a 'tit for tat' retaliation slightly in favour of the appropriate end of the appropriate–inappropriate scale.

For the second prediction based on Gouldner's norm of negative reciprocity only some support can be found in studies 1 and 2. It was found that when the data for Turkish immigrants and Dutchmen were combined, a marginally significant correlation was found between evaluation of the initial norm violation and the rating of a 'tit for tat' retaliation ($r = -0.34$, $p < 0.10$). The more inappropriate people perceived someone's norm violation, the more appropriate they judged a 'tit for tat' reaction. For employees in study 2 no similar significant relationship was found ($r = 0.04$). Even when we stretch the notion of negative reciprocity to imply that a mildly negative reaction (R−) falls under this label, the picture does not improve ($r = -0.36$, $p < 0.10$ in study 1 and $r = 0.21$, NS in study 2). The only result in line with the notion of negative reciprocity for study 2 was that employees judged a positive reaction to be less correct the more they perceived the initial norm violation as improper ($r = -0.33$, $p < 0.10$).

In sum, the results of the present studies indicate that in the groups we studied Gouldner's general norm of negative reciprocity did not hold, or at least did not manifest itself. In contrast, there appears to be a general norm to react in a positive or constructive way in the case where another person or party starts a conflict by violating a norm.

In concluding, we would like to make two points with respect to the notion of reciprocity. In the first place, the emphasis on the importance of reciprocity in anthropology (e.g. Mauss 1954; Sahlins 1972) and in sociology (e.g. Homans 1950; Gouldner 1960) for 'primitive' and 'cultured' societies is probably correct, provided conclusions are restricted to 'positive' or 'balanced' reciprocity. As Sahlins stated, negative reciprocity is the *unsociable* extreme (1972, p. 195). It is probably only found among foreigners, but not among individuals and groups that are related to one another (Bar-Tal *et al.* 1977). As a second remark, we would like to add that the idea of a general norm of negative reciprocity may be qualified as a Western invention. It is probably inspired by the existing Western culture in which uniqueness, unrelatedness, and individualism are highly cherished values.

Notes

[1] It should be noted that neither Turner and Killian (1972), nor Rabbie and coworkers (Rabbie and Lodewijkx 1986, 1987; Rabbie 1989) discuss the importance of a larger social unit for the emergence of norms in different groups. Both

approaches exclusively focus on *ingroup* processes (imitation, social comparison, communication, etc.) establishing these norms. Neither do these authors take into account the possibility of a common history and future of the two groups. Owing to the absence of these features, we believe that Lodewijkx (1989) was able to create the optimal conditions for a group's dominant ingroup norm to become one of aggressive retaliation.

[2] No distinction was made between supervisors and subordinates. All respondents except four were subordinates.

[3] The respondents also gave an *absolute* rating of the (in)appropriateness of each reaction alternative. That is, they judged the reactions independently of what happened in the item stem. The results for this rating will not be dealt with here.

[4] This was done in a pilot study with a different sample of subjects before the main investigation, reported in Chapter 4, took place. See Appendix 4.1.

[5] The only exception are Hindus' ratings of R+ and R− for Muslim victims (see Table 8.3).

PART III

General discussion

9 Norm violation and intergroup relations: conclusions and prospects

Richard DeRidder, Sandra G. L. Schruijer, and Rama C. Tripathi

The empirical studies reported in this monograph focused on reactions to norm violations in two culturally different countries, India and The Netherlands. In two studies within each culture, the effects were investigated of own group identification, intergroup attitudes, perceived power and fraternal relative deprivation on reactions to norm violations (Chapters 3–6). Additionally, three studies were conducted on the norms of redress (two in The Netherlands and one in India, Chapter 8).

From the perspective of norm violation theory presented in Chapter 1, we shall now review the findings of these studies. The following questions will be addressed. What are the strong points and the limitations of the studies that should be kept in mind? What are the main findings of the four studies reported in the Chapters 3–6? How can norms of redress be related to these findings? And, what prospects for future research on norm violation and intergroup relations can be suggested?

Empirical studies: criticism

Methodological issues

The methodological problems which can be encountered in cross-cultural research were treated in Chapter 2. The main point to be repeated here is that direct comparisons of scores on the scales tapping the different variables between groups and cultures were virtually impossible and were not attempted. Such comparisons were not necessary to meet our objectives because we were mainly interested in investigating whether the framework formulated in Chapter 1 has explanatory value for different group contrasts in different societies, and whether the relationships specified in this framework hold across groups and societies. To this end we chose to match the research method and measurement procedures as closely as possible across group contrasts and cultures. Instead of trying to achieve perfect psychometric equivalence of the scores obtained, we employed an almost identical research methodology across the four different group contrasts in India and The Netherlands. The success of this endeavour can be viewed as a considerable strength of the research presented.

Nevertheless, two issues remain. The first concerns imperfections in the instruments employed to measure the context factors. The second issue regards our main dependent variable, the reaction alternatives to the norm violations presented in the norm violation inventory.

Scales for context factors Owing to the large number of variables which were assessed and constraints imposed by the level of education of the subjects, the measurement of the context variables needed to be as uncomplicated and as short as possible. In spite of our efforts to keep the wording of the items and the response scales simple, problems occurred in one of the studies. This led Singh and Sinha (Chapter 5) to replace some of the five-point response scales (e.g. for attitudes) by a bimodal scale (yes/no) and to adapt the presentation of the fraternal relative deprivation scale. Our concern for the intelligibility and relevance of the questions led us to abandon highly sophisticated scales and procedures for the measurement of attitudes such as those suggested by Fishbein and Ajzen (1975) and by Dawes and Smith (1985). We limited ourselves to the operationalization of the essential components of each context factor. Consequently, items and response scales were less precise than they could have been.

The scales for the measurement of attitudes and own group identification were similar across the four main studies. As explained in Chapter 2 they consisted of a number of adjectives (varying between 20 and 30 across the studies) for which subjects indicated their applicability to themselves, to their own group and to the other group in the contrast pair. Approximately half of the adjectives were derived from descriptions which members of the groups typically employed in their characterization of members of their own and of the other group. This selection procedure is important because it limited the number of adjectives needed for an assessment of attitudes and own group identification.[1]

It goes without saying that the measurements of attitudes and own group identification could be improved by the inclusion of more scales and more social categories. This would enable a refinement of attitudes and identifications of individuals between and within the groups studied. Hindus for instance, can be distinguished as Hindu fundamentalists, secular Hindus and atheists. How important such distinctions are for the prediction of reactions to norm violation is left for future research.

The scales for power and fraternal relative deprivation were different. To measure perceived power, questions were answered related to the economic, political, and social influence subjects' own group and their other group had over one another (resource power) and about their power to retaliate (retaliation power). In measuring fraternal relative deprivation, the subjects assessed the relative position of their group in comparison with the other group and indicated, in Chapters 3, 4 and 6, their (dis)satisfaction with the progress made thus far and/or with the present state of affairs. Significant correlations were obtained between the composite indices of power and fraternal relative deprivation for all contrast pairs (i.e. when all items of the power scale were aggregated as well as those of the fraternal relative deprivation scale, see Table 7.7). However, a similar consistent positive relationship between power and fraternal relative deprivation was not found for all the groups studied when the separate sub-scales of these variables were considered (see Appendices 3.2, 4.2, 5.2, and 6.2). For some groups (Turks, Dutch, Muslims and subordinates) significant correlations between power and fraternal relative deprivation were found, while for others (Hindus, workers and managers in India, and supervisors in The Netherlands) the correlations were weak and insignificant.

Thus, the results for power and fraternal relative deprivation were confounded in the studies conducted. In particular, one of the essential elements of fraternal relative deprivation, feelings of resentment, should be measured more elaborately in the future. Separate assessment of power in terms of resources and retaliation may not be needed. Subjects' ratings of the two were highly correlated in most of the studies and on theoretical grounds the distinction is questionable. It can be argued that a relative advantage in resources probably implies an advantage in means of retaliation (Ng, personal communication).

Reaction alternatives in the norm violation inventory The five response alternatives provided with each norm violation in the norm violation inventory were treated in the analyses as a five-point scale ranging from a positive to an extremely negative reaction. These alternatives and their position on the scale were extensively discussed by the researchers before inserting them in the inventory. In addition, several pilot studies were conducted to find out to what extent our classification was justified. These studies revealed that the overall rank order was perceived similarly by the Dutch, the Turks, the subordinates and the supervisors on the one hand and by the research team on the other. For these groups legitimation was obtained to treat the five reaction alternatives in line with our a priori scale.[2] Still, care should be taken when assessing the reactions to *single* norm violations as the rank order of reactions belonging to some situations deviated from this a priori scale. The results in Chapter 8 show that our scale does not fully emerge from the Hindu and Muslim data. Particularly, the result that 'not showing any reaction' was rated as less appropriate than 'reacting slightly negatively' is incompatible with our a priori scale. Nevertheless, we decided to analyse the data of the Hindu–Muslim study (Chapter 4), in line with the a priori scale, as no substantial difference in results was observed when the data were analysed leaving out the R0 reactions. However, the issue remains debatable.

It should be added that the way we operationalized our reaction scale may have led to the problem that qualitatively different reactions were included in the scales (withdrawal, calling in a third party, verbal abuse, physical abuse, etc.). However, its definite advantage was that the psychological meaning of the reaction alternatives was clearly communication to the respondents.[3]

Samples and research settings

We should briefly pay attention to the comparability of the samples within each contrast. In the Hindu–Muslim contrast some demographic variables (e.g. education, income) were different. Likewise, differences existed between the workers and managers and between subordinates and supervisors. The most similar groups were the Turks and the Dutch who were matched quite carefully.

These differences should be taken into consideration when making inferences from the data. We deliberately chose groups which differed in their societal or organizational position. Some undesired differences related to these positions could not be avoided, e.g. differences in education between the high and low power groups. However, it should be pointed out that the similarities between the samples from the same contrast are probably much larger than the differences, since explicit attempts were made to make the samples as similar as practically possible.

Furthermore, it should be borne in mind that the samples drawn were not meant to be representative of the total population. Our primary concern was to establish a match as closely as possible between groups within a contrast rather than in achieving population-wide representativeness.

One of the general problems we faced was how to rule out the possibility that actual events or incidents from a recent past would affect subjects' responses. The inclusion of situations in the norm violation inventory which could directly refer to such incidents was avoided. Nevertheless, in two studies events beyond our control took place during the course of data collection which may have affected the results obtained. To some extent this may have happened in the manager–worker study (Chapter 5),[4] but it may have been particularly the case for the Hindu–Muslim contrast (Chapter 4).

At the time that this study was being conducted a near riot situation developed in the town where the data were collected (the walls of a mosque which was being constructed on a disputed land site were pulled down by the authorities, leading to the imposition of a curfew in certain parts of the city). It could be that in this study subjects found it awkward to be presented with questionnaires in which norm-violating incidents were depicted and in which they were asked to assess the relative power of Hindus and Muslims. The respondents may have become highly suspicious and may have given either socially acceptable responses, or they may have simply lied or responded randomly. Any combination of these response strategies could account for the fact that, in comparison with the other three studies conducted, only a few significant results were obtained for the Hindu–Muslim contrast (see next section). Moreover, some of the results of this study are at variance with those obtained in other studies (e.g. Ansari 1983). It therefore seems desirable to repeat the Hindu–Muslim study under more peaceful and controlled circumstances.

Main results

The methodological limitations discussed and the problems raised with respect to samples and research settings indicate that care should be taken in the interpretation of the data obtained. Therefore, we shall focus our discussion on those results which emerged most clearly.

Norm violation and intergroup reactions

In Chapter 1 it was proposed that a group's reaction to norm violation depended on (i) its perception of norm violation by an other group, (ii) the outcome of the ensuing attribution process, (iii) various intergroup context factors, and (iv) norms of redress. The empirical studies reported addressed the influence of context factors and norms of redress.

In designing the norm violation inventories employed in these studies, care was taken to keep the first two factors, perception of norm violation and attribution, constant. Before the main investigations took place, pilot studies were conducted to ensure that the behaviours described in the situations were perceived as norm infringing. Moreover, efforts were made to exclude the possibility that these behaviours would be attributed to external factors, such as environmental constraints or previous provocations by members of the afflicted group. Thus, in the main studies, subjects were presented with situations in which members of one group manifested norm-infringing behaviour for which members of the other group held the actor(s) responsible. What kind of reactions to norm violation can be expected under these circumstances?

According to the theory, the answer to this question depends on the strength of the context factors specified (own group identification, intergroup attitudes, power, and fraternal relative deprivation) within a given group contrast. The general prediction made in Chapter 1 was that escalation of negative intergroup behaviour is likely when (i) members of both groups have a strong own group identification, (ii) negative attitudes between groups exist, (iii) differences in power are small, and (iv) feelings of fraternal relative deprivation are intense (see p. 30). If the own group identification is moderately strong, if the attitudes of one group towards the other are neither extremely positive nor extremely negative, if power differences are small, and feelings of fraternal relative deprivation are relatively weak, then it can be expected that one group's norm violation will lead to a 'tit for tat' reciprocation by the other group.[5] In other words, in an economic, social, political, and historical vacuum, norm violation by members of one 'group' will be answered with norm violation on the part of members of the other 'group'.[6]

It will be evident that such a situation does not apply to relations between co-existing groups. What the argument implies, however, is a theoretical baseline against which the results obtained can be measured (see Fig. 9.1).

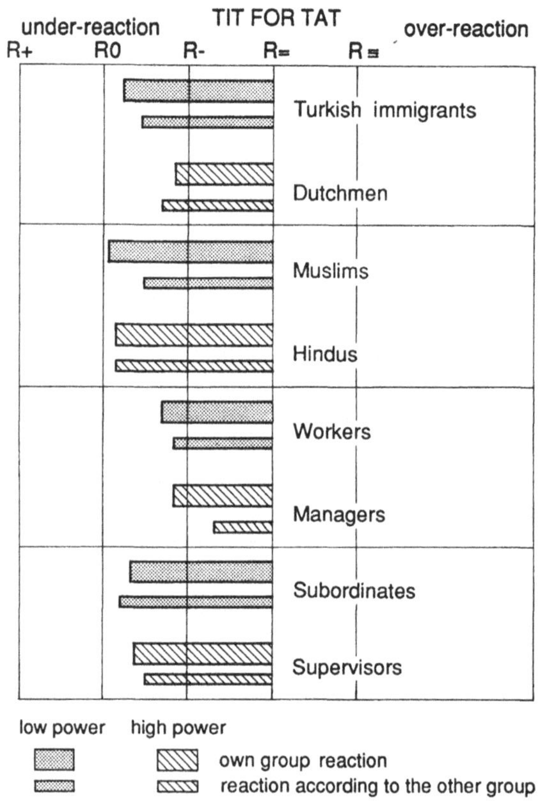

Figure 9.1 Reactions to norm violation expressed as deviations from a 'tit for tat' reaction

In Fig. 9.1, reactions to norm violation by members of the own group and by the other group are depicted as deviations from this theoretical baseline, a 'tit for tat' reaction (labelled R= in the empirical chapters). For example, the average deviation from the baseline for Turkish immigrants was −1.68 for the own group reaction. The other group in this contrast pair, autochthonous Dutchmen, anticipated an average deviation of −1.49 from Turkish victims. Both scores indicate that the Turks manifested an under-reaction, i.e. their reaction was less negative than the behaviour inflicted on them by Dutchmen. Such an under-reaction appeared to be a general finding across the studies. We will return to this phenomenon in the next section. Here, we will focus on differences between the groups with respect to the context factors measured and on their degree of under-reaction.

Power and fraternal relative deprivation

The groups studied differed with respect to their historical and cultural background and in a number of other respects (see samples discussed above). Within each contrast pair, it appeared that two context factors, power and fraternal relative deprivation, clearly differentiated between the two groups and were significant predictors of reactions to norm violation.

Members of one group were generally judged as higher in power than member of the other, by themselves as well as by members of the other group. The Turkish immigrants were perceived as having less power than the Dutchmen, the Muslims less than the Hindus, the workers less than the managers, and the subordinates less than the supervisors. Similar results were found for fraternal relative deprivation. Moreover, power and fraternal relative deprivation were the best predictors of differences in reactions to norm violation between the groups in a contrast pair (see Chapter 7). Their effects albeit less profound, also appeared when the reactions to norm violations were analysed for the different groups separately. The more power individuals judged their own group had over the other, the more negatively they expected their own group members to react (Chapters 3, 5 and 6). A similar relationship was found for anticipated other group reactions in these chapters. In some cases negative attitudes predicted reactions to norm violations (Chapter 3 and 5). In two studies (Chapters 4 and 6), some evidence was also found for the relationship between fraternal relative deprivation and reactions. For instance, the more dissatisfied employees were with their actual situation, the more negatively they expected their own group to react.

The similarity of the results for power and fraternal relative deprivation across studies does not imply that these two context factors refer to the same theoretical concept. The experience of power differences does not necessarily lead to a sense of injustice and to feelings of resentment (see Chapter 1). As long as the existing power balance is evaluated as legitimate or just, no feelings of resentment or dissatisfaction will probably be aroused. Unfortunately, feelings of fraternal relative deprivation and power cannot be disentangled in the studies conducted. Therefore, it seems most correct to conceptualize the major difference between the groups within a contrast pair as a difference in *perceived* (economic, political, and social) *power* (sometimes resented, sometimes not). In Fig. 9.1 the groups are distinguished accordingly.

It appeared that, in general, the high power groups deviated less from a 'tit for tat' retaliation than the low power groups. In three out of four instances, anticipated reactions from the low power group deviated more from a 'tit for tat' retaliation in a de-escalating direction than those of the high power group. The only exception to this overall pattern was Hindus' anticipation of Muslims' reactions.

Conclusions

Two conclusions can be drawn for situations in which the two groups clearly differ in terms of perceived political, economic, and social power. The first conclusion is that differences in perceived power lead to differences in reactions to norm violations. Members of the high power group are more likely to retaliate than members of the low power group. The second conclusion is that the more members of a group judge their group as higher in power, the more likely they are to react negatively to the outgroup's norm violation.

Two general comments should be made with respect to these conclusions. Our first comment is related to the effects of the other context factors on reactions to norm violation. A conclusion that own group identification and attitudes are irrelevant for intergroup reactions to norm violations is, in our view, not warranted. Our results showed some evidence for relationships between these factors and reactions to norm violation (in Chapters 3 and 6 for attitudes, and in Chapter 4 for own group identification). Another finding was that in three of the four studies the low power group had a more positive attitude towards their own group than the high power group members had twoards their own group (Chapters 3–5). Thus, although the results for attitudes and own group identification are less clear and less convincing than those obtained for perceived relative power, they suggest that it is too early to discard them.

Our second remark pertains to the second conclusion. It is cast in terms of 'negativity' of reaction. Although in the main studies a judgement of higher power coincided with a *relatively* more negative reaction, a 'tit for tat' reaction and a strongly negative reaction (escalation) were *not* very likely responses to norm violation. On the contrary, as Fig. 9.1 shows, we generally found a tendency towards *de-escalation*. A number of explanations can be offered for this phenomenon. One possible interpretation is that the norm infringements described in the norm violation inventory constituted, in the opinion of our subjects, 'only' a first and isolated incident. It may well be true that such a first norm violation sufficed to trigger the attribution process as norm violation theory proposes, and that the subjects held the (members of the) other group responsible for it. This attribution, however, may not have been sufficient to lead to the manifestation of 'tit for tat' reactions and escalation. Maybe a 'full-blown' attribution of malevolent and evil intent is needed for reciprocity and/or escalation to occur, and maybe such an attribution is only likely after *repeated* norm violations (Beals *et al.* 1977, p. 446). But even if we assume that members of the victim group were convinced of the negative motives of the norm-violating group, would this necessarily lead to escalation or to reciprocation in a 'tit for tat' fashion? When we take into consideration the anthropological evidence cited in Chapter 8, combined with the results of the studies in the present book, we believe that the answer is negative. It is likely that among co-existing groups norms of redress, fostering de-escalation, will become operative as soon as tendencies towards negative intergroup behaviour arise.

Norms of redress and reactions to norm violation

The operation of norms of redress is a plausible additional explanation for the general tendency of under-reaction found across the four main studies.

In Chapter 8 it was argued that Gouldner's (1960) 'norm of negative reciprocity' probably does not hold for relations among co-existing groups. This argument was based on anthropological literature on conflict and on the results of three studies reported in that chapter. For all the groups for which we checked this, it was found that a positive or constructive reaction was considered the most appropriate way to respond to norm violation. Another finding of these studies was that a minor negative response was also judged appropriate. Reciprocation in a 'tat for tat' fashion was generally disapproved of.

We should be cautious in relating these norms of redress directly to the results obtained in the main studies (Chapter 3, 4, and 6).[7] Although the norm violations presented in these chapters were identical with those in the norms of redress studies, such a comparison is not permitted. No study was conducted in which data were gathered on norms of redress as well as on reactions to norm violation using the same subjects. Therefore, no direct comparisons should be made between the average appropriateness ratings of each separate reaction alternative (summarized in Table 8.5) and the likelihood of each reaction presented in Fig. 3.1, 4.1, and 6.1. A further complication is that the number of respondents in the norms-of-redress studies (Chapter 8) is rather small and the samples are not fully comparable with those of the main studies. For these reasons, we will only mention the average percentage of reactions that corresponded to two of the general norms of redress formulated ('one should do R+' and 'one should do R−'). On average, more than 50 per cent of the reactions to norm violation in the main studies (Chapter 3, 4, and 6) fell in the categories R+ and R− (range between 46.3 per cent for Dutchmen and 72.8 per cent for Muslims). The results of Chapter 8 suggest that these two reactions are the most appropriate.

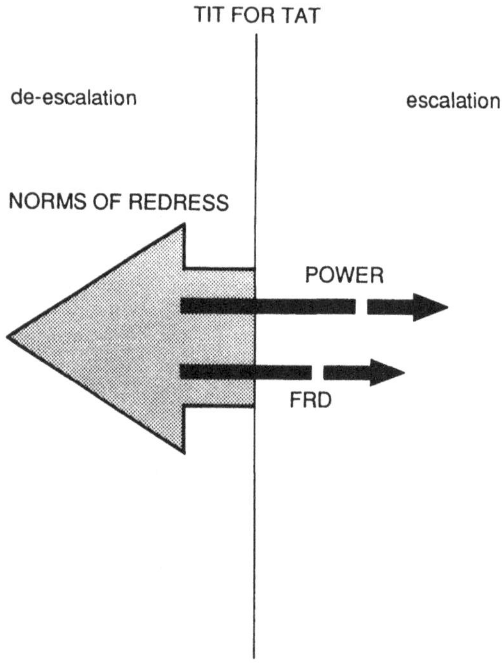

Figure 9.2 Norms of redress and power/fraternal-relative-deprivation as counterforces in reactions to norm violation

Note again that a causal effect of norms of redress on reactions to norm violations cannot be established. In combination with the effects of perceived relative power, this leads to the following general view on the results presented in this monograph (see Fig. 9.2).

When two groups have a history of co-existence within a larger cultural, political or organizational unit, norm violation by (members of) one group triggers the negatively biased attribution process proposed by norm violation theory. Within the victim group tendencies towards retaliation and escalation are aroused. These tendencies will be stronger the more members of this group judge their group's power as superior to that of the other group. Under the conditions specified in the preceding section (see p. 177), the victim group will retaliate with an equally serious norm violation. At the same time that escalating tendencies arise, however, norms of redress come into operation. These norms state that the victim group should show behaviour of a de-escalating nature ('try to solve the problem in a constructive way', 'react in a mildly negative fashion', and 'do not reciprocate the norm violation suffered in a tit for tat fashion'). The functions these norms serve are that tendencies towards escalation are restrained, the balance of power existing before the incident(s) took place is preserved, and a future co-existence between the two groups is, at least temporarily, guaranteed.

This line of reasoning, sketched in Fig. 9.2 with norms of redress and power and fraternal relative deprivation as two counter-forces, provides a parsimonious account of the results presented in this book. It suggests that power and fraternal relative deprivation are factors which instigate escalation. They are counteracted, however, by norms of redress which strongly dictate constructive or positive reactions to norm violation. The argument also emphasizes the dual function which the concept of norm fulfils in norm violation theory. Violation of norms may trigger negative intergroup behaviour, but norms of redress become operative as soon as tendencies towards retaliation or escalation are set in motion.

This overall interpretation of the results raises some theoretically interesting issues, such as the kind of norms of redress that exist, when they become salient, and the specific conditions under which the balance between norm violations triggering escalation and norms of redress stipulating de-escalation is disturbed. Limitation of space does not permit us to elaborate on these issues. Only a brief comment will be made on one of the conditions under which norms of redress may become salient and have an impact on intergroup behaviour. Although alternative interpretations are possible (see p. 176), the apparently high correspondence between Hindus' and Muslims' own group reactions to norm violation and their norms of redress (for the categories R+ and R− more than 69 per cent), could mean that norms of redress had become salient because a situation of intergroup tension or confrontation existed while the study was conducted.

This discussion leads us to the more general point of the prospects for future research on norm violation and intergroup relations.

Prospects

A substantive issue for future investigations is related to an inherent weakness in all the studies reported in this book. All studies employed self-report measures. The basic problem is whether what people said they would do corresponds with what they actually would have done in real life. Questionnaire responses are subject to phenomena like social desirability and self-presentation. Although in this chapter we have emphasized the role of norms of redress, the possibility cannot be ruled out that the high frequency of positive responses and the perceived inappropriateness of norm-violating responses are due to a desire to present oneself or one's group in a favourable way to the researchers. These phenomena may obscure what we are basically interested in, namely being able to understand and predict what people think, feel, and especially, how they behave in natural settings.

A variety of methods, to be employed under controlled conditions as well as in the field, is needed to test the validity of the claims made by norm violation theory with respect to dynamics of intergroup relationships. In particular, experimental studies need to be designed to test the central sequence involving norm violation, attribution, reaction, etc. To what extent, for instance, are the reactions of the victim group influenced by the causal factors to which, in their view, the other group will attribute their reaction? It will only be possible to answer complicated questions like this when more evidence is obtained concerning the more crucial elements of the theory, i.e. attribution, some context factors, and norms of redress.

Attribution processes

Norm violation theory postulates that attributions play a crucial role in intergroup relations. As a first step the present project chose to focus on reactions to norm violations. Focusing on both attributions and reactions within the constraints imposed by a cross-cultural project was beyond our scope. The choice for reactions does not imply that norm violation theory underestimates the influence of attributions. On the contrary, we ensured that certain types of explanations were given of the norm-violating episodes on the basis of pilot studies. Now we feel two other relationships specified by norm violation theory need to be addressed, namely that between norm-violating behaviour and attribution processes, and that between explanations given for norm violations and subsequent reactions. The results of some recent studies (Schruijer 1990*a*) are promising for future investigations into the interrelated processes of norm violation, attribution, and intergroup reaction.[8]

A closer look at the context factors

The model outlined by norm violation theory is a general one and predicts crude relationships between components by merely pointing out their directions. On the basis of the research described in this book we feel that the model can be developed further by focusing selectively on those variables which successfully predicted reactions to norm violations. From our studies it can be derived that, in particular, power and fraternal relative deprivation hold promise for a better understanding of intergroup behaviour.

Norms of redress

Research proposed in the previous paragraphs will lead to an insight into the conditions under which norm violation by one group will lead to negative intergroup behaviour or to an escalation thereof. Norms of redress, however, will in most instances constitute a strong counterforce against these tendencies (although exceptions exist; see Kuschel 1987). One of the immediate tasks within norm violation theory is to study whether these norms indeed have a causal effect on reactions to norm violation.

Evidence for the existence of norms of redress is almost exclusively found in anthropological literature. It will be a challenge to the social psychology of intergroup relations, and to those researchers interested in applying their knowledge to 'natural' groups, to study these norms.

Concluding remarks

At the end of any research endeavour one is caught between focusing on the omissions and on emphasizing the promises. Starting with the omissions, some readers may comment that insufficient attention has been paid to the phenomenon of 'group bias', i.e. intergroup differentiation in favour of the ingroup or in favour of the outgroup in terms of evaluations, attitudes or behaviour. We have deliberately avoided the labels 'ingroup bias' and 'outgroup bias' as much as possible, since the issue of what actually constitutes bias and how to measure it is extremely complex.[9]

Other readers may be of the opinion that some of the results found can be interpreted within the framework of other theories on intergroup relations.

However, such would divert the attention away from some of the most interesting and promising features of norm violation theory: norm violation as a starting point of negative behaviour between groups; attribution processes determining the positive or negative direction of reactions; power and fraternal relative deprivation as factors instigating tendencies towards escalation; norms of redress as a controlling factor of negative behaviour in relationships between co-existing groups. We hope that these features of norm violation theory will receive the attention of social-psychological theory and research.

Notes

[1] Given this procedure, it is adequate to calculate an individual's own group identification as the difference between self-rating and own-group-rating. A calculation of the 'meta-contrast ratio', proposed by Turner *et al.* (1987) as an index of prototypicality of a group member, is not necessary.
[2] For the worker–manager contrast in India no new data set was obtained to validate the scaling of the responses.
[3] One solution to the problem of the R0 reaction in future research is to present it as a separate option and not as one of the possible alternatives randomly interspersed among other reactions.
[4] Singh and Sinha report that there were 11 strikes in the coal area while they conducted their study.
[5] . . . unless norms of redress dictate otherwise (see Chapter 1, p. 000).
[6] The term 'group' is put between parentheses here because one may argue that under such circumstances it loses its meaning.

[7] For Chapter 5 no comparison is possible because a study on norms of redress with managers and workers in India was not conducted.
[8] We also want to plea for studies which relate intergroup behaviour to intragroup behaviour as for instance has been done by Rabbie and his colleagues (Rabbie and Bekkers 1976; Rabbie and Lodewijkx 1987; Rabbie 1989). More specifically, it may prove to be critical which attributions about the other group's behaviour are discussed within the victim group before overt responses are actually engaged in.
[9] One of the main problems is that one needs a standard of comparison so that any exhibited differentiation between the ingroup and a specific outgroup can be related to differentiation which would have been manifested *vis-à-vis* any other comparison group. That is, ingroup favouring behaviour by the Turks of a certain magnitude *vis-à-vis* the Dutch may have been much larger if the Turks were making a comparison between themselves and Moroccans, or between themselves and any other outgroup, except for the Dutch. Thus, apparent Turkish ingroup favouritism *vis-à-vis* the Dutch may actually constitute outgroup favouritism, favouring the Dutch! (see Schruijer 1990*a*, pp. 214–6 for a more extensive discussion).

APPENDICES

Appendix 3.1 Situation descriptions of norm violation inventory for autochthonous Dutchmen and Turkish immigrants.

For X and Y should be read 'Dutchman/Dutch' and 'Turk/Turkish' or 'Turk/Turkish' and 'Dutchman/Dutch'. Inappropriateness ratings for each situation, as obtained in the second pilot-study, are provided (1 very inappropriate, 7 very appropriate, see Chapter 3).

	Inappropriateness	
	Turks (n = 15)	Dutch (n = 15)
1 An X ridicules the Islam (Christianity)	1.20	1.53
2 At a party an X obtrudes on a married Y woman	1.13	2.07
3 An X girl is pestered by a Y who lives in the same street as she does	1.07	1.27
4 An X does not show any sign of appreciation for a present which he has been given by his Y neighbour	1.27	1.93
5 An X car driver causes through his own fault an accident with serious damage to a Y person's car	1.13	2.40
6 An X girl of age tells her parents that she is going to marry a Y man	5.47	6.21
7 An X refuses to accept a typical Y dish, specially made for him by his Y neighbour	1.13	1.93
8 An X regularly parks his car on the spot of his Y neighbour; a complaint did not help	1.33	2.33
9 An X plays loud music in the middle of the night	1.07	1.60
10 An X does not respond to the greeting of his Y neighbour, yet ignores him completely	1.33	2.47
11 In the canteen, an X takes the regular seat of his Y colleague	2.07	3.27
12 During their first acquaintance, an X newcomer in the street ignores a hand held out by a Y neighbour for a handshake	1.13	1.29
13 An X personnel manager unjustly favours unemployed X people over unemployed Y people	1.20	1.47
14 An X football-player continuously tackles a Y opponent by playing the man instead of the ball	1.53	1.93

Appendix 3.1 (*contd.*)

	Inappropriateness	
	Turks (n = 15)	Dutch (n = 15)
15 An X market trader regularly shortchanges Y customers	1.13	1.27
16 An X shopkeeper refuses to sell to Y clients	1.53	1.93
17 An X bus driver does not want to respond to the question of a Y passenger which bus he should take to reach his destination	1.07	1.47
18 An X teacher gives higher marks to X compared with Y children, although their performance is equally good	1.20	1.53
19 An X physician refuses the request of a Y patient, who is unable to go to the physician himself, to make a house call that day	1.00	1.20
20 In a factory there are a light and a heavy task; an informal agreement exists that everyone regularly should change tasks; an X worker repeatedly refuses to change his light task for the heavy task of a Y colleague	1.29	1.47
21 An X police-officer refuses to register a complaint of rape reported by a Y girl	1.00	1.07
22 Two X shop attendants continue to chat among themselves some time, while a Y customer is waiting	1.33	2.00
23 An X employee refuses to work with a Y colleague; he says: 'I do not work with lazy Y's'	1.13	2.00
24 An X butcher sells meat of lower quality to Y customers	1.13	2.33
25 An X in the neighbourhood deals in heroin	1.80	1.87
26 An X smokes a cigarette in a train carriage where this is prohibited and ignores the sign 'no smoking'	1.71	1.53
27 An unemployed X receives unemployment benefits, yet at the same time earns money from moonlighting	2.13	3.13
28 In the supermarket an X jumps into a queue of waiting people	1.27	1.60
29 An X train passenger travels without a ticket	1.93	2.73
30 An X worker steals tools from the workshop	1.27	1.64
31 An X reports to be ill, yet takes a holiday	1.73	2.53
32 An X almost always comes late at meetings of the neighbourhood society	2.00	2.33
33 In the bus an X refuses to yield his seat over to a handicapped Y	1.00	1.33

Appendix 3.1 (*contd.*)

	Inappropriateness	
	Turks ($n = 15$)	Dutch ($n = 15$)
34 A Y has a heart attack on the street; an X passer-by ignores him completely and quietly walks on	1.00	1.13
35 A leader of an X political organization insists that intergroup marriages between the Ys and the Xs should be discouraged	1.33	1.47
36 An X swindles an insurance company by claiming money for goods which in fact are not stolen as he reports they are	1.67	2.27

Appendix 3.2 Correlations between the variables for Turkish immigrants (left of diagonal) and autochthonous Dutchmen (right of diagonal)

	1	2	3	4	5	6	7	8	9	10	11	12	13	14
1 R-in	–	0.26**	0.15	−0.12	−0.23*	−0.01	−0.01	0.00	0.13	0.01	0.14	0.02	0.01	−0.11
2 R-out	0.27*	–	−0.04	0.22*	−0.25**	−0.16	−0.23*	−0.02	−0.18	0.30***	−0.03	0.30***	−0.01	−0.10
3 OGI	0.11	−0.02	–	−0.46***	−0.05	−0.03	−0.04	−0.20*	0.10	−0.01	0.04	0.17*	−0.06	0.03
4 ATT-in	−0.15	−0.09	−0.34***	–	0.49***	−0.06	−0.13	0.11	−0.13	0.26**	−0.13	0.16	0.12	−0.04
5 ATT-out	−0.05	−0.21	−0.04	0.52***	–	0.00	−0.07	0.15	0.03	−0.08	0.04	0.00	0.00	0.02
6 FRDpres	0.22*	−0.05	−0.00	0.10	0.02	–	0.63***	0.31***	0.51***	−0.50***	0.29***	−0.21*	0.00	0.20*
7 FRDfut	0.16	0.00	−0.05	0.19*	0.08	0.56***	–	0.19*	0.43***	−0.49***	0.24**	−0.28***	0.17*	0.18*
8 FRDsat	0.20*	−0.09	0.18	0.07	0.16	0.57***	0.50***	–	0.07	−0.13	0.03	−0.17	−0.04	0.02
9 RsP-in	0.34***	0.04	0.05	−0.14	−0.17	0.66***	0.44***	0.46***	–	−0.38***	0.55***	−0.14	0.04	0.17
10 RsP-out	−0.15	0.08	0.12	0.18	0.07	−0.30***	0.01	−0.06	−0.28***	–	−0.25**	0.55***	−0.15	−0.10
11 RtPh-in	0.18	0.04	0.22**	−0.25**	−0.19*	0.25**	0.12	0.33***	0.36***	−0.11	–	−0.01	0.12	0.29***
12 RtPh-out	−0.15	0.25*	−0.09	0.20*	0.04	−0.24**	0.01	−0.17	−0.28***	0.45***	0.02	–	−0.09	−0.06
13 RtPs-in	0.02	0.05	0.09	−0.06	−0.16	0.10	0.27***	0.12	0.19*	0.27***	0.10	0.19*	–	0.36***
14 RtPs-out	0.04	0.09	0.06	0.06	−0.04	0.01	0.02	0.21*	0.04	0.22**	0.18*	0.17*	−0.14	–

R-in, reaction of own group; R-out, anticipated reaction of other group; OGI, own group identification; ATT-in, attitude towards own group; ATT-out, attitude towards outgroup; FRDpres, fraternal relative deprivation present; FRDfut, FRD future; FRDsat, FRD satisfaction; RsP-in, resource power own group; RsP-out, resource power other group; RtPh-in, retaliation power own group 'harass'; RtPh-out, retaliation power other group 'harass'; RtPs-in, retaliation power own group 'sacrifice'; RtPs-out, retaliation power other group 'sacrifice'.

* $p<0.05$; ** $p<0.01$; *** $p<0.001$.

Appendix 4.1 Norm violation inventory employed for Hindus and Muslims

For X and Y should be read 'Hindu' and 'Muslim' or 'Muslim' and 'Hindu'. Inappropriateness ratings for each situation are provided (1 completely appropriate, 5 very inappropriate see Chapter 4).

		Inappropriateness
1	An X teacher attends to Muslim students more than Y students	4.85
2	An X sub-inspector refused to register a complaint from some Ys about the rape of a Y girl by an X boy of the neighbourhood	4.65
3	Some X's seduced some Y girls and forced them into prostitution	4.73
4	An X boy passed indecent remarks and teased a Y girl going to college	2.88
5	It is discovered that an X in the neighbourhood sells spurious injections to illiterate Y customers	4.30
6	The X of a locality play loud music when Ys are at prayer	4.18
7	A zealous X has been trying for some days to convert some Ys to become X	2.10
8	Some X employees did not attend the farewell function of their Y colleagues	3.85
9	In a factory some Y employees work after getting drunk	2.28
10	In a crowded railway compartment, an X traveller repeatedly blows cigarette smoke into the face of a Y passenger	3.10
11	An X shopkeeper uses pages of the Ramayana (Koran) to wrap the articles which he sells	3.73
12	An X doctor makes obscene gestures to a Y nurse	4.05
13	A Y has a 'heart attack' on the road, yet the X ignore it and silently pass by	3.90
14	An X employee fixed an appointment with a Y colleague but did not turn up on time	3.13
15	An X takes bribe in the construction of an office building but the building falls down after some time owing to its construction being substandard	3.68
16	An X shopkeeper sold adulterated ghee (butter) to his Y customers	2.68
17	Some X youngsters stand in front of a temple and make fun of the Y gods	3.55
18	An X refuses to give his seat to a crippled Y in a bus	3.25
19	The only doctor in a village who is an X refuses to attend to Y villagers who have been critically wounded in Y–X riots	2.85
20	An X worker does not maintain relations with his Y colleagues	3.28
21	An X private physician refuses to attend to Y patients	4.05

Appendix 4.2 Correlations between the variables for Hindus (left of diagonal) and Muslims (right of diagonal)

	1	2	3	4	5	6	7	8	9	10
1 OGI	–	0.11	−0.19	0.15	0.11	0.12	0.15	−0.08	−0.02	−0.04
2 ATT-out	0.27*	–	0.40**	0.17	−0.13	−0.04	0.12	−0.10	−0.19	−0.01
3 ATT-in	−0.60**	0.17	–	−0.18	−0.09	−0.35**	−0.24*	−0.07	−0.14	0.02
4 RsP-rel	0.23*	0.13	−0.20	–	0.23*	0.40**	0.48**	0.19	−0.01	−0.19
5 RtP-rel	0.18	0.15	−0.01	0.48**	–	0.03	0.01	−0.10	0.11	−0.03
6 FRDpres	0.13	0.13	−0.08	0.11	0.05	–	0.62**	0.60**	0.14	−0.15
7 FRDsat	−0.14	0.15	0.37**	−0.18	−0.10	0.22	–	0.36**	0.14	−0.14
8 FRDfut	0.02	0.05	0.10	0.02	0.09	0.26*	0.12	–	0.03	−0.08
9 R-in	−0.18	0.04	0.19	0.12	0.16	−0.06	0.23*	−0.11	–	0.44**
10 R-out	−0.34**	−0.12	0.34**	−0.11	0.01	−0.21	0.20	−0.24*	0.59**	–

OGI, own group identification; ATT-out, attitude towards outgroup; ATT-in, attitude towards own group; RsP-rel, relative resource power; RtP-rel, relative retaliation power; FRDpres, FRD present; FRDsat, FRD satisfaction; FRDfut, FRD future; R-in, reaction of own group; R-out, anticipated reaction of other group.

* $p<0.05$; ** $p<0.01$.

Appendix 5.1 Norm violation inventory for managers and workers in India

Substitute for X and Y 'manager' and 'worker' or 'worker' and 'manager'. In the formulation below norm violations are committed by managers. Items with an asterisk were slightly reformulated for workers as norm-infringing agents.

---

1 In a departmental meeting Xs were served tea after the Ys had already taken their tea.
2 A Y slanders an X saying that he comes dead drunk to work.
3 A Y suspended his steno for a small typing mistake.*
4 Some Ys do not wear uniform in the factory premises.*
5 A Y held his Xs responsible for incomplete work, although he himself had failed to give proper instructions to the Xs.*
6 Some Ys go back home during the night shift without completing the duty.*
7 In a work committee a Y sits in the chair leaving the Xs standing.
8 A Y ignored a report by the Xs that a machine was out of order.*
9 A Y coming to the factory on his motorcycle did not give a lift to an X.*
10 A Y's domestic servant threw garbage in front of an X's house.*
11 Some Ys got their children admitted to the factory school by exercising undue influence in preference to the Xs' children.
12 When the Xs went on strike, the Ys got their water and electricity connections in the Xs' colony disconnected.*
13 A Y beat up an X's son for roughing up his own son.
14 A Y's son made indecent remarks and teased an X's daughter.
15 A Y used the company account to get petrol for personal use.*
16 Some Ys make their Xs work extra hard and do not do any work themselves.*
17 During a strike by Xs some Ys got some machines broken in order to implicate the Xs.*
18 A Y does not keep his office clean.*
19 A Y spends a lot of time in the canteen.
20 A Y always comes to the factory late.

Appendix 5.2 Correlations between the variables for managers (left of diagonal) and workers (right of diagonal)

Variables	1	2	3	4	5	6	7	8	9	10
1 R-in	—	0.14	0.15	−0.09	0.15	0.39**	−0.05	−0.20*	−0.11	0.15
2 R-out	0.37**	—	−0.18*	−0.26**	−0.02	0.14	0.04	0.18*	−0.20*	0.00
3 OGI	0.07	0.07	—	−0.04	0.15	0.24**	0.02	−0.01	0.14	−0.08
4 ATT-out	−0.02	−0.23*	−0.46**	—	0.03	−0.09	−0.19*	−0.19*	0.01	0.25**
5 RsP-in	0.20*	−0.18*	−0.10	0.21*	—	0.34**	−0.26**	−0.06	0.08	−0.11
6 RtP-in	0.14	−0.26**	0.19*	0.21*	0.26**	—	−0.22*	−0.01	−0.12	0.05
7 RsP-out	−0.13	0.00	0.02	−0.15	−0.12	0.01	—	0.37**	−0.01	0.06
8 RtP-out	−0.14	0.00	−0.12	−0.06	0.01	−0.18*	0.45**	—	0.11	0.08
9 FRD-in	−0.08	0.05	−0.07	−0.13	−0.08	−0.07	−0.05	0.07	—	−0.15
10 FRDp-out	0.19*	−0.01	−0.13	0.16	0.27**	−0.12	0.23*	0.17	0.20*	—

R-in, reaction own group; R-out, anticipated reaction other group; OGI, own group identification; ATT-out, attitude towards outgroup; RsP-in, resource power own group; RtP-in, retaliation power own group; RsP-out, resource power outgroup; RtP-out, retaliation power outgroup; FRDp-in, FRD position own group; FRD-out, FRD position outgroup.

* $p<0.05$; ** $p<0.01$.

Appendix 6.1 Norm violation inventory for supervisors and subordinates in The Netherlands

Items and mean ratings of inappropriateness by employees. Substitute for X and Y 'supervisor' and 'subordinate' or 'subordinate' and 'supervisor'.

Item	Description	Mean inappropriateness
1	An X is often drunk at work and then it is impossible to get the work done	4.55
2	X has the nasty habit of laughing at Y whenever Y makes a mistake	3.71
3	X repeatedly parks his car in Y's parking space	3.51
4	In a small crowded office X is requested not to smoke; he ignores this request and continues smoking	3.67
5	X repeatedly comes to work late, although he knows that his Y is waiting for him	3.77
6	X allows Y to be blamed and fired because of his (X's) mistake	4.28
7	X employs impolite/rude language when addressing Ys	4.03
8	X interrupts a conversation with his Y for a chat with a colleague	2.83
9	An X has emphatically promised to do something important for his Y, but does not keep his promise	3.68
10	X does not react to Y's greeting	3.00
11	X does not show any appreciation for a gift received from Ys	3.03
12	At the weekly meeting X takes Y's regular seat	2.55
13	X obtrudes on Y's wife at a company party	3.65
14	X ignores Y's advice to improve the atmosphere at work	2.68
15	X repeatedly interrupts Y's work with all kinds of silly questions	2.97
16	Due to X's negligence a machine becomes completely out of order and production is stopped for some time	3.77
17	X is spotted by Y stealing tools	4.58
18	X has reported sick for quite some time and work is piling up; however, he is regularly seen in a local pub	2.93
19	Secretly an X disposes of poisonous waste	4.97
20	X neglects the safety regulations of the company	4.16
21	In a food company employees are obliged to wear caps for sanitary reasons; X refuses to do so	3.90

Appendix 6.1 (*contd.*)

Item	Description	Mean inappropriateness
22	A serious accident occurs to Y; an X who notices it does not pay any attention	4.74
23	X's regular bad moods make it impossible to work with him	3.00
24	X regularly phones his family abroad at the company's cost	3.45

Ratings of inappropriateness: 1 completely correct, 2 it's just proper enough to pass muster, 3 rather inappropriate, 4 very inappropriate, 5 completely unacceptable.

Appendix 6.2 Correlations between the variables for subordinates (right of diagonal) and supervisors (left of diagonal) in The Netherlands

	1	2	3	4	5	6	7	8	9	10	11	12
1 R-in	—	0.55**	−0.12	0.09	0.17	0.32	0.03	−0.19	0.09	0.18	0.15	0.14
2 R-out	0.79**	—	−0.48**	−0.01	0.15	0.06	0.05	−0.03	0.01	0.02	0.12	0.01
3 OGI	0.40*	0.44*	—	−0.12	−0.14	0.04	−0.05	−0.12	0.11	0.08	0.08	0.09
4 ATT-out	−0.25	−0.38*	−0.38*	—	0.17	0.36*	−0.25	0.13	−0.23	−0.38*	0.11	−0.36*
5 RsP-in	0.10	−0.12	0.11	0.34	—	0.42*	−0.13	−0.18	−0.22	−0.13	−0.03	−0.21
6 RtP-in	0.36	0.24	0.11	0.01	0.41*	—	−0.22	−0.23	−0.19	−0.23	−0.03	−0.25
7 RsP-out	−0.13	0.01	−0.35	0.20	0.05	−0.01	—	0.46**	0.56**	0.49**	−0.56**	0.44**
8 RtP-out	−0.54**	−0.32	−0.56**	0.19	−0.33	−0.14	0.49**	—	0.13	0.14	−0.11	0.02
9 FRDp-in	−0.28	−0.23	−0.37	−0.34	−0.05	−0.11	−0.04	0.10	—	0.79**	−0.72**	0.73**
10 FRDs-in	0.25	0.21	0.22	0.21	−0.06	0.27	−0.16	−0.23	−0.56**	—	−0.43*	0.91**
11 FRDp-out	0.49**	0.23	0.21	0.29	0.17	0.16	0.02	−0.16	−0.86**	−0.49**	—	−0.37*
12 FRDs-out	0.62**	0.51**	0.47*	−0.05	0.10	0.48*	−0.22	−0.40*	−0.55	0.75**	0.59**	—

R-in, reaction own group; R-out, anticipated reaction other group; OGI, own group identification; ATT-out, attitude towards outgroup; RsP-in, resource power own group; RtP-in, retaliation power own group; RsP-out, resource power outgroup; RtP-out, retaliation power outgroup; FRDp-in, FRD, position own group; FRDs-in, satisfaction with position own group; FRDp-out, FRD, position outgroup; FRDs-out, satisfaction with position outgroup. R-in and R-out, the higher the score the more negative the reaction; OGI, the higher the score the smaller OGI; ATT-out, the higher the score the more positive the attitude; power, the higher the score the more power; FRD, the higher the score the lower the position and satisfaction.

* $p<0.05$; ** $p<0.01$.

Appendix 7.1 Hierarchical regression analysis

In a first stage of the analysis the intergroup difference on the dependent variable is expressed in the form of a multiple correlation. This is computed from a simple regression equation with group membership as a dummy variable.

The second stage takes the form of a hierarchical regression equation in which the context variables are included, i.e.

$$X = a + b_1 K_1 + \ldots\ldots + b_n K_n + E \tag{7.1}$$

where X is the dependent variable,
a is the intercept,
$b_1, \ldots, b_n$ are the regression coefficients of context variables 1 to n,
$K_1, \ldots, K_n$ are the scores of a subject on the context variables 1 to n,
and E is the error term.

If appropriate context variables have been selected they will explain part of the variance on the dependent variable.

In the third stage of the analysis, group membership is entered as a dummy variable in the regression equation. The remaining intergroup difference after elimination of the effects of the context variables is now computed. This stage can be expressed in the following equation:

$$X = a' + b_1'K_1 + \ldots\ldots + b_n'K_n + b_{g,k}G + E \tag{7.2}$$

where $b_1', \ldots, b_n'$ are the regression coefficients of context variables 1 to n,
$b_{g,k}G$ is the regression effect of the variable for group after correction for the context variables (with subjects nested in groups), and
G is a dummy variable coding for group (membership).

In eqn (7.1) the proportion of variance explained by the context variables is computed. In eqn (7.2) the variance explained by the context variables in combination with the variable group membership is calculated. The difference between the two proportions is the remaining group effect after correction for the effect of the context variables.

In analysing the results of two groups, one has to test for the equivalence of the regression effects. This can be done by including product terms of the dummy variable (coding for groups) and the context variables (cf. Miller and Erickson 1981; Pedhazur 1982, Chapter 12).

With the product terms eqn (7.1) obtains the following form:

$$X = a + b_1K_1 + b_1'K_1G + \ldots\ldots + b_nK_n + b_n'K_nG + E \tag{7.3}$$

where $b_1', \ldots, b_n'$ are the regression coefficients for the product terms of the context variables 1 to n with the dummy variable G.

Equation (7.2) now takes the form:

$$X = a' + b_1K_1 + b_1K_1G + \ldots + b_nK_n + b_nK_nG + b_{g,k,k'}G + E \quad (7.4)$$

where $b_{g,k,k'}G$ is the regression effect of the dummy variable coding for group after correction for the context variables and their product terms.

A non-significant coefficient for a product term means that the groups can be taken to have identical regression slopes b for the corresponding context variable. Significant product terms can represent different forms of inequivalence, depending on the sign and the magnitude of their regression weight and the weight of the associated context variable. If the values 0 and 1 are given to the dummy variable coding for group there are three alternatives.

1. Only the product term shows a significant regression weight, but not the context variable. This means that only for the group coded 1 is there a relationship between the context variable and the dependent variable.
2. The weights for the product term and the context variable are of similar size but with opposite sign. In this case there is only a relationship between the context variable and the dependent in the group coded 0.
3. In all other instances, with significant weights for both the context variable and its product term, there exists a relationship in both groups with the dependent variable, but of a different strength.

Appendix 7.2 Interpretation of results of regression analysis

The hierarchical regression analyses for NV-own and NV-other scores were repeated with four more variables, namely the product terms of group identification (GROUPID) and each of the four context variables (cf. Appendix 7.1). In the analysis of NV-own for the Turks–Dutch contrast a significant product term, ($R^2 = 0.37$) was found for OGI × GROUPID. The interpretation of this effect is not straightforward. In our view it means that the main regression effect of the OGI variable should be interpreted with great care.

For the NV-other scores the following significant product terms were found.

(1) workers versus managers in India, FRD × GROUPID, $R^2 = 0.13$;

(2) subordinates versus supervisors in The Netherlands, ATT-out × GROUPID, $R^2 = 0.13$;

(3) Turkish migrants versus Dutch, POW × GROUPID, $R^2 = 0.13$.

The second of these three effects is found for a variable that is not interpreted because it does not contribute significantly to the explanation of the intergroup variance. The first and the third results point again to the need for a very cautious interpretation of the associated context variables.

Appendix 8.1 Correlations between appropriateness ratings of the five reactions to norm violation

Appendix 8.1.1 Correlations between the five reactions to norm violation for Turkish immigrants and Dutchmen (study 1)

	Turkish immigrants					Dutchmen				
	R+	R0	R−	R=	R≡	R+	R0	R−	R=	R≡
R+	–	0.10	0.11	−0.05	0.01	–	0.24	−0.04	0.05	−0.26
R0		–	−0.12	−0.08	−0.06		–	−0.20	−0.20	−0.16
R−			–	0.35	0.35			–	0.21	0.24
R=				–	0.51				–	0.32
R≡					–					–

Correlations greater than 0.51 are significant at $p<0.05$, two-tailed.

Appendix 8.1.2 Correlations between the five reactions to norm violation for employees (study 2)

	Employees				
	R+	R0	R−	R=	R≡
R+	–	0.57	−0.49	−0.26	−0.07
R0		–	−0.44	−0.44	−0.28
R−			–	0.82	0.66
R=				–	0.91
R≡					–

Correlations greater than 0.36 are significant at $p<0.05$, two-tailed.

Appendix 8.1.3 Correlations between the five reactions to norm violation for Hindus and Muslims (study 3)

	Hindus					Muslims				
	R+	R0	R−	R=	R≡	R+	R0	R−	R=	R≡
R+	–	−0.37	0.39	−0.42	−0.44	–	−0.10	0.12	−0.35	−0.36
R0		–	0.23	0.24	0.31		–	0.11	−0.25	−0.32
R−			–	0.35	0.35			–	0.47	0.48
R=				–	0.88				–	0.81
R≡					–					–

Correlations greater than 0.40 are significant at $p<0.05$, two-tailed.

REFERENCES

Abeles, R. D. (1976). Relative deprivation, rising expectations, and black militancy. *Journal of Social Issues*, **32**, 119–37.

Adorno, T. W., Frenkel-Brunswik, E., Levinson, D. J., and Sanford, R. M. (1950). *The authoritarian personality*. Harper, New York.

Agrawal, A. N., Varma, H. O., and Gupta, R. C. (1988). *India: economic information year book, 1988–1989*, (revised 3rd edn). National, New Delhi.

Ansari, M. J. (1983). Fraternalistic relative deprivation and styles of conflict resolution. Unpublished doctoral dissertation. Allahabad University.

Apfelbaum, E. (1979). Relations of domination and movements for liberation: an analysis of power between groups. In *The social psychology of intergroup relations*, (ed. W. G. Austin and S. Worchel), pp. 188–204. Brooks/Cole, Monterey, CA.

Apfelbaum, E. and Herzlich, C. (1970–71). La théorie de l'attribution en psychologie sociale. *Bulletin de Psychologie*, **24**, 961–76.

Argyle, M., Furnham, A., and Graham, J. A. (1981). *Social situations*. Cambridge University Press.

Aronson, E. (1984). *The social animal*. W. H. Freeman, New York.

Asch, S. E. (1952). *Social psychology*. Prentice-Hall, Englewood Cliffs, NJ.

Aschenbrenner, K. M. and Schaefer, R. E. (1980). Minimal group situation: comments on a mathematical model and on the research paradigm. *European Journal of Social Psychology*, **10**, 389–98.

Austin, W. (1977). Equity theory and social comparison processes. In *Social comparison processes: theoretical and empirical perspectives*, (ed. J. Suls and R. Miller), pp. 279–305. Hemisphere, Washington, DC.

Austin, W. and Worchel, S. (1979). *The social psychology of intergroup relations*. Brooks/Cole, Monterey, CA.

Bar-Tal, D., Bar-Zohar, Y., Greenberg, M. S., and Hermon, M. (1977). Reciprocity behavior in the relationship between donor and recipient and between harm-doer and victim. *Sociometry*, **40**, 293–8.

Beals, R. L., Hoijer, H., and Beals, A. R. (1977). *An introduction to anthropology*, (5th edn). Macmillan, New York.

Blake, R. R. and Mouton, J. S. (1962). The intergroup dynamics of win/lose conflict and problem solving collaboration in union–management relations. In *Intergroup relations and leadership*, (ed. M. Sherif), pp. 98–140. Wiley, New York.

Blake, R. R. and Mouton, J. S. (1964). *The managerial grid*. Gulf, Houston, TX.

Blau, P. M. (1964). *Exchange and power in social life*. Wiley, New York.

Bookman, L. M. (1978). Hindus and Muslims: communal relations and cultural integration. In *Cohesion and conflict in modern India*, (ed. G. R. Gupta), pp. 103–127. Vikas Publishing House, New Delhi.

Bornewasser, M. (1985). Verantwortlichkeitsattributionen im Intergruppenkontext am Beispiel deutscher Arbeiter und jugoslawischer Gastarbeiter. *Gruppendynamik*, **1**, 19–33.

Bovenkerk, F. (1978). *Omdat zij anders zijn: patronen van rasdiscriminatie in Nederland* (Because they are different: patterns of racial discrimination in The Netherlands). Boom, Meppel.

Branco, K. J. and Williamson, J. B. (1982). Stereotyping and the life cycle: views of aging and the aged. In *In the eye of the beholder: contemporary issues in stereotyping*, (ed. A. G. Miller), pp. 364–410. Praeger, New York.

Brassé, P., Sikking, E., and Bakker, J. (1986). *Positie en kansen van etnische minderheden in Nederlandse ondernemingen* (Position and opportunities of ethnic minorities in Dutch enterprises). Ministerie van Sociale Zaken en Werkgelegenheid, The Hague.

Brewer, M. B. and Kramer, R. M. (1985). The psychology of intergroup attitudes and behavior. *Annual Review of Psychology*, **36**, 219–43.

Brown, L. D. (1983). *Managing conflict at organizational interfaces*. Addison-Wesley, Reading, MA.

Brown, R. (1986). *Social psychology: the second edition*. Collier Macmillan, London.

Bulman, R. J. and Wortman, C. (1977). Attributions of blame and coping in the 'Real World': severe accident victims react to their lot. *Journal of Personality and Social Psychology*, **35**, 351–63.

Burke, R. J. (1970). Methods of resolving superior–subordinate conflict: the constructive use of subordinate differences and disagreements. *Organizational Behavior and Human Performance*, **5**, 393–411.

Cantor, N. (1981). Perceptions in situations: situation prototypes and person–situation prototypes. In *Toward a psychology of situations: an interactional perspective*, (ed. D. Magnusson), pp. 229–44. Erlbaum, Hillsdale, NJ.

Caplan, N. (1970). The new ghetto man: a review of recent empirical studies. *Journal of Social Issues*, **26**, 59–73.

Caplan, N. and Paige, J. M. (1968). A study of ghetto rioters. *Scientific American*, **219**, 15–22.

Cartwright, D. (1959). *Studies on social power*. Institute for Social Research, Ann Arbor, MI.

CBS (1986). *Statistisch zakboek* (Overview of statistics). Staatsuitgeverij, The Hague.

Centre for Monitoring Indian Economy (1985). Basic statistics relating to Indian economy, September, Tables 16.2-1/2. Based on *The Census of India, 1981*. Economic Intelligence Service, Bombay.

Child, J. (1981). Culture, contingency and capitalism in the cross-national study of organization. In *Research in organizational behavior*, (ed. L. L. Cummings and B. M. Staw), Vol. 3, pp. 303–56. JAI Press, Greenwich, CT.

Cohen, J. and Cohen, P. (1983). *Applied multiple regression/correlation analysis for the behavioral sciences*, (2nd edn). Erlbaum, Hillsdale, NJ.

Collett, P. (1977). *Social rules and social behaviour*. Basil Blackwell, Oxford.

Cook, T. D., Crosby, F., and Hennigan, K. M. (1977). The construct validity of relative deprivation. In *Social comparison processes: theoretical and empirical perspectives*, (ed. J. M. Suls and R. L. Miller), pp. 307–33. Halsted-Wiley, Washington, DC.

Constitution of India (1949). Government of India, New Delhi.

Crittenden, K. S. (1983). Sociological aspects of attribution. *Annual Review of Sociology*, **9**, 425–46.

Crosby, F. (1976). A model of egoistical relative deprivation. *Psychological Review*, **83**, 85–113.

Crosby, F. (1982). *Relative deprivation and working women*. Oxford University Press, New York.

DaGloria, J. (1975). La fréquence d'un acte d'autrui comme indice, pour un sujet, de son caractère volontaire. *Psychologie Française*, **20**, 113–32.

DaGloria, J. and DeRidder, R. (1977). Aggression in dyadic interaction. *European Journal of Social Psychology*, **7**, 189–219.

Dalal, A. K. and Pande, N. (1988). Psychological recovery of accident victims with temporary and permanent disability. *International Journal of Psychology*, **23**, 25–40.

Dansereau, F. and Markham, S. E. (1987). Superior–subordinate communication: multiple levels of analysis. In *Handbook of organizational communication: an interdisciplinary perspective*, (ed. F. M. Jablin, L. L. Putman, K. H. Roberts, and L. W. Porter), pp. 343–88. Sage, Newbury Park, CA.

Davis, J. A. (1959). A formal interpretation of the theory of relative deprivation. *Sociometry*, **22**, 280–96.

Dawes, R. M. and Smith, T. L. (1985). Attitude and opinion measurement. In *Handbook of social psychology*, Vol. 1 (3rd edn), (ed. G. Lindzey and E. Aronson), pp. 509–66. Random House, New York.

Deaux, K. and Emswiller, T. (1974). Explanations of successful performance on sexlinked tasks: what is skill for the male is luck for the female. *Journal of Personality and Social Psychology*, **29**, 80–5.

DeCarufel, A. (1981). The allocation and acquisition of resources in times of scarcity. In *The justice motive in social behavior: adapting to times of scarcity and change*, (ed. M. J. Lerner and S. C. Lerner), pp. 317–41. Plenum, New York.

DeRidder, R. (1980). Agressie in sociale interactie: waarneming en reactie (Aggression in social interaction: perception and reaction). Unpublished Ph.D. thesis, Tilburg University.

DeRidder, R. (1983). Norm violation in a dyad: the effects of the victims' attribution of malevolent intent on reactive aggression. Unpublished manuscript, Tilburg University.

DeRidder, R. (1985). Normative considerations in the labeling of harmful behavior as aggressive. *Journal of Social Psychology*, **125**, 659–66.

DeRidder, R. (1988). Review of rediscovering the social group: a self-categorization theory. *Social Behaviour*, **3**, 46–8.

Deschamps, J. C. (1973). L'attribution, la catégorisation sociale et les répésentations intergroupes. *Bulletin de Psychologie*, **27**, 710–21.

Deschamps, J. C. (1982). Social attribution. In *Attribution theory and research: conceptual, developmental and social dimensions*, (ed. J. Jaspars, F. D. Fincham, and M. Hewstone), pp. 233–40. Academic Press, London.

Deschamps, J. C. and Doise, W. (1978). Crossed category memberships in intergroup relations. In *Differentiations between social groups: studies in the social psychology of intergroup relations*, (ed. H. Tajfel), pp. 141–58. Academic Press, London.

Deutsch, M. (1973). *The resolution of conflict*. Yale University Press, New Haven, CT.

Dhingra, O. P. and Pathak, V. K. (1972). Professional background of Indian personnel managers. *PACT*, 11–17 (IPA, 5:254).

Diab, L. (1970). A study of intragroup and intergroup relations among experimentally produced small groups. *Genetic Psychology Monographs*, **82**, 49–82.

Doise, W. and Lorenzi-Cioldi, F. (1989). Patterns of differentiation within and between groups. In *Ethnic minorities*, (ed. J. P. van Oudenhoven and T. M. Willemsen), pp. 43–57. Swets & Zeitlinger, Amsterdam.

Dollard, J., Doob, L. W., Miller, N. E., Mowrer, O. H., and Sears, R. R. (1939). *Frustration and aggression*. Yale University Press, New Haven, CT.

Draper, N. R. and Smith, H. (1981). *Applied regression analysis,* (2nd edn). Wiley, New York.

D'Souza, V. S. (1983). Religious minorities in India: a demographic analysis. *Social Action,* **33,** 365–85.

Dubbelman, J. E. (1984). *Vooroordelen veroordeeld, feiten tegen vooroordelen over buitenlanders* (Prejudices convicted, facts against prejudices about foreigners). Staatsdrukkerij, The Hague.

Dubé, L. and Guimond, S. (1986). Relative deprivation and social protest: the personal-group issue. In *Relative deprivation and social comparison: the Ontario symposium,* Vol. 4 (ed. J. M. Olson, C. P. Herman, and M. P. Zanna), pp. 201–16. Lawrence Erlbaum, Hillsdale, NJ.

Duncan, B. L. (1976). Differential social perception and attribution of intergroup violence: testing the lower limits of stereotyping of blacks. *Journal of Personality and Social Psychology,* **34,** 590–8.

Engineer, A. A. (1981). The anatomy of post-partition riots. *Mainstream,* December 12, pp. 14–7.

Engineer, A. A. (1984). The causes of communal riots in the post-partition period in India. In *Communal riots in post-independence India,* (ed. A. A. Engineer), pp. 33–41. Sangam Books, Hyderabad.

Entzinger, H. B. (1984). *Het minderhedenbeleid* (Policy concerning minorities). Boom, Meppel.

Eppink, A. (1981). *Kind-zijn in twee culturen* (Being a child in two cultures). Van Loghum Slaterus, Deventer.

Evans-Pritchard, E. E. (1940). *The Nuer.* Clarendon Press, Oxford.

Felson, R. B. (1984). Patterns of aggressive social interactions. In *Social psychology of aggression: from individual behaviour to social interaction,* (ed. A. Mummendey), pp. 107–26. Springer-Verlag, Berlin.

Fishbein, M. and Ajzen, I. (1975). *Belief, attitude, intention and behavior: an introduction to theory and research.* Addison-Wesley, Reading, MA.

Five Year Plan (1977–1983). Draft, Planning Commission, Government of India, New Delhi.

Folger, R. (1986). A referent cognitions theory of relative deprivation. In *Relative deprivation and social comparison: the Ontario symposium,* Vol. 4 (ed. J. M. Olson, C. P. Herman, and M. P. Zanna), pp. 33–55. Lawrence Erlbaum, Hillsdale, NJ.

Forsyth, D. R. (1983). *An introduction to group dynamics.* Brooks/Cole, Pacific Grove, CA.

Fox, R. (1975). *Encounter with anthropology.* Penguin Books, Harmondsworth.

Frank, J. D. (1967). *Sanity and survival: psychological aspects of war and peace.* Barrie & Rockliff, London.

French, J. and Raven, B. (1959). The bases of social power. In *Studies in social power,* (ed. D. Cartwright), pp. 150–67. University of Michigan, Ann Arbor, MI.

Gergen, K. J. (1982). *Toward transformation in social knowledge.* Springer-Verlag, New York.

Gergen, K. J., Morse, S. J., and Gergen, M. M. (1980). Behavior exchange in cross-cultural perspective. In *Handbook of cross-cultural psychology: social psychology,* Vol. 5 (ed. H. C. Triandis and R. W. Brislin), pp. 121–53. Allyn & Bacon, Boston, MA.

Ghosh, E. S. K. and Huq, M. M. (1985). A study of the social identity of two ethnic groups in India and Bangladesh. *Journal of Multilingual and Multicultural Development*, **6**, 239–51.

Gibbs, J. P. (1965). Norms: the problem of definition and classification. *The American Journal of Sociology*, **70**, 586–94.

Giles, H. and Powesland, P. F. (1975). *Speech style and social evaluation*. Academic Press, London.

Gluckman, M. (1963). *Custom and conflict in Africa*. Basil Blackwell, Oxford.

Gouldner, A. W. (1960). The norm of reciprocity: a preliminary statement. *American Sociological Review*, **25**, 161–78.

Gouldner, A. W. (1975). *For sociology: renewal and critique in sociology today*. Penguin Books, Harmondsworth.

Greenberg, J. and Rosenfield, D. (1979). Whites' ethnocentrism and their attributions for the behaviour of blacks: a motivational bias. *Journal of Personality*, **47**, 643–57.

Gruisen, T., Janssen, F., and Van der Vorst, H. (1987). *Bij ons gebeurt dat niet: sociaal-kultureel werk en racismebestrijding* (Such things do not happen with us: social case work and fighting racism). Offset Kurver Sittard B.V., Sittard.

Guimond, S. and Dubé-Simard, L. (1983). Relative deprivation theory and the Quebec nationalist movement: the cognitive–emotion distinction and the person–group deprivation issue. *Journal of Personality and Social Psychology*, **44**, 526–35.

Gurr, T. R. (1970). *Why men rebel*. Princeton University Press, NJ.

Hamilton, D. L. (1981). *Cognitive processes in stereotyping and intergroup behaviour*. Lawrence Erlbaum, Hillsdale, NJ.

Harmsen, G. and Reinalda, B. (1975). *Voor de bevrijding van de arbeid: beknopte geschiedenis van de Nederlandse vakbeweging* (Towards the liberation of labour: short history of the Dutch labour union). SUN, Nijmegen.

Harvey, M. D. and Enzle, M. E. (1981). A cognitive model of social norms for understanding the transgression–helping effect. *Journal of Personality and Social Psychology*, **41**, 866–75.

Heider, F. (1958). *The psychology of interpersonal relations*. Wiley, New York.

Helm, B., Bonoma, T. V., and Tedeschi, J. T. (1971). Counter aggression as a function of physical aggression: reciprocity for harm done. In *Proceedings of the 79th Annual Convention of the American Psychological Association*. APA, Washington, DC.

Hewstone, M. (1989). *Causal attribution*. Basil Blackwell, Oxford.

Hewstone, M. and Jaspars, J. M. F. (1982). Intergroup relations and attribution processes. In *Social identity and intergroup behaviour*, (ed. H. Tajfel), pp. 99–133. Cambridge University Press, MA.

Hewstone, M. and Jaspars, J. M. F. (1984). Social dimensions of attribution. In *The social dimension: European developments in social psychology*, Vol. 2 (ed. H. Tajfel), pp. 379–404. Cambridge University Press, MA.

Hewstone, M. and Ward, C. (1985). Ethnocentrism and causal attribution in southeast Asia. *Journal of Personality and Social Psychology*, **48**, 614–23.

Hofstede, G. (1980). *Culture's consequences: international differences in work-related values*. Sage, Beverly Hills, CA.

Hogg, M. A. and Abrams, D. (1988). *Social identifications*. Routledge, London.

Homans, G. C. (1950). *The human group*. Harcourt Brace Jovanovich, New York.

Homans, G. C. (1961). *Social behavior: its elementary forms*. Harcourt Brace and World, New York.

Howard, J. A. and Pike, K. C. (1986). Ideological investment in cognitive processing: the influence of social statuses on attribution. *Social Psychology Quarterly*, **49**, 154–67.

Hraba, J., Hagendoorn, L. and Hagendoorn, R. (1989). The ethnic hierarchy in The Netherlands: social distance and social representation. *British Journal of Social Psychology*, **28**, 57–69.

Industrial Dispute Act (1947). Ministry of Labour, Government of India, New Delhi.

Industrial Policy Resolution (1956). Ministry of Labour, Government of India, New Delhi.

Jablin, F. M. (1979). Superior–subordinate communication: the state of the art. *Psychological Bulletin*, **86**, 1201–22.

Jain, L. C. (1971). *The Indian Manager*. Somaiya, Bombay.

Jaspars, J. M. F. and Warnaen, S. (1982). Intergroup relations, ethnic identity and self-evaluation in Indonesia. In *Social identity and intergroup behaviour*, (ed. H. Tajfel), pp. 335–66. Cambridge University Press, MA.

Jaspars, J. M. F., Hewstone, M., and Fincham, F. D. (1983). Attribution theory and research: the state of the art. In *Attribution theory and research: conceptual, developmental and social dimensions*, (ed. J. M. F. Jaspars, F. D. Fincham, and M. Hewstone), pp. 3–36. Academic Press, London.

Jha, H., Sinha, J. B. P., Gopal, S., and Tiwary, K. M. (1985). *Social structures and alignments: a study of rural Bihar*. Usha Publishers, New Delhi.

Kerssemakers, L. and DeRidder, R. (1989). The aggravation of intergroup conflict: effects of pre-existing negative attitudes. Paper presented at the 2nd Regional Conference of the International Association for Cross-Cultural Psychology, Amsterdam.

Krishna, G. (1985). Communal violence in India: a study of communal disturbance in India. *Economic and Political Weekly*, **20**, 117–31.

Kuschel, R. (1987). Twenty-four generations of intergroup conflicts on Belona Island (Solomon Islands). In *Ethnic conflict: international perspectives*, (ed. J. Boucher, D. Landis, and K. A. Clark), pp. 280–96. Sage, Newbury Park, CA.

LaPiere, R. T. (1934). Attitudes versus actions. *Social Forces*, **13**, 230–7.

Lautmann, R. (1971). *Wert und Norm: Begriffanalysen für die Soziologie*, (2nd edn). Westdeutscher Verlag Opladen, Opladen.

Lewin, K. (1948) *Resolving social conflicts*. Harper, New York.

Lieberson, S. and Silverman, A. R. (1965). The precipitants and underlying conditions of race riots. *American Sociological Review*, **30**, 887–98.

Lodewijkx, H. (1989). Conflict en agressie tussen groepen en individuen (Conflict and aggression between groups and individuals). Unpublished Ph.D. thesis, University of Utrecht.

Lucassen, J. and Penninx, R. (1985). *Nieuwkomers, immigranten en hun nakomelingen* (Newcomers, immigrants and their offspring). Meulenhoff, Amsterdam.

Majeed, A. and Ghosh, E. S. K. (1981). Ingroup and outgroup violation in intergroup context. *Psychological Studies*, **26**, 34–40.

Mann, J. F. and Taylor, D. M. (1974). Attribution of causality: role of ethnicity and social class. *Journal of Social Psychology*, **94**, 3–13.

Martin, J., Brickman, P., and Murray, A. (1984). Moral outrage and pragmatism: explanations for collective action. *Journal of Experimental Social Psychology*, **20**, 484–96.

Mauss, M. (1954). *The gift: forms and functions of exchange in archaic societies*. Free Press, Glencoe, L.

McGuire, W. J. (1985). Attitudes and attitude change. In *The handbook of social psychology*, (ed. G. Lindzey and E. Aronson), pp. 233–346. Random House, New York.

McPhail, C. (1980). Civil order participation: a critical examination of recent research. In *Collective behavior: a sourcebook*, (ed. M. D. Pugh), pp. 157–174. West, St. Paul, MN.

Messick, D. M. and Mackie, D. M. (1989). Intergroup relations. *Annual Review of Psychology*, **40**, 45–81.

Miller, J. L. L. and Erickson, M. L. (1981). On dummy variable regression analysis: a description and illustration of the method. In *Linear models in social research*, (ed. P. V. Marsden), pp. 44–62. Sage, Beverly Hills, CA.

Milner, D. (1975). *Children and race*. Penguin Books, Harmondsworth.

Ministerie van Binnenlandse Zaken (1987). *Notitie voor de bestrijding van de werkloosheid onder etnische minderheden* (Note for fighting unemployment among ethnic minorities). Ministry of Interior Affairs, The Hague.

Ministerie van Sociale Zaken en Werkgelegenheid (1988). *Rapportage arbeidsmarkt 1988* (Report on the 1988 labour market). Ministry of Social Affairs and Employment, The Hague.

Mischel, W. (1973). Toward a cognitive social learning reconceptualization of personality. *Psychological Review*, **80**, 252–83.

Mohsin, S. M. (1984). Secularism and ethnic prejudice on the Indian scene. Presidential address to the Bihar Psychological Association, Ranchi University.

Morris, R. T. (1956). A typology of norms. *American Sociological Review*, **21**, 610–3.

Moscovici, S. (1976). *Social influence and social change*. Academic Press, London.

Moscovici, S. (1981). On social representation. In *Social cognition: perspectives on everyday understanding*, (ed. J. P. Forgas), pp. 181–209. Academic Press, London.

MOW International Research Team (1987). *The meaning of working*. Academic Press, London.

Mummendey, A., Linneweber, V., and Löschper, G. (1984*a*). Actor or victim of aggression: divergent perspectives—divergent evaluations. *European Journal of Social Psychology*, **14**, 297–311.

Mummendey, A., Linneweber, V. and Löschper, G. (1984*b*). Aggression: from act to interaction. In *Social psychology of aggression: from individual behavior to social interaction*, (ed. A. Mummendey), pp. 69–106. Springer-Verlag, Berlin.

Naqvi, N. (1980). Relative deprivation and attribution of blame in communal riots. Unpublished doctoral dissertation, Allahabad University.

Naqvi, N. and Tripathi, R. C. (1980). Predicting attributions of blame in communal riots. Paper presented at the seminar on Caste and communal intergroup relations, Department of Psychology, Allahabad University.

Newcomb, T. M. (1950). *Social psychology*. Dryden, New York.

Ng, S. H. (1980). *The social psychology of power*. Academic Press, New York.

Ng, S. H. (1982). Power and intergroup discrimination. In *Social identity and intergroup behaviour*, (ed. H. Tajfel), pp. 179–206. Cambridge University Press, MA.

Oakes, P. J. and Turner, J. C. (1980). Social categorization and intergroup behaviour: does minimal group discrimination make social identity more positive? *European Journal of Social Psychology*, **10**, 295–301.

Paicheler, G. and Darmon, G. (1978). Réprésentations majoritaires et minoritaires et relations intergroupes. *Bulletin de Psychologie*, **31**, 170–80.

Pedhazur, E. J. (1982). *Regression in behavioral research*, (2nd edn). Holt, Rinehart & Winston, New York.

Penninx, R. (1983). *Migration, minorities and policy in The Netherlands: recent trends and developments*, SOPEMI report for the OECD. Ministry WVC, Rijswijk.

Penninx, R. (1985). Onderzoek en beleid met betrekking tot minderheden in Nederland (Research and policy regarding minorities in The Netherlands). In *Buitenlandse minderheden in Vlaanderen-België; Wetenschappelijke inzichten en overheidsbeleid*, (ed. A. Martens and F. Moulaert), pp. 233–53. De Nederlandse Boekhandel, Antwerp.

Penninx, R. (1988). *Minderheidsvorming en emancipatie* (Minority formation and emancipation). Samson, Alphen aan de Rijn.

Pepitone, A. (1976). Toward a normative and comparative biocultural social psychology. *Journal of Personality and Social Psychology*, **34**, 641–53.

Pepitone, A. (1981). The normative basis of aggression: anger and punitiveness. *Recherches de Psychologie Sociale*, **3**, 3–17.

Pettigrew, T. F. (1964). *The profile of the Negro American*. Van Nostrand, Princeton, NJ.

Pettigrew, T. F. (1967). Social evaluation theory: convergences and applications. In *Nebraska symposium on motivation*, (ed. D. Levine), pp. 241–315. University of Nebraska Press, Omaha, NB.

Pettigrew, T. F. (1979). The ultimate attribution error: extending Allport's cognitive analysis of prejudice. *Personality and Social Psychology Bulletin*, **5**, 461–76.

Petty, R. E. and Cacioppo, J. T. (1981). *Attitudes and persuasion: classic and contemporary approaches*. Wm. C. Brown, Dubuque, IA.

Poortinga, Y. H. (1989). Equivalence of cross-cultural data: an overview of basic issues. *International Journal of Psychology*, **24**, 737–56.

Poortinga, Y. H. and Jansen, X. H. M. (1991). Expected reactions to norm violations: an interpretation of results from India and The Netherlands. Unpublished manuscript. Tilburg University.

Poortinga, Y. H. and Malpass, R. S. (1986). Making inferences from cross-cultural data. In *Field methods in cross-cultural comparison*, (ed. W. J. Lonner and J. W. Berry), pp. 17–46. Sage, Beverley Hills, CA.

Poortinga, Y. H. and Van de Vijver, F. J. R. (1987). Explaining cross-cultural differences. *Journal of Cross-Cultural Psychology*, **18**, 259–82.

Poortinga, Y. H., Schruijer, S. G. L., DeRidder, R., and Jansen, X. H. M. (1990). Reakties op normschendingen: verschillen tussen Turkse migranten en autochtone Nederlanders (Reactions to norm violations: differences between Turkish immigrants and autochthonous Dutchmen). *De Psycholoog*, **25**, 451–9.

Pospísil, L. (1971). *Anthropology of law, a comparative theory*. HRAF Press, New Haven, CT.

Price, R. H. and Bouffard, D. L. (1974). Behavioral appropriateness and situational constraint as dimensions of social behavior. *Journal of Personality and Social Psychology*, **30**, 579–86.

Rabbie, J. M. (1982). The effects of intergroup competition and cooperation on intragroup and intergroup relationships. In *Cooperation and helping behavior: theories and research*, (ed. V. Derlega and J. Grzelak), pp. 123–49. Academic Press, New York.

Rabbie, J. M. (1989). Group processes as stimulant of aggression. In *Aggression and war: their biological and social bases*, (ed. J. Groebel and R. H. Hinde), pp. 141–56. Cambridge University Press.

Rabbie, J. M. and Bekkers, F. (1976). Threatened leadership and intergroup competition. *European Journal of Social Psychology*, **31**, 269–83.

Rabbie, J. M. and Horwitz, M. (1988). Categories versus groups as explanatory concepts in intergroup relations. *European Journal of Social Psychology*, **18**, 117–23.

Rabbie, J. M. and Lodewijkx, H. F. M. (1986). Aggressive reactions to the violation of justice norms by individuals and groups. Paper presented at the East–West Meeting of the European Association of Experimental Social Psychology, Graz, Austria.

Rabbie, J. M. and Lodewijkx, H. F. M. (1987). Individual and group aggression. *Current Research on Peace and Violence*, **2–3**, 91–101.

Radcliffe-Brown, A. R. (1952). *Structure and function in primitive society*. Cohen & West, London.

Renwick, P. A. (1975). Perception and management of superior–subordinate conflict. *Organizational Behavior and Human Performance*, **13**, 444–56.

Rommetveit, R. (1955). *Social norms and values*. University of Minnesota Press, Minneapolis, MN.

Rosenberg, M. J., Hovland, C. I., McGuire, W. J., Abelson, R. P., and Brehm, J. W. (1960). *Attitude, organization and change: an analysis of consistency among attitude components*. Yale University Press, New Haven, CT.

Runciman, W. G. (1966). *Relative deprivation and social justice*. Routledge and Kegan Paul, London.

Sachdev, I. and Bourhis, R. Y. (1985). Social categorization and power differentials in group relations. *European Journal of Social Psychology*, **15**, 415–34.

Sachdev, I. and Bourhis, R. Y. (1987). Status differentials and intergroup behaviour. *European Journal of Social Psychology*, **17**, 277–93.

Sagar, H. A. and Schofield, J. W. (1980). Racial and behavioral cues in black and white children's perceptions of ambiguously aggressive acts. *Journal of Personality and Social Psychology*, **39**, 590–8.

Sahlins, M. (1972). *Stone age economics*. Aldine Atherton, Chicago, IL.

Saiyadain, M. S. and Manappa, A. (1977). *Profiles of Indian managers*. Vidya Vahini, New Delhi.

Saxena, N. C. (1984). The nature and origin of communal riots in India. In *Communal riots in post-independence India*, (ed. A. A. Engineer), pp. 51–67. Sangam Books, Hyderabad.

Schein, E. H. (1980). *Organizational psychology*, (3rd edn). Prentice Hall, Englewood Cliffs, NJ.

Scheme of Workers Participation (1975). In *Industry at shopfloor and plant level*, (No. S. 60611 (4) 75-DK, iB). Government of India, New Delhi.

Schiffman, R. and Wicklund, R. A. (1988). Eine Kritik der social identity theory von Tajfel und Turner. *Zeitschrift für Sozialpsychologie*, **19**, 159–79.

Schruijer, S. G. L. (1989). The relationship between kind of attribution and behaviour in an intergroup context. Paper presented at the 2nd Regional Conference of the International Association for Cross-Cultural Psychology, Amsterdam.

Schruijer, S. G. L. (1990*a*). *Norm violation, attribution and attitudes in intergroup relations*. Tilburg University Press.

Schruijer, S. G. L. (1990*b*). Review of social identifications. *Social Behaviour*, **6**, 66–7.

Schruijer, S. G. L. and DeRidder, R. (1988). Evaluation of norm violations and reactions to norm violations by members of different 'cultural' groups. In *Ethnic psychology: research and practice with immigrants, refugees, native peoples, ethnic groups and sojourners,* (ed. J. W. Berry and R. C. Annis), pp. 297–307. Swets North America, Berwyn, PA.

Schruijer, S. G. L., DeRidder, R., Poortinga, Y. H., and Tripathi, R. C. (1986). Norm violations and intergroup relations: a framework for research. In *Ethnic minorities and immigrants in a cross-cultural perspective,* (ed. L. H. Ekstrand), pp. 67–76. Swets & Zeitlinger, Lisse.

Schumacher, P. (1987). *De minderheden: 700.000 migranten minder gelijk.* (The minorities: 700,000 migrants less equal). Van Gennep, Amsterdam.

Schwartz, S. H. (1977). Normative influences on altruism. In *Advances in experimental social psychology,* Vol. 10 (ed. L. Berkowitz). Academic Press, New York.

Seth, B. R. (1940). *Labour in Indian coal industry.* Taraporevala Press, Bombay.

Shaffer, L. S. (1983). Toward Pepitone's vision of normative social psychology: what is a social norm? *Journal of Mind and Behavior,* **4,** 275–94.

Sharma, B. R. (1979). *Organizational correlates of indiscipline in Bokaro Steel Plant.* Bokaro, Research Cell, Personnel Department.

Sherif, M. (1962). *Intergroup relations and leadership.* Wiley, New York.

Sherif, M. (1967). *Group conflict and cooperation.* Routledge & Kegan Paul, London.

Sherif, M. and Sherif, C. W. (1953). *Groups in harmony and tension.* Harper Brothers, New York.

Sherif, M. and Sherif, C. W. (1969). *Social psychology,* (3rd edn). Harper & Row, New York.

Sherif, M., Harvey, O. J., White, B. J., Hood, W. R., and Sherif, C. W. (1961). *Intergroup cooperation and competition: the robbers' cave experiment.* University Book Exchange, Norman, OK.

Shimanoff, S. B. (1980). *Communication rules: theory and research.* Sage, Beverley Hills, CA.

Singh, A. K. (1985). Developing secularism and national integration in India. Presidential address to the Section of Psychology and Educational Sciences, the 72nd Session of Indian Science Congress, Lucknow.

Singh, A. K. (1988). Intergroup relations and social tensions. In *Psychology in India: The state of the art,* Vol. 2 (ed. J. Pandey), pp. 159–223. Sage, New Delhi.

Singh, R. B. P. (1988). Intergroup relationship in a work setting. Unpublished Ph.D. thesis, Magadh University, Bodh Gaya.

Singh, S. (1988). Power relationship between managerial and nonmanagerial personnel in banking organizations. Unpublished Ph.D. thesis, Patna University.

Sinha, J. B. P. (1980). *The nurturant task leader.* Concept, New Delhi.

Sinha, J. B. P. (1982). Power in Indian organizations. *Indian Journal of Industrial Relations,* **17,** 339–52.

Sinha, J. B. P. (1986). Emerging power patterns in work organizations. *Management and Labour Studies,* **11,** 86–96.

Sinha, J. B. P. *Work culture in the Indian context.* Sage International, New Delhi. (In press.)

Snyder, M. and Swann, W. B. (1978). Behavioural confirmation in social interaction: from social perception to social reality. *Journal of Experimental Social Psychology,* **14,** 148–62.

Statistical Abstracts: India (1984). New Series, No. 27, Central Statistical Organization, Ministry of Planning, Government of India.

Steiner, I. D. (1974). Whatever happened to the group in social psychology? *Journal of Experimental Social Psychology*, **10**, 94–108.

Stephan, W. (1977). Stereotyping: role of ingroup–outgroup differences in causal attribution of behaviour. *Journal of Social Psychology*, **101**, 255–66.

Stephan, W. (1985). Intergroup relations. In *The handbook of social psychology*, (ed. G. Lindzey and E. Aronson), pp. 599–658. Random House, New York.

Stouffer, S. A., Lumsdaine, M. H., Williams, R. M., Smith, M. B., Janis, I. L., Star, S. A., and Cottrell, L. S. (1949). *The American soldier: combat and its aftermath*, Vol. 2. Wiley, New York.

Subramaniam, V. (1971). *The managerial class in India*. All India Management Association, New Delhi.

Sussman, M. B. and Weil, W. B. (1960). An experimental study on the effects of group interaction upon the behaviour of diabetic children. *International Journal of Social Psychiatry*, **6**, 120–5.

Tajfel, H. (1957). Value and the perceptual judgement of magnitude. *Psychological Review*, **64**, 192–204.

Tajfel, H. (1969). Cognitive aspects of prejudice. *Journal of Social Issues*, **25**, 79–97.

Tajfel, H. (1970). Experiments in intergroup discrimination. *Scientific American*, **223**, 96–102.

Tajfel, H. (ed.) (1978*a*). *Differentiation between social groups: studies in the social psychology of intergroup relations*. Academic Press, London.

Tajfel, H. (1978*b*). Social categorization, social indentity and social comparison. In *Differentiation between social groups*, (ed. H. Tajfel), pp. 61–76. Academic Press, London.

Tajfel, H. (1980). Experimental studies of intergroup behaviour. In *Psychology survey*, Vol. 3 (ed. M. Jeeves). George Allen & Unwin, London.

Tajfel, H. (1981*a*). *Human groups and social categories: studies in social psychology*. Cambridge University Press, MA.

Tajfel, H. (1981*b*). Social stereotypes and social groups. In *Intergroup behaviour*, (ed. J. C. Turner and H. Giles). Basil Blackwell, Oxford.

Tajfel, H. (ed.) (1982). *Social identity and intergroup relations*. Cambridge University Press, MA.

Tajfel, H. and Turner, J. C. (1979). An integrative theory of intergroup conflict. In *The social psychology of intergroup relations*, (ed. W. G. Austin and S. Worchel), pp. 33–47. Brooks/Cole, Monterey, CA.

Tajfel, H. and Wilkes, A. L. (1963). Classification and quantitative judgement. *British Journal of Psychology*, **54**, 101–14.

Tajfel, H., Billig, M. G., Bundy, R. P., and Flament, C. (1971). Social categorization and intergroup behaviour. *European Journal of Social Psychology*, **1**, 149–78.

Taylor, D. M. and Doria, J. R. (1981). Self-serving and group-serving bias in attribution. *Journal of Social Psychology*, **113**, 201–11.

Taylor, D. M. and Jaggi, V. (1974). Ethnocentrism and causal attribution in a south Indian context. *Journal of Cross-Cultural Psychology*, **5**, 162–71.

Taylor, D. M. and Moghaddam, F. M. (1987). *Theories of intergroup relations: international social psychological perspectives*. Praeger, New York.

Tedeschi, J. T., Schlenker, B. R., and Bonoma, T. V. (1973). *Conflict, power, and games: the experimental study of interpersonal relations*. Aldine, Chicago, IL.

Teulings, A. W. M. (1981). *Ondernemingsraadpolitiek in Nederland: een onderzoek naar de omgang met macht en conflict door de ondernemingsraad* (Works' Council politics in The Netherlands: a study on dealing with power and conflict by the Works' Councils). Van Gennep, Amsterdam.

Thaper, R. (1981). Communalism and the writing of ancient Indian history. In *Communalism and the writing of Indian history*, (ed. R. Thaper, H. Mukhia, and B. Chandra), pp. 1–23. Peoples Publishing House, New Delhi.

Thibaut, J. and Kelley, H. (1959). *The social psychology of groups*. Wiley, New York.

Topragin, H. and Van Baardewijk, C. (1987). *Als Turken zich organiseren* (When Turks get organized). Compuprint, Tilburg.

Tripathi, R. C. and Ansari, M. J. (1980). Resolution of communal conflicts: relating ethnicity and relative deprivation to conflict resolution modes. Paper presented at the seminar on Intergroup Relations, Department of Psychology, Allahabad University.

Tripathi, R. C. and Srivastava, R. (1981). Relative deprivation and intergroup attitudes. *European Journal of Social Psychology*, **11**, 313–18.

Turner, J. C. (1978). Social categorization and social discrimination in the minimal group paradigm. In *Differentiation between social groups*, (ed. H. Tajfel), pp. 101–40. Academic Press, London.

Turner, J. C. (1981). The experimental social psychology of intergroup behaviour. In *Intergroup behaviour*, (J. C. Turner and H. Giles), pp. 66–101. Basil Blackwell, Oxford.

Turner, J. C. and Giles, H. (1981). *Intergroup behaviour*. Basil Blackwell, Oxford.

Turner, J. C., Hogg, M. A., Oakes, P. J., Reicher, S. D., and Wetherell, M. (1987). *Rediscovering the social group: a self-categorization theory*. Basil Blackwell, Oxford.

Turner, R. H. and Killian, L. W. (1972). *Collective behavior*, (2nd edn). Prentice-Hall, Englewood Cliffs, NJ.

Tweede Kamer der Staten-Generaal (1988). *Financiële nota sociale zekerheid 1989* (Financial note on social security 1989). Staatsdrukkerij, The Hague.

Tyerman, A. and Spencer, C. (1983). A critical test of the Sherif's Robber's cave experiments: intergroup competition and cooperation between groups of well-acquainted individuals. *Small Group Behavior*, **14**, 515–31.

Van de Vijver, F. J. R. and Poortinga, Y. H. (1982). Cross-cultural generalizability and universality. *Journal of Cross-Cultural Psychology*, **13**, 387–408.

Van Heck, G. L. (1989). Situation concepts: definitions and classification. In *Personality and environment*, (ed. P. J Hettema), pp. 53–69. Wiley, New York.

Van Knippenberg, A. and Ellemers, N. (1990). Social identity and intergroup differentiation processes. In *European Review of Social Psychology*, Vol. 1 (ed. W. Stroebe and M. Hewstone), pp. 137–69. Wiley, Chichester.

Vanneman, R. D. and Pettigrew, T. F. (1972). Race and relative deprivation in the United States. *Race*, **13**, 461–86.

Van Praag, S. C. P. (1981). *Allochtonen: huisvesting en spreiding* (Allochthones: housing and dispersal) (SCP Cahier no. 22). Staatsuitgeverij, The Hague.

Vermeulen, H. (1985). *Etnische groepen en grenzen: Surinamers, Chinezen en Turken* (Ethnic groups and boundaries: Surinamese, Chinese and Turks). Het Wereldcentrum, Weesp.

Vroom, V. H. (1964). *Work and motivation*. Wiley, New York.

Walker, I. and Pettigrew, T. F. (1984). Relative deprivation theory: an overview and conceptual critique. *British Journal of Social Psychology*, **23**, 301–10.

Walraff, G. (1985), *Ganz unten*. Kiepenheuer & Witsch, Cologne.

Weber, M. (1947). *The theory of social and economic organization*, (trans. A. M. Henderson and T. Parsons). Oxford University Press, New York.

Wentholt, H.(1982). *Massamedia en buitenlandse werknemers in Nederland* (Mass media and foreign workers in The Netherlands). NOS programmadiensten en programma onderzoek, Hilversum, The Netherlands.

Williams, R. M. (1975). Relative deprivation. In *The idea of social structure: papers in honor of Robert K. Merton*, (ed. L. A. Coser), pp. 355–78. Harcourt Brace Jovanovich, New York.

Wish, M.; Deutsch, and Kaplan, S. J. (1976). Perceived dimensions of inter personal relations. *Journal of Personality and Social Psychology*, **33**, 409–20.

Wong, P. T. P. and Weiner, B. (1981). When people ask 'why' questions, and the heuristics of attributional search. *Journal of Personality and Social Psychology*, **40**, 650–63.

Woonsituatie (1982). *Woon- en leefsituatie etnische minderheden in Utrecht* (Housing and living situation of ethnic minorities in Utrecht). Dienst Ruimtelijke Ordening, afdeling Onderzoek, Utrecht.

Worchel, S. and Austin, W. G. (1986). *Psychology of intergroup relations*. Nelson-Hall, Chicago, IL.

Wright, Q. (1965). *A study of war*, (2nd edn). University of Chicago Press, IL.

Zajonc, R. B. (1966). *Social psychology: an experimental approach*. Brooks/Cole, Belmont, CA.

Zillmann, D. (1979). *Hostility and aggression*. Lawrence Erlbaum, Hillsdale, NJ.

AUTHOR INDEX

SUBJECT INDEX

The manufacturer's authorised representative in the EU for product safety is Oxford University Press España S.A. of El Parque Empresarial San Fernando de Henares, Avenida de Castilla, 2 - 28830 Madrid (www.oup.es/en or product.safety@oup.com). OUP España S.A. also acts as importer into Spain of products made by the manufacturer.

Printed and bound by CPI Group (UK) Ltd, Croydon, CR0 4YY

14/09/2026

02216286-0001